BRINGING HOME THE BIRKIN

"Funny, whip-smart. . . . Both a hilarious raid on fashion's strongholds and a memoir that satisfies like a novel. Fashion die-hards, and many others, will be delighted from beginning to end." —*Publishers Weekly*

"Hermès' worst nightmare." —*New York Daily News*

"The perfect, fluffy, and fun beach read." —glamour.com

"I devoured and adored *Bringing Home the Birkin*, the story of how one man turned the fashionable set's obsession with Hermès' signature handbag into a handsome, globe-trotting career."

—JENNIFER WEINER, author of
Good in Bed and *In Her Shoes*

"[A] sunny memoir. . . . The prose is vivid, the tone lighthearted. Mr. Tonello comes off as the fantasy gay best friend immortalized in contemporary women's fiction: sassy, plucky, optimistic—oh, and he can get you a Birkin." —*Wall Street Journal*

"Tonello recounts the strange and serendipitous tale of how he went from cleaning out his closet to being one of the busiest Internet resellers of Birkin bags in the world." —*Globe and Mail*

"Fascinating. . . . The sassy and resourceful Tonello built a very lucrative eBay resale business from his apartment, specializing in Hermès scarves and the French luxury purveyor's highly desired Birkin bag. It's hard not to be swept up in his delightful one-man Birkin Brigades." —*Minneapolis Star Tribune*

"Witty and engaging." —*Pittsburgh Post-Gazette*

"The deliciously quick nonfiction read is almost too good to be true. While living abroad and paying the rent by selling off his luxe goods on eBay, Tonello unlocks the secret to buying the famed Hermès Birkin bag and turns it into a profession. As he country-hops and shops his way across Europe, Tonello exposes an ultra-luxury world that isn't as exclusive as they'd like us to believe." —*Charlotte Observer*

"Funny, thrilling, chock-full of great cocktail-party stories told with the flair of a natural raconteur." —"The Year in Books 2008," Chicago Center for Literature and Photography

"A deliciously addictive true tale of continent-hopping, celebrity-schmoozing, and a crazy-like-a-fox quest for that Hermès 'it' bag, the Birkin. Haute read, indeed." —straight.com

"In his peppy, addictive memoir . . . [Tonello] details the comical lengths to which he's gone to snag hundreds of Birkins that he then sells (with a steep mark-up) on eBay." —moderntonic.com

"The one-step, one-stop shop guide to buying a Birkin." —*Huffington Post*

About the Author

MICHAEL TONELLO grew up in Massachusetts. He traveled the world as a makeup artist and hairdresser until a chance job assignment in Spain proved fateful, and he resettled in Barcelona. Pressed to find a profession that didn't necessitate working papers, he started a lucrative business on eBay as a reseller of all things Hermès. Michael lives in Barcelona with his partner, Juan.

BRINGING HOME THE BIRKIN

MY LIFE IN HOT PURSUIT OF THE WORLD'S MOST COVETED HANDBAG

Michael Tonello

HARPER

NEW YORK · LONDON · TORONTO · SYDNEY

For Marilyn

THE NAMES AND IDENTIFYING DETAILS OF SOME CHARACTERS IN
THIS BOOK HAVE BEEN CHANGED TO SAFEGUARD THE INDIVIDU-
ALS' PRIVACY. ALL THE EVENTS ACTUALLY OCCURRED. I WAS NOT
WEARING A WIRE WHEN I TRAVELED, SO SOME OF THE DIALOGUE
IS A RE-CREATION.

HARPER

A hardcover edition of this book was published in 2008 by William Morrow, an imprint of
HarperCollins Publishers.

BRINGING HOME THE BIRKIN. Copyright © 2008 by Michael Tonello. All rights reserved.
Printed in the United States of America. No part of this book may be used or reproduced
in any manner whatsoever without written permission except in the case of brief quotations
embodied in critical articles and reviews. For information address HarperCollins Publishers,
10 East 53rd Street, NY 10022.

HarperCollins books may be purchased for educational, business, or sales promotional
use. For information please write: Special Markets Department, HarperCollins Publishers,
10 East 53rd Street, New York, NY 10022.

FIRST HARPER PAPERBACK PUBLISHED 2009.

Designed by Kris Tobiassen
Illustrations by Muntsa Vicente

The Library of Congress has catalogued the hardcover edition as follows:

Tonello, Michael.
 Bringing home the Birkin : my life in hot pursuit of the world's most coveted handbag /
Michael Tonello.
 p. cm.
 ISBN 978-0-06-147333-3
 1. Tonello, Michael. 2. eBay (firm). 3. Internet auctions. 4. Selling—Handbags.
5. Businesspeople—Biography. I. Title.

 HF5478.T66 2008
 381'.177092—dc22 2007042550

ISBN 978-0-06-147334-0 (pbk.)

 10 11 12 13 OV/RRD 10 9 8 7 6 5

Contents

HERMÈS

PARIS

Dear Sir:

Owing to serious problems with the supply of skin qualities necessary to the manufacture of your items as well as of production, we are really sorry to inform you that we have today no other options than canceling your orders, i.e.:

1 Fuchsia lizard Kelly clutch bag

1 White bull calf, 30cm, Birkin bag

1 Fuchsia goatskin, 36cm, Haut à Courroie bag.

With our most sincere apologies for not being able to give you satisfaction and thanking you in advance for your understanding, we remain,

Sincerely yours,

Serge de Bourge
Leather Department

Prologue

The sound of the fax machine drew me to the other side of the room. I saw the Hermès letterhead and scanned the letter peremptorily, then read it again, comprehension dawning. I thought it fairly unlikely that the largest luxury leather goods company in the world was having "serious problems" with its leather supply. Come on. That excuse was about as real as their two-year waiting list for Birkins. I had a sneaking suspicion that my globe-trotting and Hermès-hopping days were numbered.

The only "problem" Hermès had was with me—they must have come to the conclusion I was a reseller. (I preferred the term "leather liaison," but why quibble?) It was pretty unbelievable to have arrived at this point, especially since five years ago I hadn't known what a Birkin was. Since then, I had managed to buy them in such quantity that now I had been banished to the Birkin "blacklist." I'd come into this by serendipity; encountered blackmail, bribery, and fraud, all in pursuit of a coveted handbag that the world had an insatiable appetite for. Millions of dollars later, maybe it was time to get off the Birkin roller coaster. Maybe I needed a new start.

Who could I call with my quandaries? Who did I know that truly understood how crazy this all had gotten? Well, Kate *had* been there from the beginning . . .

1

Barcelona on the Brain

I've always thought the use of a ringing phone to symbolize the onset of great personal change was a cheap plot device, and a gross oversimplification of the various factors that inspire human metamorphosis. However, now I know better: sometimes you really *can* trace it all back to a phone call.

In my particular case, that life-changing phone call came early one wintry Cape Cod day—early enough that my roommate, Kate, and I were still cheerfully ensconced in our morning routine of Peet's coffee, PJs, and Rosie O'Donnell. Neither the caller nor the subject matter was by any means unusual—it was the Boston-based agency that represented me, giving me my newest assignment. A weeklong hair and makeup job for IBM in Barcelona, it had the allure of an escape from the drab and drear of mid-March Provincetown. The call certainly felt routine at the time, but we don't always know our Rubicon when it rings . . .

At least workwise, things weren't so shabby. I had a career that people who didn't know better might consider glamorous. As a beautician who specialized in commercial photography, I had spent most of the last decade trigger-happy with a can of hairspray and a powder puff.

And somehow, along my merry way, I had also cofounded a company. Named TEAM, it was an agency that represented artists who worked, in one capacity or another, in the photography and advertising industries. The concept was both convenience and strength in numbers. Normally, an advertising exec needed to make about half a dozen phone calls to pull together a photo shoot. What my company did was turn those six calls into one. Makeup artists, hairstylists, wardrobe stylists, location scouts, production managers, food stylists—we had it all under one roof. But good as it had been to me, my initial euphoria at being part of the fashion industry I had always worshipped as spectator was starting to wane. I had learned that celebrities were just people with name recognition, and photo shoots were as tedious as board meetings, once you had been to hundreds of them. Ten years of crafting updos and vanquishing shiny noses had driven me to uncharacteristic self-analysis. Was this really how I wanted to spend the rest of my life? Maybe not, but for now I knew one thing: I was going to Spain.

I loved traveling for work, eagerly snapping up what the industry called "go-away jobs." Nomadic by nature, I took the adage "home is where the heart is" literally—a hotel room morphed into home as long as I was in it (with the added bonuses of crisp sheets, fresh towels, and chocolates on my pillow). But lately I found myself becoming more jaded by my globe-trotting. Not because of the silly things you always heard those bridge-club biddies bemoaning in the airport—it wasn't lost luggage or the lack of a proper bagel that had me down. I didn't mind the calculus of currency conversion or the etymology of exotic entrées. No, it wasn't the inconvenience inherent to travel that was burning me out. It was boredom. I had increasingly noticed a sinister sameness about each of these foreign cities. Before my very eyes, every place was turning into every place else. I fervently hoped that Barcelona would prove to be the exception.

I sighed with disappointment and slumped against the hot vinyl seat of the taxi. Other than the flamenco music on the radio and the blinding glare of the Catalan sun, so far Barcelona felt about as foreign to

me as Boston. Tacky billboards advertising electronics and cheap hotels flashed by my window at an alarming rate. Was there any place left in the world that didn't look like one giant strip mall? Maybe it *was* time for me to settle down. Maybe I needed the white picket fence and the Weber grill after all.

A mere five minutes later, my cynicism forgotten, I was as mesmerized by the view as a midwesterner crossing the George Washington Bridge into Manhattan. I didn't know which way to look. To my left loomed the impressive bulk of the 1992 Olympic Stadium, capped off by a towering white spire that was an unlikely mating of futuristic space station and computer-generated sculpture. To my right, the Mediterranean. I was dazzled not only by the turquoise shimmer of the sea but by the hundreds of boats lining the docks. Luxury cruise ships, privately owned yachts, behemoth tankers, modest sailboats—somehow, *seeing* one of the world's biggest ports was far more impressive than *reading* about it in *Fodor's*. Suddenly, I was as excited as a little kid on his first field trip.

But it wasn't until we left the highway and entered the city's perimeter that I truly fell under its spell. None of my extensive jet-setting had prepared me for Barcelona's unique urban landscape—palm trees edged the narrow streets, ornate buildings leaned companionably against each other, and laundry adorned nearly every balcony. The architecture spanned centuries of design—gothic intermingled with modernist, contemporary coalesced with classic. It could have been jarring to the senses, but as I would later learn, Barcelona had a way of turning the incongruous into the harmonious. It looked like the European city I had always dreamed of but, of late, had despaired of ever finding. I was captivated.

My eight-hour days of grooming models and painting faces put a dent in what little time I had to prowl the city. However, even with the constraints of the IBM gig cutting into my tourist time, I still sampled enough of the Barcelona lifestyle to grow ever more enamored. My first instincts about the city's physical charm had been wrong—it was far more spectacular than I originally supposed. With a population of

nearly two million spread out over sixty square miles, Barcelona is segmented into dozens of neighborhoods, each possessed of its own particular charm. I was hard-pressed to find an undesirable location; the place was a real estate agent's wet dream.

Then there was the food. I feasted on shrimp the size of lobster, tomatoes sweet enough to eat like an apple, crusty Catalan bread hot from the oven, Torta del Casar cheese (enjoyed best with a spoon), and countless pans of paella in every variety imaginable, all accompanied with sumptuous local wine from the world-famous Rioja region. For dessert, *crema Catalana*—a heady, velvety mixture of cream, eggs, and vanilla that made crème brûlée seem about as appealing as fruitcake. I was in fat-person heaven.

But it wasn't just the food that gave the city its distinct flavor. Even the most mundane detail of day-to-day life had an artistic flair. I found myself transfixed by the most ordinary objects. Lamps were suddenly elevated to high art. Salt and pepper shakers were crafted with an attention to detail usually reserved for Fabergé eggs. Doorknobs stylishly adorned doors rather than simply opening them. It's no wonder that Jean Paul Gaultier loves to visit Barcelona.

Admittedly, the city had fantastic flying buttresses and fragrant frying *botifarra*, but rave reviews in *Architectural Digest* and *Zagat* only go so far. I'd always thought of writing a guidebook that rated the one thing in a city that can make it or break it—the people. Let's start with the French. Consider this:

"The charm of this petite Parisian bistro derives from its baby vegetable–laden pot-au-feu and year-round crackling hearth. It certainly isn't from the locals who frequent here for lunchtime rendezvous. Unabashedly elitist and arrogant, they embody (and loudly embrace, much to other patrons' dismay) all the worst qualities of the French. Still a solid choice, but bring lots of backbone—and your ear plugs."

My review of Barcelona's people would read a little differently:

"Perfect paella and plentiful pots of peonies make for positively passionate patrons of this new Mediterranean marvel. Even better,

the clientele is largely indigenous. Visiting foodies will find themselves surrounded by the beautiful, charming, and amiable (but never overbearing) locals. Their Catalan conversations and lighthearted laughter pleasantly permeate every corner of this restaurant's cathedral ceilings."

All kidding aside, these were my kind of people. Once I breached the initial cautious but gracious reserve, I found them to be warm, kind, and generous to a fault. Plus, they were fun. Any place where the average Joe gets six weeks of vacation was a place after my own heart. The Spanish, unbeknownst to me, had for centuries embodied my personal mantra: Work to live, don't live to work.

I didn't speak the language, I knew no one, and my family was thousands of miles away. However, I had a sneaking suspicion that my white picket fence was destined to have a Spanish motif.

2

The Spanish Indecision

When I returned home, it was like *The Wizard of Oz* in reverse—my Technicolor trip was replaced by Boston's black-and-white bleakness. One look at the piles of dirty snow beside the airport runway and I was frantically searching my carry-on for ruby red Spanish slippers. Driving back from Logan Airport to Provincetown through the "spring" sleet, I was a hair's breadth from pulling a U-turn and hopping the next flight back to Barcelona. Only the realization that I had no clean underwear brought me back to my senses.

I thought my infatuation with Barcelona might pass, but instead, I became increasingly consumed with the idea of moving there.

I plotted it out in my journal:

REASONS TO MOVE	REASONS TO STAY IN PTOWN
Near-perfect weather	Friends
Awesome food	Too much shit to move
Beautiful city/people	Work
Always wanted to learn Spanish	Family
I fucking love it there!	Lease on house
	Car
	No one just up and moves to Spain

I started with the anti-Spain column. All right, the car was no big deal, and Kate could very easily find a new roomie. I'd miss the house, but I had never been one of those people defined by their front yard. The "too much shit" factor was more a reflection of my loathing of packing than it was a real obstacle. So, no biggie. The "friends" item was a little trickier—my friends were everything to me. But I had moved from New York to San Francisco to Boston to Ptown, and I still kept in touch with those who had mattered most. No, it was never the same when you weren't right around the corner, but friendships, like relationships, were best if they weren't built solely on convenience. Moving to Spain didn't have to mean I'd lose anyone I was close to. And, really, that philosophy sort of transferred itself to the family angle too. My parents were exceptionally adventurous, and had made the journey from their home in Florida to wherever I was at least twice a year. I was sure that wouldn't change, and I smiled as I pictured them pricing Spanish phrasebooks at the local Borders. My sister was also living in Florida, married, with a daughter, and we, like many adult siblings, had a pretty much holiday-based relationship at this point. So I guessed I wouldn't pine away of loneliness in Spain.

I sat at the kitchen table, staring at the list. Then, like the madman I occasionally was, I started laughing. Who was I kidding? Lists? Pros and cons? I never should have watched those asinine Tony Robbins infomercials—I think they altered my brain chemistry. With the Michael Motivational Method, it all boiled down to five simple words: I fucking loved it there. Life was too short for list making and excuses. After all, millions of people live in Europe; how difficult could it be?

That evening I girded my loins and told Kate what I'd been pondering. We were sitting at The Mews, our favorite watering hole, and I think she assumed someone had slipped a Mickey in my margarita. After all, she was used to my incurable optimism and flights of fancy. What she didn't know about was an afternoon phone call from my good friend Ward. A former designer at Tiffany, he'd recently taken the plunge and embarked on his own journey, launching a company that

designed and manufactured high-end ladies' jewels. This is where it all got a little weird—Ward needed a contact in Barcelona and offered me a position as middleman to the manufacturer (let me mention here I hadn't spoken with Ward in months—talk about out of the blue). All right, I'd be a jewelry salesman, but I'd unexpectedly cleared my greatest hurdle, getting a European work visa. To me, this was a fluke to end all flukes. But when I told Kate, instead of being floored by my good fortune, she simply laughed and calmly ordered another round. I guess when your brother was Beaker on *The Muppet Show*, weird becomes relative. I sipped my fresh margarita and dropped the subject. I'd tried.

It wasn't like I was unhappy where I was. I had a house, and in Provincetown, a three-bedroom ranch like the one Kate and I shared was the equivalent of a castle. I guess it was only fitting—Kate was lovingly nicknamed "the Empress" by the locals. Her late brother, Richard, was an original Muppeteer and had owned an unpretentiously stellar beachside home on the bluffs of North Truro (a scant few miles from Ptown). Everyone assumed his untimely death (he had been taken far too soon by AIDS) had made Kate a wealthy woman. In reality, all it had made Kate was heartbroken. But instead of wallowing in grief, Kate decided the best way to honor her brother was to carry on his legacy of kindness and generosity. She never let on to most people what his death had cost her—an empress always holds her head high. I was more than honored to play her court jester. It was this dynamic that made our life together in Ptown so exceptional.

We had been happily making the "scene" and hosting dinner parties for half a decade now, and couldn't be more contented as roommates. (Our biggest disagreement was usually about who would play us in the movie version of our Ptown years—I was holding out for James Spader, she Dyan Cannon, but the debate was ongoing.) And, besides my comfy quarters, just living in Ptown was a luxury. There were only three thousand of us "townies," versus the sixty thousand "day-trippers" who made the trek to the tip of the Cape on an average day in August. I secretly reveled in the sense of privilege that accompanied staying after

Columbus Day, and in being one of the only witnesses to the scope of season in a town ruled by ocean. (This may be slightly less than honorable, but I also loved sitting next to the radio on Race Point Beach on Labor Day, enjoying one of the last days of summer and hearing the reports on the miles of traffic backed up on the bridges that led off the Cape.) But truly, there is an austerity to the winter bleakness of a tourist town, and a ghostly specter of summer that makes the wait for spring bearable. If you have borne the chilling winds and gray skies and white capped views, you know yourself more deserving of the easy charm of June, July, and August. But as noble as we year-rounders felt, there is no question that Ptown remains a New England summer haven, a combination of Martha's Vineyard and Key West, with a well-deserved history of harboring artists of every imaginable persuasion. (I never tired of knowing that on any given night I could brush shoulders with Norman Mailer or Michael Cunningham.) But I was starting to have qualms about the impermanency of life there, maybe a reflection of my late onset of adulthood. Everyone I met was on their way to somewhere else. At one time this had been exciting, but now it just made me wonder—where was *I* going?

It wasn't until the packing boxes arrived the following week that Kate panicked. Despite our conversation the other night, I could tell she had still assumed I was taking a sabbatical, not becoming an expatriate.

"My Lord, just how long are you planning to be gone?" she asked, sounding more emotional than her normal low-key self.

I almost responded sarcastically, something along the lines of "Forever, hopefully." But when I glanced up from the box I was packing and saw the look on her face, I immediately bit my tongue. Judging from her forlorn expression, Kate needed a hug, not a funny rejoinder. I suddenly felt sad too, not just for her, but for us.

"Kate, you know I will always come back to visit . . . but I think I really need to do this Spain move." I tried to sound as gentle as possible, but firm too. I didn't want her waiting for me to come back, when I was determined to make a new life for myself in Europe.

"Well, I guess we'll just have to make this summer the best one ever," she said, smiling wanly as she spoke. She was finally accepting my departure, but it wasn't easy for her. I could sense that it was going to take everything she had to accept the end of our years together. Knowing Kate, I'd bet good money that our Provincetown phone line is still in my name.

I'd begun the arduous process of putting my affairs in order. My half decade in Provincetown coming to a close, I realized how much fun I'd had. Accustomed to being surrounded on nearly every side, not only by icy Atlantic waters but by a warm circle of friends, I would miss it here. My days of wining, dining, and carousing at the Atlantic House were almost over. My friends, grief-stricken by the news of my impending departure, did what you'd expect. They nearly killed me with a never-ending stream of chemical toxins ingested nearly nightly at all my favorite bars around town. It's a summer I will long remember, or, more accurately, wish I could. The weeks flew by in a blur of bubble wrap and bottles of bubbly. Andy Warhol had his fifteen minutes, John Lennon had his lost weekend, and I had my summer of living in oblivion. But when crunch time arrived, I realized something else that summer

too. Although I did enjoy life's simple pleasures, I wasn't exactly Amish when it came to accumulation. I went on a rampage through the house. I Dumpstered, I divvied, I divested.

In the end, I stashed my remaining worldly possessions into a U-Haul storage facility. Boxes and boxes of books and photographs, enough designer clothing for a runway show, a couple dozen pieces of Roseville pottery, miscellaneous antique mahogany furniture, and my two Martin Friedman oil paintings were crammed into the tiny space. Boston's real estate market being what it was, I briefly considered renting it out as a somewhat cozy, but really luxe, studio apartment, best suited for petite masters of feng shui. Hey, I needed to be creative; I was still ironing out my financials.

Standing there looking at it all stacked like cordwood, I took pause. As George Carlin puts it, it was just "stuff." But it was *my* stuff, and none of it was going to Spain. Oh well, in for a peseta, in for a pound. I returned to my car (already sold), where two jumbo suitcases sat in the trunk, bursting at the seams with all the Prada, Ralph Lauren, and Jil Sander I would need for the time being. I hoped Barcelona was as ready for me as I was for it.

3

Vespas and Vespers

After a couple weeks of sightseeing and forays into Barcelona's nightlife (conveniently, my hotel served continental breakfast at six A.M.—right after last call), I suddenly remembered I wasn't on vacation. I needed to get an apartment.

At $120 a night, the Hotel del Pi wasn't exactly within my budget. Of course, I didn't really know my budget, but dropping $4,000 a month for bed and bath seemed a little high. It was time to go house hunting.

At the real estate office I was handed a form on a clipboard to complete, and I obediently sat down in the row of vinyl chairs that the receptionist had indicated. I felt unusually anxious and I thought it could be the vibe in there, which was reminiscent of a DMV or the waiting area in a hospital. As I puzzled over the questionnaire (written in Spanish, of course), I realized what *actually* was bugging me. Up until this day, I had been but a return ticket away from going home. Now, answering questions like *¿cuántos dormitorios?*, I realized that no matter how many bedrooms I settled on, I was going to be sleeping in Spain. Once I found my apartment, there'd be no flying over the Atlantic to get home—instead,

I had to make my own home across the Atlantic. I had to grow up, and really commit to my new life, once and for all—of course I was anxious. But then again, they say the chemicals your body produces when anxious are the same ones it produces when you are in love. And what I felt for Barcelona sure seemed like the real thing to me.

None of the nightmare scenarios many people had predicted had yet befallen me, either. I had been able to connect with people, regardless of the language barrier. In Spain every person takes English in school, although I should note that getting them to actually use it is another matter. I broke the code pretty quickly, though: only their embarrassment held them back, so if I used my really rotten Spanish, people were more than happy to use their not-so-rotten English. I was finding the "barrier" something that I could easily hop. (Additionally, as Barcelona was already well on its way to being the "new Paris," I met people from all over Europe all the time, and most spoke English to one degree or another.) I wasn't lonely, or isolated, or homesick; I didn't miss drive-thrus, strip malls, trailer parks, or open-container laws. I never pictured myself as someone who would make the move to Europe, but there I was, and I couldn't be happier. Yet even with all my rationalization, and my burgeoning love of Barcelona, it was still very strange to be in that office, sitting on a vinyl chair, peering at a form in black and white, and knowing a single irrevocable fact: once I signed a lease, I would truly be an expatriate.

With a building boom going on in Barcelona, literally hundreds of apartments were available, but I was distinctly unmotivated to settle on one. There were a couple of reasons for this. One of them was my handsome Spanish real estate agent. I had grown somewhat addicted to bouncing over Barcelona's cobblestone streets on the back of his Vespa. The main reason, though, was the simple fear of making a mistake—a standard apartment lease in Spain is five years long (and unlike marriage, there is no way out). I was shown many beautiful apartments, but for me the decision boiled down to a real estate cliché: location, location, and location. I couldn't for the life of me settle on a neighborhood.

I narrowed it down to the Eixample, the Borne, and the Barrio Gottico. The Eixample was Barcelona's "gay ghetto"—a smooth transition from Provincetown, plus I could easily walk home after clubbing. The Borne boasted cutting-edge galleries, trendy boutiques, and avant-garde eateries, all nestled around the Picasso Museum—creating a Spanish SoHo that never failed to charm me. My hotel sat squarely in the Barrio Gottico, which was home to Barcelona's famous Las Ramblas, a kilometer-long pedestrian mall lined with sycamore trees. I had already gotten into the habit of taking my morning constitutional there, replete with iced *cortado*. (I really dug that in my new city September was still summer.) I wavered daily between these three near-perfect choices. I tried to come up with a scheme to leave my housing quandary to fate, and failed even at that. I would have flipped a coin, but I couldn't find any three-sided ones; my crystal ball was back in my storage unit in the States; and I didn't know enough Spanish to explain to anyone the concept of drawing straws. I was stuck. I started to wonder if my commitment phobia was about to land me in the poorhouse.

I needn't have worried. Cupid struck in the form of a two-hundred-year-old, recently renovated apartment building. I've always been a romantic, and it was truly love at first sight. The building sat directly on the Ramblas and was a postcard of everything I liked most in Spanish architecture. Six stories of glass and stone, adorned with wrought-iron balconies and newly installed French glass doors, it exuded both Old World charm and the aroma of fresh paint. The first two stories of the ancient façade had been converted into a glass-enclosed atrium, accommodating a sumptuous marble-and-mahogany entrance lobby. It was I. M. Pei meets Saint Patrick's Cathedral. My heart was already pounding as I stepped off the elevator and walked across a steel-and-glass footbridge. The massive apartment door opened on crisp white walls and brand-new light oak hardwood floors. Huge windows (a rare feature in Spanish-style architecture) flooded the apartment with daylight. They overlooked the adjacent rooftops, providing both a charming exterior view and an immediate sense of interior expanse.

When I stepped out the double-glass doors from the living room onto the large balcony and spotted the Olympic Tower, I knew I'd be signing a lease. My Vespa-riding days were officially over.

The Hotel del Pi was only two blocks from my new home. However, when you added in the hotel's five flights of stairs, my two jumbo suitcases (which weighed more than me), the crowds of tourists aimlessly meandering on the Ramblas, and the goddamn cobblestones, it felt more like two miles. I arrived sweaty but triumphant. Home sweet home. I spent the afternoon cleaning and settling in—mapping out a furniture floor plan, drafting a list of immediate necessities, and weighing my options on various window treatments.

The day whizzed by, but then at dusk, disaster struck. I flipped a switch and discovered my recessed lighting system was lacking two essential components—lights and electricity. Hm. On a whim, I went to the kitchen and tried the sink. No water. Still, no real biggie—I figured I needed to make some calls in the morning. I could tough it out for a night. Hell, I was already resigned to a sleeping bag—it would be like camp, minus the evening vespers and the marshmallows. I ran down to the corner store and bought a couple boxes of votives, a case of bottled water, and some wine. Nothing was going to ruin the first day in my new apartment. I'd already devised a master plan: takeout by candlelight.

Feeling ludicrously pleased with myself for my unflagging optimism, I snagged some menus from the lobby. But when I picked up the phone, my plan—and my optimism—crumbled. No dial tone. I opened the bottle of wine. Hm again. My evening vespers were turning into taps. Try as I might to positively spin this new development, halfway through the bottle of wine I had still only come up with one truly cheering thought—the suitcases could stay right the hell where they were. I decided that sitting in the dark drinking was getting me nowhere, so I packed a carry-on and headed back to the hotel.

The next morning, after yet another bleary-eyed continental breakfast, I made some calls from the room. I discovered that my utilities

would not be functioning for quite some time—nine or ten days, to be exact. And as far as the light fixtures went, apparently they were the tenant's responsibility. The moving-in experience was undoubtedly one of the few cultural differences between Spain and the States that I found slightly less than charming. No wonder their leases were five years long—no one ever wanted to have to move again.

4

Warding Off Trouble

Less than two weeks later, my apartment had all sorts of newfangled modern conveniences: water, electricity, telephone, lights, and a bed. I was thrilled to be finally feathering my nest. Not that it was all wine and roses. Those initial housing cultural differences were more numerous than I had first supposed. I had been so thoroughly infatuated and blindingly starry-eyed on that original visit, I had failed to note a somewhat glaring architectural omission—a complete lack of closets. For anyone else, this would be highly problematic, but for me it was near catastrophic. The only thing I currently had a lot of was clothes, and I shuddered to think about what I had in storage. Fortunately the Aussie who installed the lights did double duty as a carpenter (he also did the window treatments—go figure). I was already hemorrhaging money, what was another couple grand for the glory of closet privileges? And I reasoned that one of the freshly acquired armoires could double as a coffin when I retired to my pauper's grave. Don't get me wrong, normally I reveled in excessive leisure time, but at the rate I was spending money, I was more than ready to see a paycheck again. Now that I was (mostly) settled in, I was eager to start slinging jewelry.

Then Ward called. He sounded a little weird, and almost imme-diately launched into a lengthy, complicated speech about businessy things like logistics and cost analysis. I gradually realized that beneath the surface of his convoluted language choices and purposefully indi-rect delivery lurked two rather salient facts, one of which piggybacked on the other. Fact one: he wasn't going to move his manufacturing to Barcelona, hence, fact two: I wasn't going to be working for him. This led me to a personal fact three—I was screwed.

I managed to subdue my growing panic and assured Ward I'd be okay. We exchanged good-byes, and as soon as the receiver was in its cradle, I calmly assessed the situation. Okay, that's a huge lie, I totally freaked. Here I was with a five-year lease, no work visa, and a rather significant language barrier. Unless I could find an under-the-table job that only involved asking people their name and ordering a beer, I was up the shit creek without a *paleta*.

I was going to handle this like a man. I called my mother. Lucky for me, my mother was not the normal kind of mom. She wasn't going to freak out at the idea of her firstborn stranded in a foreign country with-

out any way to earn an honest buck. No, my mother had unflappable poise and a matter-of-fact approach to dilemmas. People sometimes remarked on the resemblance she bore to the actress Tyne Daly, from that old cop show *Cagney and Lacey*. And, like Lacey, my mother never missed a trick—and she could detect a lie a mile off. Now, this may not sound so comforting (and when I'd missed curfew at sixteen it sure wasn't), but at times like this it was exactly what the doctor ordered. I wanted some down-to-earth advice, not someone who would reinforce my panic. And as always, she came through, cool as a cucumber.

She reminded me I still had my hair and makeup skills, and, more important, a history of "stepping in shit and coming out roses" (no *paleta* necessary in that analogy). We also decided I'd come to Florida for Christmas. Besides getting to see much-missed family and friends, it would give me an opportunity for a side trip up north to raid my storage locker. (I was determined to get my money's worth out of those damned Aussie armoires.) I got off the phone before she ran out of good bolstering material and mentioned that I still had my health—that would be too depressing. As it was, I felt marginally better after our talk.

I had barely hung up the phone when it rang again. It was my dad, the comedian in the family. He managed to fit a lot of personality into a somewhat shorter-than-average Italian frame. Although he wasn't usually the one I called for advice, he came through big that night with a story about my youthful ambition, one that I had almost forgotten.

When I was fifteen, what I wanted more than anything was to go on the Paris trip with the rest of my French class. My parents, who had never been to Europe themselves, told me that in order to go, I needed to earn my own way. To come up with the $900 or so, a veritable fortune to me at the time, I would need to be creative. After much brainstorming, I hatched a plan, one that required a little financial investment and a lot of time investment. For me and my limited teenage resources (time I had, money—not so much), it was ideal. On weekends, my dad used to golf at Halifax Country Club (about an hour's drive from Boston), and that became the venue. For three months of summer

weekends, I rode to the course with him at the rather unpleasantly early hour of six A.M., rented a golf cart, and threw my "coolers" (two trash cans full of ice) into the back. I was a moving concession stand—I sold potato chips, sandwiches (freshly made by yours truly), and sodas. All day long I simply drove the course, selling everything at a considerable markup to red-faced golfers. Did my plan work? *Oui*, and it created a lifelong belief in creative enterprise. I think my dad's point was, if I could get to Paris at fifteen, I could probably survive in Barcelona more than twenty years later. But, knowing my dad, it could also have been his way of telling me that if all else failed, I could always break into the Spanish golf-course concession scene.

Either way, survive I did, and thanks to Mom's suggestion of a trip home, that year I got to have Christmas twice: once with my family, and then again when the mailman started delivering my storage-unit bounty. I had spent nearly an entire day in that dusty storage room, handpicking my most prized possessions. All in all, I shipped twenty-seven boxes. If nothing else, at least now my home looked as though I was gainfully employed. All those years in the advertising industry taught me nothing if not the importance of appearances. Surrounded by my collection of modern first editions and Macintosh stereo equipment, I was able to convince myself (however temporarily) I was doing okay.

But the bills kept rolling in. One day, as I was rearranging my sweaters for the eight hundredth time, I realized I was staring at a herd of cashmere I never wore anymore. I was deep in the throes of a Barcelona winter, and temperatures had plummeted to nearly fifty degrees, not exactly snowsuit-and-mittens weather. It was time to thin the herd. My eyes fell upon a luxurious Polo Ralph Lauren plaid cashmere scarf I had purchased a year ago and worn only once. My first thought was to find a local consignment shop. But hello, if I didn't need it to brave the elements here, then probably no one else did either. Then I thought of eBay. I'd always been a buyer, never a seller, but how hard could it be? I already owned a great digital camera. Snap a couple of pictures, write

a couple of lines . . . I figured if Velma Vinklemeyer from Vinalhaven, Vermont, could make a killing with her hand-crocheted scripture-inspired tea cozies, then I had a somewhat decent shot of selling a designer scarf (although our client base was probably not the same). What did I have to lose?

5

Career Chop Suey

You know how when you try to master a new skill it takes a while to get good at it? That's the exact opposite of my very first foray into the world of the eBay entrepreneurship. My scarf, originally $99 at a Polo Ralph Lauren outlet in Connecticut, sparked a passionate rivalry among online bidders, and sold inexplicably for $430 to some guy in the Midwest. I guess he really liked plaid (or maybe he was just cold). After this rather surprising success, I began to look at my possessions in a whole different light. Now, I wasn't close to starving—thankfully, as a cofounder of TEAM, I was pretty much guaranteed $2,000 a month in company revenues. I knew, however, that it sure wasn't going to cut it for me long-term, so it was time to triage. At first it was only clothes that went on the chopping block, but eventually I started scrutinizing other items. I mean, how many times can you read the same book? And honestly, there's always the library. I soon listed a number of my books on eBay, some of them first editions.

Okay, if I'm to tell the whole truth, I wasn't quite as blasé about selling my books as I wanted to be. I loved clothes, sure, but clothes are . . . clothes. And books . . . well, they're more like friends. I had two favorite

writers, Lillian Hellman and Truman Capote, and I owned a number of first editions of both. *Pentimento* was, and is, my single favorite book of all time, and I reread it at least once a year, marveling each time at the dry wit of the author. Something about Lillian Hellman's brash, superbright, somehow courageous style struck a serious chord in me. And Capote always amazed me—how his acerbic humor and understated emotion formed a perfect counterpoint to his highly charged subject matter. How many writers can write a true crime book about a tragic family massacre and still pull off a couple of one-liners in the process? Obviously, the common bond was that sense of humor that peeked out from their plotlines in often surprising ways. Humor is the ultimate survival skill, and when I read these guys, I knew I was learning from the masters. Ironically, it was the recognition of this fact that made it easy for me to decide to sell off my copies of their works. I had already learned what I needed—I had taken their lessons of humor, courage, and creativity to heart. What better way to emulate my teachers than to use them to launch what was fast becoming both my funniest and bravest episode to date? (I kept one copy of *Pentimento*, however—you never know when you'll need a refresher course.)

I quickly realized it had been neither my amazing business acumen nor my acute sense of style that had snared me that first sizeable profit. In reality, there just wasn't that much you had to know about eBay in order to use it successfully. I would set an opening bid for the item, and also a reserve (the lowest price I was willing to sell for). I was partial to either a seven- or ten-day auction, timed to end on Sunday evening, when most people would be at home. (I based these calculations on "eBay time," aka Pacific Standard Time, since the greatest number of eBay users are in the USA.) Then I'd sit back and wait. The exciting part would usually come in the final few minutes. That was when a "bidding war" could break out. I was always riveted by the last sixty seconds of an auction, hitting the refresh button on my computer's browser repeatedly as the bids (I hoped) soared.

My first edition of Truman Capote's *Breakfast at Tiffany's* (autographed and in mint condition) fetched nearly a grand. I was on a roll. I

found that the sting of sacrifice lessened with every dollar I made. Another trip to the storage unit in Boston beefed up my "inventory" nicely (and took yet another chunk out of my TEAM-accrued frequent-flier miles). I sold off whole closets' worth of designer winter clothes and a veritable library of books. My new "career" was proving quite lucrative.

In those early days of my eBay adventures, I'm pretty sure everyone involved in my personal life thought I was certifiable. I'm positive my parents cringed every time one of their neighbors asked them what their son did for a living. In Florida retirement communities, "eBay guru" doesn't have the same cachet as doctor or lawyer. But Mom still sent me monthly care packages, so I guess they weren't that fazed. My friends back in the States were never surprised by anything anymore, especially after my emigration to Barcelona. However, I sensed from their lackluster responses to my stories of auction success that they believed this was just another one of my passing fancies. After all, I really didn't have a business plan or a mission statement. My 401(k) prospects weren't that hot either. But what everyone seemed to overlook was that I spent my days in my pajamas and still got a paycheck. Now to me, that trumped any Fortune 500 benefits package.

I hit some serious pay dirt when I listed a pristine copy of Bruce Weber's *O Rio de Janeiro*. It went into a major bidding war, eventually selling for about $500, and prompted a number of e-mails begging me for more Weber books. His newest—*Chop Suey Club*—had barely hit the shelves and was already completely sold out in the States. I hotfooted it to a local bookstore and found a treasure trove of about a dozen copies. Hesitant to overinvest, I bought one and listed it. Bingo! The book sold for $245 . . . not bad for a short-term $65 investment. Nobody's fool, I hustled back and bought the rest. I didn't get to keep even one. Maybe I did have a business plan after all.

After this success, I made a final trip to Boston. It seemed a little silly to be paying storage rent in Boston when I could be paying apartment rent in Barcelona. The contents of those boxes, with any luck at all, were going to take me from storage vault to bank vault. Since I

knew that storage unit had been my last tie to the Boston area, I figured it was a good time to jaunt down to my old stamping grounds and pay Kate a visit. Spring was beginning to poke its green nose out from under the frozen ground, and I knew everyone would be in a positive frame of mind.

At my former front door, I was greeted with a shriek and a huge hug. Kate was more than eager to hear all the details of my new venture, and I wanted all the newest gossip, of course. It felt strange, though—in a few short months, my life had radically changed, but hers was precisely the same. Driving the long, gray highway down, I had wondered if I would feel regretful when I saw everyone and everything I had left behind. Instead, although I still loved the house, and Kate, and Ptown, it was definitely a love that felt more like a reminiscing than a rekindling. Even if I had to sell the shirt off my back to stay in Spain (not just a cliché, in my particular case), I knew there was no future for me here. Home was Barcelona—I knew it for sure right then, and even more so a few days later. Nothing convinces you so thoroughly that you truly belong to a place as when your heart beats faster at the thought of being back on its familiar ground once more. And on that day, when my plane touched down on the tarmac in my chosen city, mine was thumping like a jackrabbit's.

On an afternoon not long after, I was sorting through the last remaining piles of clothes and books when I spotted a box I hadn't seen in years. As soon as I saw the orange, I remembered the Hermès scarf housed within. I had bought it almost a decade ago in New York, to wear to a black-tie New Year's Eve party at La Caravelle. I hadn't touched it since. I pulled it out of the box and recalled immediately why I had bought it—100 percent heavy silk twill with an intricate, striking black-and-gold design of spurs and ribbons, it was the height of understated elegance. My current mind-set being what it was, however, it looked more like dollar signs than anything else. Either way, it was beautiful.

6

Horseshoes and Handkerchiefs

I had long taken the Julius Caesar/Gaul view of life; I saw it divided into three parts—home, work, and social. But either way, my life in Spain was definitely two for three at this point. I had an intriguing new job (it was paying the bills; ergo, it was a job) and my apartment had finally reached a level approaching stylish. As I am an unapologetic homebody (blame it on astrology: I'm a Cancer), my apartments were never really *done*; they were a nest I would forever be feathering. But by now, my current nest was certainly more than tolerable, if the neighborly compliments I got in the elevator after my housewarming party were any indication. This, of course, left just one missing member of my guiding triumvirate—my social life.

With my time clock–free work front, I was having no problem devoting a more than average amount of energy to socializing. However, it wasn't panning out *quite* as easily as the other arenas. While I had made a bunch of party pals, I hadn't come close to finding anyone who was as indispensable as any one of my close friends back in the States. The people I'd met so far in Spain were the kind of friends you put in your address book in pencil (especially if their last names started with

one of the more popular letters). And, of course, there was always that pesky "quest for a soul mate" thing. Even with my considerable prowess in the area of bullshitting, I couldn't convince myself that I was content spending the rest of my life single. So I persevered with the night-life—not that I found it that arduous to go out drinking when mixed drinks in Barcelona were so cheap. In fact, at two bucks for an Absolut and tonic, I felt guilty not going out. I was *trying* to be a social animal, that's for sure. Alas, after four months in Barcelona, my little life stool was still leaning to the side, but I knew I would find something good to prop it up with eventually.

Until then, I had other things to focus my OCD on—like scarves, say. All week I had watched in amazement as the number of "hits" on my Hermès scarf auction increased to well over three hundred (nearly double any of my previous listings). More important, there was aggressive bidding within moments of the scarf's debut on eBay. By the time the auction hit "prime time" (those final sixty seconds I loved), the price of the scarf was already up to $300. In that one minute, I watched the fierce bidding drive the price up over a dollar a second, as eighteen people aggressively vied for my ten-year-old scarf.

I had barely stopped gloating over my $400 victory when my inbox started to fill up. It was all the "losers" from the auction imploring me to help with their Hermès "wish lists." It was obvious these people were serious collectors, and I didn't let my ignorance get in the way of my avarice. I intimated that this was "only the tip of the iceberg." Well, I've always been a strong believer in the power of positive thinking—I really *wanted* it to be only the tip of the iceberg.

I was on a mission: find more scarves. I whipped out the phone book. Hermele, Hermenegildo, Hermens, there it was . . . Hermès . . . Oh, cool, it was relatively close; I could take a cab. Ten minutes later I was already in front of the store, smack-dab in the middle of Barcelona's richest residential neighborhood. I approached the plate-glass storefront with no small measure of curiosity. What was it about this brand that was causing such neediness in my eBay bidders? It was

a corner location, bigger than I had expected, and I strolled around the building, taking in the visual. Their windows were full of luxurious leather goods, couture clothing, and equestrian-inspired jewelry and scarves. I stood outside for a moment, perusing. Although I sensed real marketing genius in their whimsically alluring displays, I gradually realized something surprising. Personally, I just wasn't allured—however opulent this merchandise, I didn't see a single thing that I wanted. I'd never really been the horsey type, I guess. If I hadn't been on my mission, I would have headed to the Louis Vuitton store across the street. On the bright side, temptation wouldn't be an issue.

I sensed the doorman's silent appraisal as I walked in. I ignored it. I couldn't let anything distract me from my desire to find more of these magical scarves—I was determined to incite another eBay feeding frenzy. Armed with the wish lists of my potential "clients," for once I actually wanted help shopping. I glanced around, but only spotted one saleswoman, and she certainly had her hands full. The customer she was dealing with was probably in her sixties, dressed like a publicity still of Jackie O having high tea at the Ritz. "Jackie O"'s demeanor, however, was more Imelda Marcos—she was loudly carrying on about some pink leather shoes that the poor beleaguered saleswoman couldn't find in her size. I gave them a wide berth and pretended to browse.

I started in menswear—who knew, maybe if I looked hard enough, I would unearth some items that didn't scream polo match. What with all my auctioning, the armoires had started to get downright barren (by barren, I mean I could open them now and nothing fell out). After a few minutes of thumbing through largely uninspiring racks of cotton and silk, I saw a shirt that didn't look half bad. The design was black and blue geometric H's on a pale gray background—nary a horseshoe in sight. I could dig it. But then, for possibly the first time in my life, I felt the blood drain from my face when I looked at a price tag: $690—for a cotton shirt? Was that a misprint? And it's not as if I generally shopped at Kmart—I was used to paying designer prices. But . . . come on! It was a shirt, for crissakes. I half seriously checked the sleeves for dia-

mond cuff links and slowly backed away. Then my hand brushed across a jacket, the leather soft as butter . . . I fished around for the price tag. Oh . . . my . . . God . . . $4,770. I already owned what I considered an "investment-quality" Prada leather jacket. This item of mine had, thus far, performed all its myriad jacket duties—keeping me warm, say, and sometimes providing me someplace to put my hands—with admirable reliability and unfailing competency. (And it was pretty damn stylish-looking too.) At a good $3,000 more, what could this one do? Take out my fucking trash for me? Shine my shoes? Maybe it doubled as a parachute.

Then it dawned on me. I was in a whole new league. Suddenly, I couldn't stop obsessively pricing everything in the store. Men's cotton boxers? Only $295 each. My Ralph Lauren underwear became about as designer as Fruit of the Loom. The cheapest thing I could find in menswear was the $110 handkerchiefs. I tried my luck in housewares. A brightly colored cotton beach towel with an elephant motif caught my eye: $450. I think I'll just drip-dry, thanks. I stopped at a small table set up with a brandy snifter, playing cards, and an ashtray . . . total price tag for a night of Hermès hold 'em? $700 (without the brandy or cigars). I liked the looks of the cute little stuffed horses. Mama horse? $830. Baby horse, maybe? $340. Whoa, Nelly. I decided to be more practical. How 'bout a blanket? $940. Where were they getting their wool, from caviar-fed sheep? Must be from the same dude rancher who raises the cotton for their handkerchiefs.

I probably would have dazedly wandered the store all afternoon, playing *The Price Is (Can't Be) Right*, but fortunately a salesman materialized at my elbow. Before he could try to sell me a horse, I handed him the list. He read it, brow furrowed, although whether in concentration or confusion I wasn't initially sure. Probably confusion, I guessed, when he awkwardly excused himself after a minute and went over to the saleswoman (who had finally extricated herself from Customer of the Day, Imelda). I sure hoped that she would know what was going on—somebody around here had to, and I knew it wasn't me. I edged closer

and overheard the phrases "older designs" and "check the back stock." He disappeared into the back. When he returned, he was holding two scarves of the dozen or so on the list. My heart sank a little—but all, as it turned out, was not lost.

"Sir, we may have more of these in another stockroom, but I can't get in there without my manager, who I am sorry to say is not here right now. Can I get your name and number, or perhaps you can come back in a couple of days? Whatever is best for you." He was almost excessively polite, but I never minded that quality in a salesman.

"I can come back, not a problem, I live locally—I'll take these two for now."

I rang out (feeling like a cheapskate for only dropping $450) and breezed out of there. I floated down the street, swinging the signature bright orange shopping bag. Wouldn't be the last time.

7

Silk Serendipity

After a victory dinner, I listed my two hard-won treasures on eBay and retired to bed soon after. I'm sure my dreams were of scarves, not sugarplums, but either way, the following morning I awoke refreshed. Happy to be able to keep my pajamas on for a day of work at home, I puttered around the kitchen while my computer booted up. I had several e-mails, but one in particular piqued my interest.

From: GraceoftheGarden@yahoo.com
Subject: eBay Item/Question For Seller: HERMÈS Silk Scarf
 PEONIES mint/new
To: Armoire_Auctions@yahoo.com

Hi there—This scarf (with the pink and green Peonies) has very special meaning to me, it was truly one of my favorites. A couple of years ago, I left mine in a NYC taxi and it was never recovered. Would you consider adding a Buy-It-Now to your listing? I would be greatly appreciative if you could help me to get this design back in my collection, especially considering the near-impossibility of finding the older Hermès designs in the States. Cordially, Grace

From: "michael" <armoire_auctions@yahoo.com>
To: "GraceoftheGarden" <graceofthegarden@yahoo.com>

grace, thanks for your email and interest in my auction. i'm not too
enthusiastic about adding a Buy-It-Now, however, would you like to
make me an offer? michael

At $225 a pop, I couldn't help wondering how many scarves this
woman had in her collection. These scarf people really were serious.
Whatever. I was content to help assuage their burning desire to spend
suitcases full of money so long as some of it landed in my wallet.

I checked on my auctions. There were no bids yet. However, there
were a dozen or more "watchers." A "watcher" is basically someone who
is worshipping your listing from afar, but afraid that expressing their
interest through a bid will cause others to notice how pretty it is too.
Bad news (sort of) for me, but good news for Grace. Since there were
no bids on the Peonies scarf, I could legitimately end the listing. I had
a hunch her offer would be fair, maybe more than fair.

My instincts were good.

From: GraceoftheGarden@yahoo.com
To: Armoire_Auctions@yahoo.com

Thank you for your kind reply. If the scarf is truly pristine and new I
would be comfortable with an offer of $350. Grace

From: "michael" <armoire_auctions@yahoo.com>
To: "GraceoftheGarden" <graceofthegarden@yahoo.com>

grace, it's a deal. i like knowing that it's going to a good home. ☺

michael

p.s. I will need your details for shipping, are you okay with sending a
check?

I was still adjusting to the weird brand of intimacy that eBay necessitated. I had not yet met face-to-face anyone whom I had sold to, and I didn't know if I ever would. (Obviously, geography played a part in this—many of my buyers lived half a world away.) But even though I couldn't pick them out of a lineup, the whole process of buy-and-sell often offered me little tidbits of information in passing. For example, I knew which women had to hide their Hermès habit from their husbands (they usually paid by money order) and which ones had no such concerns (they paid by check or credit card). I had a feeling this woman was sure to be the latter.

From: GraceoftheGarden@yahoo.com
To: Armoire_Auctions@yahoo.com

Michael, lovely! I will post a check to you today and all of my information will be on the check. You are most kind indeed. Grace

p.s. Are you receptive to some constructive criticism?

Bingo. This woman hid nothing, it seemed . . . (including her opinions, apparently). I was actually superinterested to hear what she had to say, since I had no clue how I was doing this whole eBay thing so successfully. It was a no-brainer, making money like this—why was I the only person (practically) doing it on such a large scale? Maybe my girl Grace had some insider info.

From: "michael" <armoire_auctions@yahoo.com>
To: "GraceoftheGarden" <graceofthegarden@yahoo.com>

constructive criticism??? sure . . . why not. michael

From: GraceoftheGarden@yahoo.com
To: Armoire_Auctions@yahoo.com

I've reviewed a number of your auctions, both current and previous, and you've sold some exceptional pieces . . . however, your

descriptions are quite bare bones and not terribly informational. You should also include more photos than you have been. This is especially important if you are going to be showcasing more scarves to serious buyers. Do you indeed have more scarves? Grace

Okay, judging by her eloquence and formality, Grace probably wasn't exactly a "girl." More of a barrister, maybe, or CEO of a Fortune 500. Either way, she was definitely more scarf-savvy than I. I briefly worried about eBay espionage (maybe she worked for Hermès?) but decided I was probably being a wee bit paranoid. It wasn't like I was the keeper of the goddamn Hermès Holy Grail or something. And, really, she had the sweetest e-mail address in the world. As if that actually ensured she wasn't a spy, but—GraceoftheGarden? It didn't exactly have the ring of dishonesty. (I pictured a kindly woman in a field of lilies, Hermès scarf over her gray hair, "My Favorite Things" gently playing in the background.) At any rate, she was so incredibly polite I couldn't *help* but like her. Indeed.

From: "michael" <armoire_auctions@yahoo.com>
To: "GraceoftheGarden" <graceofthegarden@yahoo.com>

grace, I must be honest and tell you that I know nothing about Hermès scarves, except that they are silk and cost about $225.

I'M GREEN. Michael

I bet the only thing green about Grace was her garden.

She definitely had an expert's approach to this whole eBay scarf scenario. I went to the kitchen to brew up another pot of tea. It was thinking time—Sherlock had his opium pipe; I have my Earl Grey. I reread the e-mail while sipping, and the most salient point Grace was oh-so-gently trying to make leaped out at me: don't come off as a scarf schmuck. This was serious business here, and I needed to upgrade. These people obviously were deeply committed to this brand,

and if I was going to find "serious buyers," as she called them, I needed to be a serious seller.

From: "michael" <armoire_auctions@yahoo.com>
To: "GraceoftheGarden" <graceofthegarden@yahoo.com>

grace, wow! i had no clue . . . i thought they were just 3 foot squares of silk (albeit pricey ones). in all honesty i would LOVE any and all information/help.

your new student, michael

From: "GraceoftheGarden" <graceofthegarden@yahoo.com>
To: Armoire-Auctions@yahoo.com

Michael, after helping me reunite with my beloved Peonies I feel I will be forever in your debt. No, seriously, I would be more than happy to help you. Grace

p.s. an Hermès scarf is NOT three feet square, it is 35.4 inches square. (or more accurately, 90 centimeters, it's French, after all.)

For once Mom was wrong. Apparently, when you stepped in *Spanish* shit everything came up peonies, not roses. Through no fault of my own, I had miraculously stumbled upon what was proving to be an incredibly lucrative commodity. I had always known about coin collectors and philatelists, but silk-scarf aficionados? Never would have guessed it. Bizarrely enough, I might even be in the exact right place at the exact right time for supplying the demand—apparently, some of these scarves were easier to find in Europe. And, to top it off, I had formed a burgeoning e-mail friendship with an amazing potential mentor. Did this aptly named Grace have some sort of PhD in Hermès? She was so well versed in this stuff that I thanked my lucky stars we had crossed paths. If my orange-tinted visions of the future weren't too far off, I wouldn't be getting back out of my pajamas anytime soon.

8

Le Monde d'Wish Lists

A month later, I didn't have my Hermès doctorate yet but I was well on my way to earning my bachelor's. I did get out of my pajamas (sometimes), but mostly just to go to *correos* (the post office). Of course, I was still enjoying the nightlife. However, I had realized that no time clock at my workplace also meant no water cooler. Somehow, it wasn't the same to go out and get drunk if you had no one to commiserate with over your hangover. And frankly, I wasn't all that great at sleeping in—I was like a little kid with these auctions.

I marveled at how different my life here truly was. Not that I had been mired in a nine-to-five at any point, but still, this was over the top, freedomwise, even for me. I could work a lot or a little; I could work at noon or midnight. Some days I made no money, other days my bank account swelled by thousands. And I realized that as soon as I got a laptop, I could even choose *where* I worked. I envisioned sitting on the beach later that summer, margarita at my side, watching my auctions over the tops of my Trussardi sunglasses. As much fun as Labor Day in Ptown had been, this time I'd actually be getting *paid* to bask in the sun. Maybe I would even buy an Hermès towel.

Subsequent trips to the Hermès shop in Barcelona had yielded nearly two dozen scarves, which netted me a sizable profit. On my last visit, the salesman handed me a copy of *Le Monde d'Hermès* (The World of Hermès). Nestled amid glossy photographs and consumer-oriented vignettes, this luxe catalog contained a directory of all the Hermès stores worldwide. A few weeks later, my *Le Monde* was already as dog-eared as my teenage copy of *Catcher in the Rye*. I worked the phones. I was determined to find as many of the items from my clients' wish lists as possible. On a couple of occasions, my trips to the Hermès shop in Madrid proved fruitful. Then I discovered Andorra.

Andorra is a tax-free principality, tucked in the Pyrenees Mountains, between France and Spain. It's a tiny country—California's Yosemite National Park is nearly seven times larger. More important, an Hermès scarf costs $30 less in Andorra than in Barcelona, and that savings alone made it worth the two-hour drive. It was also here that I learned the valuable difference between a franchise Hermès store and a "regular" Hermès store. Because the franchise stores like Andorra's didn't ship their scarves back to Paris at the end of a season, their backroom was a veritable wish-list bonanza. Being able to find the older, out-of-production designs coveted by serious collectors was the name of my eBay game these days. I lived for the bidding wars a highly-sought-after scarf could incite. All in all, I probably bought close to a thousand scarves there.

All of my earlier sarcasm about Hermès U aside, it turned out this whole scarf thing really was almost indescribably complicated. I had learned in my tutorials from Grace that Hermès issues two new scarf collections a year, often by several different designers. In addition, there are reissues of older scarves, recolorations of preexisting designs, and, naturally, any number of "special edition" scarves. (Examples of those included the Mozart scarf, only available at the Salzburg store, and designs the company had issued to commemorate the Olympics—1980 Lake Placid, for example.) A true collector also knows to look for certain telltale hallmarks of authenticity and condition—such as copyright

symbols (only on scarves issued after 1976) or care labels (which needed to be intact if, like me, you wanted to command top dollar). Although, I have to admit, as complex as the whole market was overall, for me it was pretty simple. If my clients put it on a wish list, and I found it, I bought it. Then I sold it. End of story. And in Andorra, I found a lot.

Business was booming! The months quickly vanished and, with them, the scarves. With fifty or sixty eBay auctions running round-the-clock, it was not unusual for me to sell twenty or thirty scarves on any given Sunday. With Grace's help, I had "graduated" (magna cum laude) and had magically become the reigning online Hermès scarf mogul. Before too long, Grace was tipping me off to scarf designs that were hot among the collectors. I now knew firsthand how brilliant this woman was, and she hadn't steered me wrong yet. If she so much as murmured the name of a scarf, it got quickly added to my pile of rapidly growing wish lists. One such scarf was the "Kachinas"—designed for Hermès by a postal worker/artist from Texas, with the unlikely name of Kermit Oliver. This scarf featured American Indian dolls and had quickly sold out in the United States. Europeans, logically enough, had little interest in Kachinas; hence, this scarf was readily available anywhere in Europe. (Good luck finding one now!) To me, Kachinas sounded an awful lot like $ka-ching$. I made a profit of anywhere between $100 and $200 on every one I sold.

Besides the scarves, there was one other fun little way Hermès helped me make a buck or two. One day, when I bought a scarf, after the saleswoman finished wrapping it up in the ceremoniously ornate way that they do, she pulled out this little bitty book. (Need I even mention it was orange?) Full of photographs and simple line drawings, this book gave you every conceivable option on how to tie a scarf, and then some. As odd as the concept initially struck me, on further consideration, I realized it was pure genius. You see, if you had two hundred of these things, it was inevitable that you would eventually run out of ideas. And it was free for the asking, although customarily given with a scarf purchase. Once I knew about them, I made sure to ask for one

whenever I checked out. I started auctioning these as a sideline. People would pay around $30 for them, and I didn't have to be a CEO to calculate that particular profit margin. I figured it was my version of a business perk.

My guest room had transformed into Scarf Central. Piled around the armoires were hundreds of bright orange boxes, each of them housing a wish-list treasure. With no exaggeration, at that point, serious scarf collectors visiting Barcelona would have done better to swing by my apartment than the local Hermès store. (Especially since I had already cleaned those guys out.) I felt bad for anyone actually *staying* in my guest room, since it was now my shipping and receiving department. I definitely would have to do a major cleanup before my parents visited; Mom had implied they might make the trip over sometime soon. Next to the boxes were precarious stacks of the how-to-tie-a-scarf book, cartons and cartons of padded envelopes, and roll upon roll of packing tape. The only bedside reading material was *Le Monde d'Hermès*. Not exactly fodder for a spread in *Architectural Digest*. On the whole, though, I was exceedingly pleased with my new lifestyle. Fingers crossed, pretty soon I would be able to spring for a couple of pairs of those snazzy Hermès boxer shorts. But I still had to pull in the reins on buying those stuffed horses—maybe next year.

9

The Pyrenees Passing

I was drowning in silk by the time I realized I was in uncharted waters. I had figured out one of the reasons I was so wildly successful was that Hermès didn't have a Web site yet. I figured this out around the same time that I became the world's first accidental workaholic. I bought the goods, sold the goods, packed the goods, shipped the goods . . . my lark was becoming an aviary. I guess the soul mate search was going to wait, unless I was destined to end up with a scarf fanatic. At any rate, the time had clearly come to diversify my wares. Enamel bracelets, playing cards, Ulysses (leather notebooks), desk accessories—if it had the "Hermès Paris" logo, it sold. I could see why the CEO's dictum was rumored to be "Hermès should never make anything ugly, because someone might buy it." *My* dictum was "Get it while the getting is good." And at Hermès Andorra, the getting was *always* good. I never had even the hint of a problem, until one particular afternoon.

My trips to that store were like clockwork—three or four times a month, I made the two-hour trek over the mountains in my Hertz rent-a-car (due to my upgrades, almost always a Mercedes, thank

you kindly). I was now largely financially dependent on my Hermès eBay earnings—I was essentially a small business owner, and these trips were my version of warehouse deliveries. So it was more than a small hitch when the credit card machines were down that one day. I was bleakly contemplating the $10,000 worth of merchandise I'd have to leave behind when the owner, Carmen, suggested I just pay her on my next visit. (Carmen had *employees* who were less reliable than me.)

Initially overwhelmed by relief, I was halfway through my journey home before it really hit me. I grabbed my cell phone.

"Mom, you're not gonna believe what just happened." (Although probably, at this point, nothing about this Hermès saga would have surprised her.) I spilled the entire story, ending with my grand exit in a Mercedes crammed full with over ten Gs of unpaid-for merchandise. While I had her on the phone, I gave her more good news. This month I had become a Platinum PowerSeller on eBay, which meant that I was regularly surpassing the $25,000 mark in monthly sales. Like the supportive mother she was, she oohed and aahed in all the right places, and couldn't wait to get off the phone to tell my dad.

I never even contemplated ditching my Andorra tab. That would be like shooting the goose that laid the orange egg. Besides that, I would never get a decent night's sleep again, regardless of my high-thread-count sheets. Ever since my mother had made me return a stolen half-eaten Heath bar to a supermarket cashier (at the ever-so-impressionable age of four), the idea of stealing anything was psychologically insurmountable. Well, as complexes go, that one has served me well. It went right along with the idea of selling anything inauthentic—that would be the same as theft to me. No knocking over and no knockoffs, and that's final. On a more practical note, inured as I usually was to the lure of Hermès products, every once in a while that Andorra store would yield up something I wanted for myself. (This was partially owed to their franchise status. Remember, they never sent anything back.) They should have had a docent, considering the Hermès museum their back

room was. I was back there, idly touring the exhibits one day, when I found a set of teacups I loved. They were cobalt blue and gold, made of an eggshell porcelain so fine that light passed through it. The design included flourishes of ribbon, in representation of the prize bouquet given the winning horse of the Prix de Diane. Win, place, or show, I knew my Earl Grey would taste better from one of those cups. I had to have them. I piled them on top of the rest of my loot, and Carmen started wrapping everything up for me. She picked up a cup and casually commented that Hermès no longer produced the china pattern Cocarde de Soie (Ribbons of Silk). I now knew enough about Hermès that I perked up my ears at even the mere insinuation of rarity. I ended up leaving that day with enough Cocarde de Soie to host a holiday banquet for Harvard's Equestrian Club. Tempting as that would be, I just couldn't say no when some guy in New Jersey offered me twice what I paid for the entire lot. (I kept the teacups, though.)

Andorra had always seemed too good to be true, and sadly, in the end, it was. Hermès had started its franchised stores at a time when it was unsure of its potential to flourish on a worldwide level. Now, given its unbelievable success in the global market, the company had no need to keep locations like this one open. Quite simply, franchised stores did not earn Hermès the same kind of revenue as corporate-owned locations. One day, about a year after I had first started raiding Andorra's bounty, the other (horse)shoe dropped. I had barely gotten out of my car (parked as usual in the loading zone right in front) when a visibly distraught Carmen came out the front door of the store. She immediately launched into a lengthy tale of woe.

"Michael, it's horrible, you won't believe it, Hermès is forcing me to close down. My husband and I went to Paris last week for a meeting at headquarters. I think I may have mentioned last time I saw you that we haven't been getting our shipments these past couple months?"

I numbly nodded.

"Well, we've made all these appointments to talk to the Hermès powers that be about our situation, and they all keep canceling out on

us at the last minute. We finally get to the boardroom this time, and they tell us that they won't be able to supply us with goods any longer. Of course, I can't exactly sell Hermès product if I can't get any! We considered suing for breach of contract, but what's the point? I'm better off without the hassle."

I was, naturally, quite dismayed at all this. This woman, and her store, had been exceedingly good to me. I also didn't like seeing this side of Hermès. I had always distrusted large corporations, but oddly enough, I hadn't really given too much thought to the possible machinations of Hermès in particular. (Quite probably because I was too damn busy with my own Hermès business . . . FYI, Hermès does have an official Web site now; like a lot of luxury brands, they had just been a little slow on the uptake, not launching one until 2002.) But now it came home to me . . . I was something of a persona non grata to a company like Hermès. They wanted to control their market utterly, that much was now obvious. Up until now, I had cast myself as someone who made Hermès accessible to those who couldn't run out to one of their stores themselves. (Which, with only fifteen or so stores in the U.S., was a lot of people . . . plus, many of the designs that kicked around the older European stores were simply not available in the American locations.) But to Hermès, I was a rogue warrior, reselling to the masses. It was the difference between wearing the cowboy hat or the dark moustache. Still, if I wanted to continue paying the rent, I had to keep a low profile. I wasn't doing anything illegal, certainly, but neither was Carmen, and they shut her down without even a second thought. Well, at least I could take comfort in the knowledge that Carmen wasn't exactly headed to the breadline. Her husband owned several hotels and Peugeot dealerships. The biggest economic impact would be weathered by Carmen's wardrobe budget—she was the store's best customer.

"Michael," she continued, "I don't want those bastards, pardon my vulgarity, buying anything back that I can sell to you at the same price, so today, anything you want, I will sell to you at cost. I would rather see you with it than them."

Wait a minute—at cost? Like, 50-percent-off-the-list-price cost? Okay, maybe I was slightly self-interested, but her offer did take out a little bit of the sting. I tried not to look too happy.

I had hoped for one last nostalgic glimpse of the store in my rear-view mirror, but $30,000 worth of Hermès items obstructed my sight-line. I thought about calling my mom; I knew she'd be all excited about my windfall. I got as far as the first three digits and put the phone back down. I wasn't in a celebratory mood. Despite the significant money I would make from Carmen's generosity, today's experience had been bittersweet at best. It wasn't really the loss of my favored location—after all, there were lots of other Hermès stores I could buy from. No, it was that in some weird way it was the end of an era. It wasn't all a caprice anymore, as it had been when I'd first crossed Andorra's border. Carmen's story made me realize this was business, and business could be ruthless. I also realized something else very important—I'd have to get nicer pajamas.

10

Living It Up Between the Birkin and Barcelona ("Michael's Theme")

I finally decided that I needed to take back my life from eBay. I had become something of an auction addict, and it was making me a little uncomfortable. Remember, work to live, not live to work . . . I kept reminding myself of my mantra. So one evening, after a particularly long stretch of nights at home watching my watchers, I wrenched myself away from the screen. An hour or so later, Michael had left the building. I felt absurdly proud of myself as I rode the elevator down to the lobby. At this point, I had no BlackBerry, so I was truly liberated from the virtual marketplace. I hailed a cab and headed to one of my favorite haunts.

I think I love hanging out at the Hotel Arts because it's like going away on vacation and paying only five bucks for "airfare." Housed in the Port Olympic complex, it was constructed as part of the massive urban overhaul that preceded the 1992 Olympics. I now understood why cities competed so heavily for the athletic invasion of the Games. It was

like hosting a giant party, but instead of just having an empty keg the next day, you netted a whole bag of municipal goodies built off tourist dollars. And Port Olympic is undoubtedly Barcelona's poster child for that whole concept. Impeccably planned and superbly architected, it is a virtually flawless inner-city Mediterranean sanctuary. Admittedly, the main draw is not man-made—it is the two stunning public beaches that run through the area. However, the renovators wisely built on nature's glory, and those clothing-optional beaches are now paralleled by a palm tree–shaded boardwalk that hosts crowds of midday inline skaters and joggers. The revitalization effort also added beach bars, restaurants of every imaginable sort, a gigantic marina, funky sculptures, nightclubs and discos, two hotels, and even a casino. But the crowning glory, in my eyes at least, is the Ritz-Carlton Hotel Arts.

On my first visit there, I had been both surprised and charmed to walk inside a giant luxury hotel and be greeted by the soothing sound of running water and the wafting scent of flowers. I was now used to that slightly disconcerting moment of "outdoors brought indoors" when I entered the hotel and knew it was provided by the rock-embedded waterfalls and arrangements of highly sought-after species of orchids. It gave the whole lobby area a tranquil vibe that subtly relaxed your mind (and, presumably, your grip on your wallet). On a less ethereal note, I also dug the custom-made furniture designed by Jaume Tresserra (a Catalan designer who is clearly a disciple of Ruhlmann's Art Deco genius). But arguably the coolest aspect of the whole place is the outdoor Frank Gehry whale sculpture, literally bigger than most homes. The sculpture's woven metallic curves are a Pink Floyd song brought to life, the color constantly changing under the natural and artificial lights playing over its surface. (Timothy Leary would have had a field day.) It's considered the magnum opus of Gehry's "fish period." But since I had seen it all before, that night I was considerably more interested in the fish I was going to eat.

The Arola restaurant is my personal favorite among the various dining choices in the building. Massive sliding glass walls serve a dual

purpose—to allow a breathtaking view of the manicured gardens that lead down to the omnipresent backdrop of ocean's edge, and to provide a seamless border to alfresco dining. On warm evenings, which are the majority, the walls are left wide open and the candlelit terrace forms a natural extension of the indoor area. I also groove on the high-visibility kitchen—as an aspiring gourmet cook myself, I love seeing how the professionals do it in a critically acclaimed establishment. Additionally appealing to my voyeuristic tendencies is the wine cellar, which is a large glass enclosure in the center of the room, a transparent cube showcasing thousands of bottles. So I was more than a little excited to be back here in Arola, finally at large in the world again, and about to make up for some of the past few weeks of hermetic scarf-mongering.

As the hostess wound us both through the crowded dining room over to my table for one, the mouthwatering smells and fleeting glimpses of succulent entrées awakened my hunger. By the time I was seated, conveniently adjacent to the wine cube, I was more than ready to pore over the eclectic offerings on the *pica pica*. The *pica pica*—a colloquial variation on the word *picar*, meaning "to pick"—is not really a menu. It's a written description of that particular night's surprise mini-dishes, available à la carte for the adventurous diner. Since it gives you more than a dozen courses of small portions of exquisitely wrought food, I'm a *pica pica* patron, that's for sure.

I reveled in the thought of culinary delights on their way and ordered a bottle of 200 Monks Rioja from my gracious waitress. My one big decision of the evening—the wine, of course—thus made, I was free to people-watch. My eyes were drawn to a particularly handsome quintet (three men and two women) seated diagonally from me. They were clearly Catalan, not Spanish, as evidenced by their lighter complexions and more European bone structures. They were also clearly bent on celebrating, although in Spain excuses to celebrate include getting out of bed that morning and the ability to breathe for long periods of time. Then my first parcel of *pica pica* arrived, and I was distracted from my spying. But a few glasses of wine later, I made the journey to

the little boys' room, and almost ran right into one of the trio of men I'd surveyed. He smiled, introduced himself, and initiated conversation, feigning mock surprise over my dining alone. Over the course of our small talk, I was struck by two things: how fun it was to flirt again, and how perfect his English was. Clearly younger than me, Juan exuded kindness, and I wasn't surprised to learn he was a teacher at a private high school in Barcelona. After speaking for only those few minutes, I already wanted to know more about him, and amazingly enough, he also seemed interested in little ol' me. Determined not to blow things by seeming too eager, I coolly dropped a hint about my later club destination, and returned triumphantly to my table to drain my final glass and head out.

Later that night, sipping a fresh drink at Celtes, I made a conscious effort not to babysit the door; I didn't want to overindulge my hopes of seeing my new acquaintance, Juan. Somehow, though, I was still looking right at the entrance when he and his friends strolled in. I saw him casually scan the crowd, and then smile widely when he spotted me by the bar, and at that sight of him the floor under my feet seemed to quake slightly. As I watched him make his way over to where I stood expectantly, I had a premonition that his was one name I would have no problem entering into my address book in nonerasable ink.

A few weeks later, my new romance in full bloom, it took extreme effort to stop mooning around the apartment aimlessly, a blissful grin on my face. But time and eBay stop for no man, and I determinedly tethered myself back to my work. Continents were about to shift pretty drastically there too, but in my love-induced stupor, I heard nary a rumble. I was happily listing and auctioning, not a care in the world. When one day I sold a set of pretty Hermès playing cards, I was simply happy that someone had elected to "Buy It Now" and give them a new home. (Any time I could get an item out of the guest room, I felt I had accomplished something.) Little did I know—like any Old West cowboy who lost his horse in a poker game—my life was destined to be changed forever by that single deck of cards. Of course, I hadn't

thought anything important rested on my restaurant choice a couple of weeks ago, either, so obviously my Spidey-skills were on the fritz.

And then I got an e-mail.

From: CBShelper@yahoo.com
Subject: endofauction: payment details
To: Armoire_Auctions@yahoo.com

Armoire-Auctions: I am the assistant to Carole Bayer Sager and will be making payment and shipping arrangements with you. Please confirm your mailing address for remittance. Cordially, Tori

Oh wow, my first famous client! Carole Bayer Sager! That woman wrote songs for *everyone*. Barbra Streisand, Aretha Franklin, Frank Sinatra, Bette Midler, Whitney Houston, Ray Charles . . . not to mention that she is Burt Bacharach's ex-wife. I called Juan's cell phone immediately, bubbling with excitement.

"Juan, you will never believe this . . . I sold a deck of Hermès cards to CAROLE BAYER SAGER!" Right after the words left my mouth, I wondered whether he would even know who she was. I mean, I wasn't sure how big she was in Spain. Oh, me of little faith.

"In good times, in bad times, I'll be on your side forevermore . . ." Juan immediately began singing "That's What Friends Are For" (one of her eight billion hits), in a surprisingly strong baritone voice, and then he laughed. "Really, Mikey, are you sure it's her?"

"Well, I don't have any reason to think that it isn't her . . . I'm going to e-mail her back right now . . . talk later?"

"Yeah, but keep me posted . . . I always thought I belonged in theater, maybe this could be my big break?" Juan's voice was faux-pleading.

"I'll see what I can do." I laughed. "Get some kind of routine together, just in case."

He hung up, singing his good-byes, and I laughed for a minute after putting down the phone. He was pretty funny, and more than that, I loved that we could be silly and goofy together, even this soon in the

relationship. Smiling and humming to myself, I got down to business and typed a reply. (I reminded myself to play it cool—I didn't want to come off all googly-eyed and starstruck.)

From: "michael" <armoire_auctions@yahoo.com>
To: "Tori" <CBShelper@yahoo.com>

hi tori, the address you received in the end-of-auction notice is correct. i will send the item out by registered mail upon receipt of your payment. thanks for your help, michael

My celebrity excitement rekindled when I got the payment. The check was drawn on a trust at some fancy-pants L.A. law firm, and I was damned sure it would clear. I pretty much forgot about the whole thing once I shipped out the cards. I figured that one e-mail was the last of my brush with fame and fortune. Happily, I was mistaken. About a week later I received the following e-mail:

From: lyricalCarole@yahoo.com
Subject: Hermès Birkins
To: Armoire_Auctions@yahoo.com

Hi Michael, thanks for the cards, they're perfect!!! I've looked at your ebay listings, you have some great things. keep me in mind for any Birkins. I'm always interested (especially croc!). carole

From: "michael" <armoire_auctions@yahoo.com>
To: "CBS" <lyricalCarole@yahoo.com>

hi carole, i'm thrilled that you are pleased. do you want me to start a wish list for you? i do that for lots of my clients. michael

I had no idea what a Birkin was. I promptly fired off an e-mail to Grace, explaining the situation. Then I Googled Birkin. I couldn't for

the life of me understand why Carole Bayer Sager wanted me to find CDs by some French singer and actress named Jane Birkin. (And what the hell did "croc" mean?) Maybe this Birkin chick's CDs were out of print in the States or something. Hey, this could be my new sideline. I figured I'd wait to hear back from Grace before I cleaned out France's Amazon site. I didn't want to jinx things.

From: GraceoftheGarden@yahoo.com
Subject: Hermès Birkin
To: Armoire_Auctions@yahoo.com

Michael, a Birkin is a famous handbag made by Hermès. Croc refers to crocodile (which the most expensive Birkins are made of). Not to worry . . . you won't be getting any Birkins, croc or otherwise. Grace

In and out of the music business before I even got started. Damn. Poor Jane.

From: "Michael" <armoire_auctions@yahoo.com>
To: "GraceoftheGarden" <graceofthegarden@yahoo.com>

grace, what do you mean I won't be getting any? do they not make them anymore??? but I want to get one for CBS. michael

From: GraceoftheGarden@yahoo.com
To: Armoire_Auctions@yahoo.com

Michael, a Birkin is THE celebrity it-bag and literally impossible to get . . . which is EXACTLY why she is asking you to get her one . . . even she can't get one. It's well known amongst a certain class of woman that there is a two or three year waiting list to get a Birkin. The joke goes that there is even a waiting list to get on the waiting list. Grace

p.s. Did I mention that they can cost as much as a car?

From: "michael" <armoire_auctions@yahoo.com>
To: "GraceoftheGarden" <graceofthegarden@yahoo.com>

grace, are we talking Hyundai or Hummer? michael

From: GraceoftheGarden@yahoo.com
To: Armoire_Auctions@yahoo.com

Either. Birkins range in price from about $7000 (the basic leather model) on up to about $100,000 (the Persian Princess model). And trust me, there are Birkin collectors just as there are Hermès scarf collectors. Grace

Man alive, these purses made everything else at Hermès look reasonably priced.

(I flashed back to my first day in the Barcelona store and was grateful I hadn't seen them then—I probably would have run out screaming.) Which did make me wonder . . . where did they keep these bags, anyway? In solitary confinement? I had to at least *see* one . . . I was already way beyond intrigued. Because in the midst of all this e-mailing, my mind had started calculating (I'd always been pretty decent at word problems). If a $225 scarf doubled in price at auction it made me . . . $225. Now, if a $7,000 handbag doubled in price it made me . . . wow. So one Birkin equaled . . . a shitload of scarves. But even with math on my side, a couple of things weren't adding up so nicely. Like, where would I get $100,000 to buy a handbag? How come Carole Bayer Sager couldn't get her own Birkin? Who the hell was in charge of these waiting lists? (In a restaurant you just slipped the maître d' a twenty and got the best table—I wasn't sure that would work here.) I was determined to get to the bottom of this Birkin thing, for my sake, and for Carole's—after all, that's what friends are for.

CHAPTER 11

Birkin Bankruptcy

For all the luck I was having telephoning the Hermès shops looking for a Birkin, I might as well have asked if their refrigerator was running (or if they had Prince Albert in a can). Madrid's salesperson kept it short and sweet; all I got was a "Sorry, no Birkins here." My call to Barcelona marked a milestone, the first time I actually heard those infamous words . . . (drumroll, please) . . . "the waiting list." They said two or three years, but I put my name on it anyway. I wasn't going anywhere. Subsequent calls to Marbella, Lisbon, and Biarritz were the same; I always dead-ended at one of those two responses. (I took some comfort in the knowledge that in two or three years I'd be *rolling* in Birkins.) Undeterred, I planned a summer trip, half business, half pleasure. It was time to go straight to the source—France.

Le Monde d'Hermès at my elbow, I mapped it out. It was an easy trip: first stop Montpellier, then a hop, skip, and a jump to Aix-en-Provence, which is very close to Avignon, which is a short drive to Marseille, which is not far from Cannes, which is only down the road from St. Tropez, which is just across the border from Monte Carlo (technically Monaco, but no one really knows that), which is on the way to Milan (I've always loved Italian food). I printed it all off MapQuest and laid it

next to my already-packed-to-the-hilt jumbo suitcase. I would embark the next morning. I woke up in the middle of the night, disoriented—I had dreamed of a two-year waiting list to cross France's border.

My first destination, the Montpellier Hermès shop, was located in the Place de la Comédie. This centuries-old stone town square, surrounding a fountain, was home to the city's finest boutiques. The saleswoman, who looked barely out of her teens, was sweet, but she scampered off at the first mention of a Birkin. She returned with a young man, presumably her manager, who apologetically offered up a consolation prize—a Kelly bag. I didn't know what a Kelly bag was (more questions for Google and Grace), but I knew it wasn't a Birkin. I pulled out my wish lists and went scarf shopping. Something had to pay for this trip.

Next stop, Aix-en-Provence. I'd read the Peter Mayle books, but I was still unprepared for anything *this* picturesque. It was like a *Twilight Zone* episode where the main character gets trapped in a Paul Cézanne painting . . . and I happened to be the main character. The shop here was really tiny—like, changing-room tiny. I had not spotted a Birkin in the seventeen seconds it took to look around, and my spirits sank. If they had one, it was in their secret Birkin Batcave in the basement. As I'd suspected, it was *"Aucunes Birkins, désolé"* (No Birkins, sorry). With a sigh of resignation, I handed over my wish lists. Scarves, *s'il vous plaît*.

In Avignon, an ancient walled city, the Birkins were as well fortified as the city perimeter. (Scarves, scarves, scarves . . . I was getting sick of scarves.) Down but not out, I bravely soldiered on to Marseille, second in population only to Paris. Shiploads of cargo arrived daily in this massive port city; surely *some* barge held a Birkin. I walked into their Hermès store full of vim and vigor. This store visit marked another milestone: the first time I left a store angry. I asked a kind-looking older saleswoman for help immediately after I entered the store. Upon hearing the word "Birkin," another saleswoman came (or, more accurately, stormed) over. This woman was not so kind looking—in fact, Leona Helmsley sprang to mind. My original saleswoman immediately evacuated (no dummy, she). When I repeated my request to this presumably self-appointed

guardian of the Birkingdom, her expression became so suspicious and snide I wondered if I'd accidentally said "Fendi Baguette," not "Birkin."

"Sir, that waiting list is closed." She managed to fit a lot of loathing into six words. What I couldn't figure out is why she hated me so much. I mean, I was in Hermès, right? It wasn't as if I'd ordered a Big Mac at Burger King. They did sell Birkins, after all, didn't they? (I was beginning to wonder . . . maybe a Birkin was like a phoenix or a unicorn . . . you heard about them, but you never saw one.) Imaginary bag or not, I didn't deserve this kind of treatment asking for an Hermès handbag at an Hermès store. After days of canvassing the French countryside, I hadn't come this far to be condescended to by a homely woman in a company-issue scarf.

"What do you mean the waiting list is closed? It's a *waiting list.* So I can't *wait*? You're telling me I can't *wait*?! This isn't a restaurant, it's not like you're gonna stop serving. I am in Hermès, right? You do make something called the Birkin, right? Oh, wait a minute, I get it . . . you *make* them, you just don't *sell* them . . . that makes perfect sense. Hey, I have an idea, why don't you charge people to get on the waiting list? Oh that's right, the waiting list is closed." I let out a full month's worth of fruitless-Birkin-hunting frustration on this miserable woman. I didn't regret it, especially when all the other employees looked ready to circle around and applaud.

"Sir, if you don't stop yelling I will be forced to ask you to leave." Her tone was smugly triumphant. I could tell she loved nothing more than forcing her customers out the door.

"First off, I wasn't yelling, and I don't appreciate your insinuation that I was. Second of all, I was working nicely with another saleswoman before you decided to storm the beaches at Normandy and drive her off . . . may I please be excused to talk with her about some scarves I'm interested in? Or do you guys not have *scarves*, either?" My voice dripped with sarcasm. At my last sally about the scarves, she turned on her heel and marched off. My original saleswoman, you ask? Well, she couldn't get me a Birkin either, but she treated me like a hero for the rest of the afternoon.

Ten days later, in Milan, I wasn't experiencing anything that re-sembled frustration. No, I hadn't fulfilled my Birkin destiny—not in

St. Tropez, not in Cannes, not in Monte Carlo. But as I sat in Boeucc, a restaurant more than three hundred years old, idly sipping my Amarone and nibbling on my fettuccine with truffles, it was impossible to be unhappy. Let's be honest, touring the south of France wasn't exactly torturous, even if you couldn't find the handbag you wanted. I decided I'd make one last-ditch effort at the local Hermès store the next day, but held no great hopes. I had to revise my original percentages: for my trip to be viewed as a rousing success, I should have projected 75 percent pleasure, 25 percent business. This was owing to a distinct lack of Birkins in their native France—someone should put them on the endangered list, and quick, before they had to be mated in captivity. On the bright side, the scarf population was flourishing; they were a scrappy little species. (At least I knew my wish-list clients would be pleased with my vacation—my trunk was full of scarves.) But, however content I was at the moment, some small part of me couldn't stop obsessing over my failure. Was Grace right—was I destined to live Birkinless forever? I pondered purses—and possible plans—as I savored my *panna cotta*.

What happened next reminded me of the Christmas the year I was eight. I had become suspicious that Santa wasn't some guy in a red suit (come on, that's a lot of presents to fit in a sleigh). My parents took drastic measures. On Christmas Eve, my father, against my mother's better judgment, actually climbed onto our roof to make enough noise to reconvince an eight-year-old of the reality of Saint Nick. It was that feeling—the exact feeling I had lying in my bed, hearing reindeer scramble on the eaves—that surged through me in Milan that night. It had appeared out of thin air—on the arm of an elegant woman who walked by my table—a Birkin bag (I recognized it from photographs). I immediately believed in them again. I wondered—Who *was* this woman? What did she know that I didn't? Did she actually wait two years for a handbag? And on the heels of these questions came a solution so simple I couldn't believe I hadn't thought of it already. I'd ask Santa for one—I bet *he* didn't have to bother with waiting lists.

Anatomy of a B*irk*n

plaqué

poignées

ponTeT

ToureT

TireT

Lock

sangles

cLocheTTe

cLou (4)

InTerior

Large zippered
pockeT

open
pockeT

12

Orange You Glad You Asked?

I returned from vacation late on Saturday night, to an in-box crammed full of e-mails. I had lots of scarves to ship, and I'd be making more than one trip to the *correos* on Monday. Wait till all those Hermès-happy people get a load of my new listings. I also had a blinking answering machine light, with a message from Juan, reminding me about our date for tomorrow. He dropped a bit of a bomb on the message: instead of our typical Sunday brunch together, it was to be a Sunday lunch at his parents' home in a suburb of Barcelona. Oh boy, meeting the parents. Big step, although it did seem a natural thing, given our accelerated courting—I had seen Juan almost every day since we had met, other than when I had been out of town. So even though I really shouldn't be doing anything tomorrow but starting the process of unloading my scarf merchandise, I wasn't going to let my Birkin aspirations get in the way of my burgeoning romance. Plus, I was eager to tell him about my . . . well . . . failure, I guess. But that's okay, I knew he was a good listener. It already seemed as if I had known him forever.

I still did feel somewhat nervous, though, waiting next to Juan outside his parents' apartment door, after he had rung the bell. How could

I charm them when neither of them spoke a word of English? What if they didn't like me because I didn't speak their language? What if they just didn't like me, period? I knew how important they were to Juan. He must have seen some of these anxious thoughts on my face, because he managed to give my hand a reassuring squeeze before the door swung open. I knew *he* liked me, at least for now.

I couldn't have been sillier, in retrospect. Juan's parents were the embodiment of hospitality, and somehow their personality came crashing right through that language barrier between us. His dad, Juan Sr., was clearly the comedian in the family, and managed to tell his stories and make his little asides in such a way that between his gestures and Juan's quick translations, I was laughing through most of the meal. Carmen, his mom, was the epitome of a gentle soul, always shaking a smiling head at her outgoing husband. She was a gracious and attentive hostess, and an unbelievable cook in the bargain. We ate like kings, starting with native cheeses served with Spanish ham, or *jamón*. The expensive *jamón* Carmen served was made from black pigs that are raised on a diet of only acorns, which results in a particularly sweet and nutty-flavored meat. Then we had white asparagus with homemade *alioli* and baby artichokes—and this wasn't even the main course. For that, Carmen had made her special paella, called *mar y montana*, or "the sea and the mountains." This was made with rabbit, wild mushrooms, tiny clams, shrimp, langoustines, and assorted vegetables. Dessert was fresh sliced pineapple and homemade *coca*—a sweet flatbread topped with toasted pine nuts. All these delicious courses were accompanied by Juan Sr.'s one culinary accomplishment: *cava sangria*. He took a bottle of the best local champagne, added apples, oranges, lemons, and peaches, and more than a splash of Grand Marnier. After eating all that food and drinking my share of the sangria, I was more than relaxed at the end of the meal—I was nearly comatose. Apparently, in Juan's family, you had Thanksgiving dinner every Sunday afternoon, which seemed like a great idea to me. But we had a train to catch back to the city, so instead of some sleepy

sofa-time, I got hugged and kissed and told to come back soon, and we made our exit. As we headed across the square in front of their apartment building, Juan suddenly stopped, turned around, and pulled my sleeve to do the same. When I did, I saw why we had paused—both his parents stood on their apartment balcony. We waved, they waved back, and Juan said, "They always watch me leave, so I wave to make them happy." Although he seemed almost embarrassed to admit this, I couldn't think of anything I had seen him do that had made me like him more. And I found out something else that day too—trains are great for napping.

My romance on track, Monday morning I was back in the thick of it, first dealing with Grace's correspondence.

From: GraceoftheGarden@yahoo.com
Subject: Welcome home/Your trip
To: Armoire_Auctions@yahoo.com

Michael, I hope your trip was successful. So, is your backseat full of Birkins? Teehee.

Any new scarf treasures? Oppressively hot here in Manhattan . . . I may be heading off to Montauk later in the week. Grace

Yeah, teehee.

From: "Michael" <armoire_auctions@yahoo.com>
To: "GraceoftheGarden" <graceofthegarden@yahoo.com>

grace, trip was a major success on a culinary level (haha), however a total birkin bust, although I did manage to actually see one at a restaurant (but the woman who owned it had no interest in selling). tons of great new scarves which I'll list tomorrow on five day auction (to end on sunday). mt

From: GraceoftheGarden@yahoo.com

To: Armoire_Auctions@yahoo.com

Michael, Did you at least get on some waiting lists? They say good bags come to those who wait! Grace

From: "Michael" <armoire_auctions@yahoo.com>

To: "GraceoftheGarden" <graceofthegarden@yahoo.com>

I'm on waiting lists all over the south of france, except for Marseille (their waiting list is closed, remind me to tell you that story later.) mt

Grace and I had decided to make our relationship unique. When I said I'd "tell" her the Marseille story later, I actually meant that I'd e-mail her. We had agreed to only communicate by e-mail or fax. No phone time. No face time. I thought it odd when Grace first suggested it, but now I totally understood. It was like having a pen pal, only better, because it was moments between "letters," not months.

From: GraceoftheGarden@yahoo.com

To: Armoire_Auctions@yahoo.com

Michael, Lots of "chatter" on the boards about Carnaval de Venise scarf (especially in the black colorway). Suggest you add this to your wish-lists . . . could be the next Kachinas. Grace

"The boards" referred to three or four Yahoo chat rooms, all devoted entirely to Hermès scarves (or HS, as those in the know called them). Grace, obviously, was one of their frequent visitors/contributors, and anytime she passed on a tip from them, I got out my scarf-shopping sneakers, and fast. (If you were dedicated enough to sit around and cyber-chat about rare "HS" all day, you were definitely dedicated enough to spend the money on them.)

From: "Michael" <armoire_auctions@yahoo.com>
To: "GraceoftheGarden" <graceofthegarden@yahoo.com>

Thanks for the tip . . . a-shopping I will go! mt

I learned from experience that calling around didn't cut it when it came to older scarf designs. It was inevitable—I'd call, and get some salesperson Hermès had just hired about three days ago, who had only *skimmed* the scarf chapter in the employee handbook. But if I went there in person, I could talk to the "scarf ambassador." (Yes, I think that's really what they are called, and every Hermès has one.) Now, the "scarf ambassador" knows not only what scarves are *in* the glass case at the front of the store, but also what scarves are *under* the display, hidden in the wooden drawers. Generally, I was after the latter—that's where the older designs were stashed.

Armed with this breaking news from Grace, I planned a weekend outing to Madrid. (I'd already seen to it that Barcelona's drawers were so empty they rattled.) That Saturday morning I walked into Hermès Madrid and was greeted by name. I whipped out my wish lists.

I immediately hit pay dirt on the Carnaval de Venise—the "ambassador" said she was positive they had it in several colors. That wasn't all she had either, and soon there were ten or so primo scarves stacked by the register. Emboldened by my success, and my VIP status at the store, I went for it.

"This is great, thanks so much, I'll take all these . . . Oh, and if I could, a scarf book to go with each . . . Yes, one in each of the boxes is fine . . . oh . . . and one more thing . . . do you have a Birkin?" I tried to sound casual.

"Let me look." With that she disappeared into the back. I couldn't believe it. This was the first time someone didn't immediately say no or bring up the waiting list. Could it really be? I concentrated on not staring at the door marked EMPLOYEES ONLY. But then, at the edge of my peripheral vision, came a flash of orange. The saleswoman had reemerged, and was barely visible behind the enormous, traffic-

cone-colored box in her arms. It looked about two feet square, and my mouth went dry at the thought of what it contained. She gestured me over to join her at one of the many little island counters every Hermès store has.

"Mr. Tonello, I have one if you are interested. It's an anthracite 35cm crocodile Birkin. Shall we take a look at it?" Um, yes. I nodded. I didn't trust myself to speak.

She opened a drawer in the counter, and donned a pair of spotless white cotton gloves. She removed the lid, and placed it gingerly beside the box. Under the lid were four layers of white tissue, tissue so stiff it looked starched (I'd later learn Hermès had their tissue custom-made, to ensure that it was acid-free). She carefully negotiated the barriers of white, draping them in such a manner that each sheet lay perfectly suspended over the edge of a corresponding cardboard wall—north, south, east, west. Then, with utmost care (like picking up a newborn from a bassinet), she lifted out the Birkin and placed it in front of my wondering eyes. It was still hidden, though, snug inside a dun-colored dustcover. She unlaced the drawstring, and peeled back the cloth. (I almost expected them to pipe in some burlesque music.) Once she had unveiled it, I couldn't stop gawking, although I don't think I was that obvious. The charcoal-gray (I guess that's what "anthracite" meant) crocodile bag gleamed richly. She kept talking.

"As you can see, the hardware is palladium. I think this juxtaposes nicely with the warmer-looking charcoal." With that, she picked up the bag and stepped out from behind the case. She crossed in front of me to use the mirror on the opposing wall. Holding the bag down at her side, she pivoted back and forth slowly in her four-inch heels, so that

the bag swayed slightly by her knee. Her expression, visible in the mirror, was that of someone sharing a delightful secret. After a moment of this, she extended her arm, the bag's handles resting gently atop her two fingers—clearly offering me a chance to hold it myself. My initial thought was how *light* it was—I guess they didn't charge by the pound. My second thought was whatever this purse cost, it was going home with me.

"I'll take it."

Thankfully, they didn't make me sign away my soul (at this point, I probably would have). They did, however, produce a document from the Department of Fish and Wildlife, a kind of "passport" for the transport of exotic leather (I found out crocodiles are under some sort of protective measure—my thought was it couldn't be too protective if they ended up as handbags all the time). I also, naturally, had to sign a credit card slip, which I was too scared to look at . . . I had averted my eyes and put it in my wallet to contemplate later. The bag itself had been priced at a reasonable $18,000, then you added in the scarves . . . oh boy.

Twenty minutes later, I was walking down the street, sipping my complimentary bottle of Evian, a ludicrously large shopping bag hanging from my hand. What had happened in there? I wanted to tell everyone I knew about my Birkin victory—but I couldn't figure what I would say when they asked me how I had done it. I had no goddamn clue. Had I performed a secret handshake without realizing it? I looked down at my clothes—same stuff I always wore. I had a nice tan from France, but a Birkin seemed like an awfully big present for being a little sun-kissed. And on top of all this, another mystery—how come a Birkin's dustcover wasn't Hermès orange?

1 3

The Formula

A week later I was en route to Paris, trying to think like Nancy Drew, desperate to solve the mystery of the Madrid Birkin. I was playing Pony Express, Air France–style, hand-delivering the anthracite croc bag to Carole Bayer Sager at the Hotel Ritz. Upon receiving my "got one!" e-mail, she immediately responded with a very generous offer (through her assistant, of course) that netted me a tidy profit of almost $5,000.

The question remained: what purse potion had I used to work such magic in Madrid? After all, I needed the recipe for that elixir in order to conjure more Birkins. Maybe I could land a security job at Hermès Madrid—that way I could hunt for the clues to my success in the surveillance tapes from that fateful Saturday. Or how about arranging for a covert rendezvous with that saleswoman in some shady bar. I could wear a trench coat and dark glasses, and our password would be "crocodile." Or what if I staked out the store from across the street, and did exit interviews with everyone who left with a Birkin? Okay, so I wasn't coming up with the most realistic scenarios—I guess you shouldn't try to channel your childhood sleuth hero at 25,000 feet.

At first I felt conspicuous entering the hotel lobby with a giant (orange) shopping bag. Then I realized: at the Ritz Paris, *my* Hermès bag was just one of countless dozens that revolved through the seemingly featherlight mahogany-and-glass door each and every day. Carole was staying in the Coco Chanel suite and had instructed the front desk to send me right up. She opened the door with a big smile, the warmth of her welcome catching me slightly off guard. You'd think she'd known me for a dozen years, rather than through a dozen e-mails. But she seemed nothing if not sincere—the first word I would have used to describe her was "kind." I felt immediately at ease with her. I had agonized over what to wear, but needn't have; she was dressed casually in a white cotton blouse and jeans, although both the sheen of the cotton in her shirt and the tailor-made fit of her jeans hinted at money. (The huge pink diamond on her hand hinted at nothing.) Once I had unearthed the bag from its box, and handed it to her, Carole immediately stepped over to the nearest Tiffany-shaded lamp to inspect the skin. She examined the size and symmetry of the crocodile scales, and finally smiled broadly, praising both the color and overall quality of the bag. I got the feeling this wasn't her first Birkin, that's for sure.

The suite itself was what you would expect from the Coco Chanel suite at the Ritz Paris . . . At $4,500 a night, I knew it wouldn't be Motel 6. The sitting room I was in was roughly the size of an Olympic swimming pool. However, it had the intimacy of a Renaissance tearoom and was decorated with the exquisite taste of a baroness. It was full of authentic Louis antiques, their dark carved wood covered in sumptuous, down-filled pillows. The atmosphere of luxury was reinforced by the richness of the heavy grosgrain cloth in the giant draperies that framed the view of the Place Vendôme. However, what struck me most was the oh-so-elegant touch of silver trays piled high with red strawberries. I waited, but the whole time I was there, as hospitable as she was, Carole never offered to feed me one.

I returned to the lobby without a bag of any sort. I had handed over that hard-won handbag without even a twinge of loss. Despite my

lingering questions about how I would repeat the feat of buying one, I had newfound confidence in the ease of selling one. After my afternoon sojourn in Coco's old stomping grounds, I wasn't quite ready to leave the opulence of the Ritz. I decided to celebrate my Carole coup with a glass of Champagne in Bar Hemingway. After a moment spent studying the writer's artifacts and photos that were framed on the back wall of the tiny bar, I settled in on one of the tall stools. I realized it wasn't quite right to order Champagne in this place (I don't think old Ernest would have approved) and ordered a sidecar instead. Since my mom was the best-read person I knew, it was only appropriate that I call her from this literary landmark.

"Mom, hi . . . I'm at Bar Hemingway, at the Ritz. Yup, I'm already in Paris. Just brought Carole her bag . . . Oh my God, the suite was amazing . . . and she's the nicest person on the planet . . ." I couldn't get my story out fast enough, but, excited as I was, I tried to keep my voice discreet. In this bar, you could be sitting next to *anyone*—I didn't want to give some Parisian Liz Smith her scoop of the week. (I knew if *I* were a gossip columnist, I'd be sure to hit the Hemingway on my way home.) I wasn't about to lose my best (and only) Birkin client.

"What did she say? Did she like the bag? What was the suite like?" My mom was all questions, so I dished her all the details, right down to the strawberries I didn't get to eat. But there was something else on my mind.

"You know, it's funny, I still am not sure how I actually *got* the bag in the first place." I laughed a little as I said it, but I think Mom heard the frustration I couldn't help feeling.

"Michael, give it time and I'm sure it will come to you. Just think it over, think about every detail, and you'll stumble over it eventually." Her voice was calm, as always, but instead of soothing me as it usually did, for some reason I got a little testy.

"Mom, listen, I walked into the store like I always do. I was greeted by name, sure, that was new, but I don't think they sell you a Birkin because they recognize you. If so, Barcelona would have handed it over

a *lonnnng* time ago. I walked in, I handed them my wish . . . lists . . ." I stopped. I really hoped my mother hadn't noticed how small my voice had gone, or, if so, that she would blame it on the overseas connection. Unfortunately, this was the age of the cell phone, and she wasn't fooled for a second. (She also, having given birth to me, knew me better than anyone in the world. I hate to sound cliché, but come on, this was my mother.)

"Michael, what is it? Something wrong? Or did you think of something with the bags?" I could hear her trying not to sound too smug. I knew that she could see my mental lightbulb through the phone somehow.

"Nothing's wrong, Mom . . . yeah, I might have figured it out. I'll let you know tomorrow. Bye, love you . . . Bye." It was one of those moments when putting it into words might make it sound ridiculous. (Although really, what about this whole Birkin thing wasn't ridiculous?) The simple fact was, this entire time I'd been thinking about the ingredients, and all the ingredients were *exactly* the same. Every time I went to Hermès, there were wish lists, and scarf ambassadors, and my plea for a Birkin. I *knew* I shouldn't have cut all those chemistry classes in tenth grade to smoke in the parking lot. Because I'd almost forgotten that in chemistry, the order in which you add the ingredients to the formula is as important as the ingredients themselves.

14

Smoke and Mirrors

The following morning I awoke bright-eyed, bushy-tailed, and bursting to buy a Birkin. I decided that the Hermès flagship store at 24 Rue du Faubourg Saint-Honoré was not the right place to try out my Birkin-buying hypothesis for the first time. That six-story building housed not only two floors of Hermès products, but also corporate offices, design workshops, and a private museum. At this point in my purse game, I found the place a teeny bit intimidating. I decided to start small (at least square-footage-wise): I'd go to the Hermès store on Avenue George-V. It would be a perfect staging area for my revised Birkin-buying script.

As I cabbed over, I tried to find the holes in my theory. Last night, the sidecar swimming through my veins, the breakthrough moment I'd had while chatting with Mom had been flawless—inarguable in its logic. Of course, it had also seemed like a good idea to drunk-dial Juan at one in the morning, even though he had to teach English to high schoolers at some ungodly hour (thankfully, he hadn't minded, or at least pretended not to). So, I supposed it was possible that my judgment had been a wee bit skewed in other ways as well. Minutes before trying out my new plan, I had doubts—did all of my agonizing and analyzing *really* distill into a conclusion this banal? Because the "formula," as it were, was simply

this: *first* the wish lists, *then* the Birkin. I'd been going about it all wrong. Trying to get an Hermès employee to sell you a Birkin before dropping a bundle on other things was like trying to sleep with your prom date before you'd even complimented her hair. That's how I'd nailed it in Madrid . . . I'd gone scarf shopping first. Once that Hermès employee saw I was already dropping well over a grand, she was more than happy to put a Birkin right on top of that pile. You needed an initiation fee, a qualifying purchase. (This is what I was hoping, anyway. I was about to see how my scientific stratagem held up to experimentation.)

When the cab pulled up in front of Hermès, I wiped my sweaty palms on my Bottega Veneta jeans, swallowed the knot of anxiety in my throat, and strolled through that door like I owned the place—and every Birkin in it.

A salesman smelled money and immediately approached me.

"Good morning. I have a rather long list of scarves I'm looking for, and perhaps you can make this easier for me," I said as I handed him my wish lists.

"Certainly," he said, his manner immediately obsequious, no doubt his natural response to the length of the list. "Most of these scarves are older issues, I'll have to look in the back."

I refrained from saying "Surprise, surprise." My MO in stores was to appear as "fish out of water" as possible. I wanted everyone to assume I was on a mission for my mom. Part of that whole low-profile thing. I was standing there, trying to look uncomfortable yet arrogant, when my salesman returned bearing a tray full of scarves. As he touched each scarf, he indicated its position on the wish list. He had about seven or eight of the designs I was after. I hoped it would be enough. (The precise amount I needed to "qualify" was, of course, still a gray area.)

"Okay, great, perfect . . . I'll take all of them . . . [here goes nothing] . . . and do you have any Birkins?"

"Sir, I'll have to go check. I won't be a moment."

Surprise, surprise—again. Did these guys work from a script or what? I just hoped there wasn't going to be a plot twist at the end. All

I wanted was a sequel to Madrid. When he returned bearing a large orange box, I knew all my hopes had been answered. And formula or no, I was loving this movie. He performed the whole grand show I had seen a week or so ago (no white gloves, though—those were just for croc bags). My bag this time was a 30cm blue jean leather Birkin. I didn't care if it was a six-inch rainbow plastic Birkin—I wanted to buy it and get the hell out of there before some kind of double-dipping alarm went off in the store. And that's exactly what I did.

Safely back at the hotel room, I put the bag on the bedside table and waited for it to do something. Surely these bags had some kind of magical powers. I knew now that *I* did—today, I was the Harry Potter of handbags. I had the ability to perform a trick that was much better than pulling rabbits out of hats—I knew how to pull Birkins out of Hermès. (I mean, we all know how rabbits are—you never had to wait two years to get more of them. More like two minutes.) It was like any other sleight of hand—once you knew how it was performed, you couldn't remember why it had mystified you in the first place. And simple as "the formula" was, there sure were a lot of people on "the waiting list," languishing away quietly, tortured by their unfulfilled quest for pricey leather purses. Well, languish no more, people— help was on the way. I couldn't wait to start my new life as an Hermès Houdini—I was going to make Birkins appear all over the world.

1 5

Road Trip Redux

I decided to "redo" the south of France trip. I was hoping, just this once, that the second time would be the charm. I was still nervous about whether I would be able to keep pulling off this Birkin-buying thing. It was so absurd, really—worrying about whether you could buy a purse. But, I should confess, it wasn't just the money I was anxious about . . . I definitely dug the idea of beating Hermès at its own game. Maybe it was silly, but I found it exciting to think I had knowledge that had eluded even the wealthiest people in the world. I had never equated money directly with power, but if you are over ten years old, you can sense that there is a connection. And any human who could pay $20,000 for a purse was in the ninety-ninth percentile of income, no doubt. An Hermès customer, at least a repeat one, was someone who rarely looked at price tags, or worried about bills, or thought about money at all, really. But for all that, Hermès still had their "waiting list." You almost had to respect the company for its sheer balls: their customer base was not a demographic that was accustomed to waiting. But they waited for Birkins. And I didn't—or so I hoped.

I dug through an armoire drawer and fished out the MapQuest route from my last trip. I threw together some outfits and packed up the suitcase. Now that I finally had a laptop, I could keep an eye on my eBay auctions . . . this trip was going to be purely business (except, perhaps, for the cuisine). Three hours later, I walked into the Hermès Montpellier shop. Thirty minutes later, I walked out with a Birkin ($7,500). An hour later, I walked into Aix-en-Provence Hermès. Thirty minutes later, I walked out with a Birkin ($7,500). One hour after *that*, I walked into Hermès Avignon. Thirty minutes later, I walked out with a Birkin ($7,500). On my way out of that third store, I couldn't help but do a little gleeful math. If most people wait two years for a Birkin, and I can get one in about a half hour, that meant I'd trimmed the wait time by about 17,519 hours (and a half). Then my mind, without a hint of glee, coughed up some other inarguable figures. Between my three credit cards, each with a $10,000 limit, I had about $5,000 worth of credit still available. In one day, I had maxed out two credit cards (and half of another).

I was almost out of credit and almost out of daylight (and completely out of energy). I checked into a hotel. As soon as I was alone in the hotel room, just me and the Birkins, I booted up my computer. I had the supply, and now I just needed to create the demand. I fired off an e-mail to everyone in my Hermès wish-list Rolodex:

From: Armoire_Auctions @yahoo.com
Subject: BIRKIN AVAILABLE
To: "everyone"@my-yahoo-address-book.com

Hi everyone, AVAILABLE TODAY:

BIRKIN 35CM, TOGO LEATHER, BLACK WITH GOLD HARDWARE. BIRKIN 30CM, TOGO LEATHER, VERT ANIS GREEN, SILVER "PALLADIUM" HARDWARE. BIRKIN 35CM, TOGO LEATHER, ROUGE VIF WITH GOLD HARDWARE.

ALL THREE BAGS ARE BRAND-NEW, UNUSED AND TOTALLY

STORE-FRESH. GUARANTEED AUTHENTIC. AVAILABLE ON A
FIRST COME, FIRST SERVED BASIS.

CALL OR EMAIL ME.

All the best,

michael

I looked at the trio of Birkins to relay the exciting news about their
impending adoptions, but they weren't acting so enthusiastic, so I called
my mom to give her the good news.

"Hey, Mom, it's me. Just wanted to let you know I solved the mys-
tery about buying these bags."

"Oh, good, I knew you would. So you're home now?"

"Um, actually, I'm in Provence, but I'm sitting here looking at the
three purses I just bought today. Turns out if I spend a lot of money
first, it's a lot easier to get the bags."

"Well, that's great, sweetie . . . I can't talk right now, though, your
father and I have a tee time in about six minutes. I'll catch up with you
later and you can tell me the whole story . . . Love you . . . Bye."

I tried to call Juan and tell *him* all about it, but he wasn't home. I
sat there, deflated. All pursed up and nowhere to go. I guess it isn't that
much fun to be Houdini unless you have a lovely assistant at your side,
or at least a rabbit to talk to. But, realistically, I knew I should be con-
centrating on banking, not bragging. Within ten minutes of hanging up
the phone, I had transferred $10,000 from my bank account to pay off
a MasterCard. I could get a couple more Birkins now—crisis averted.
The credit thing was going to be an issue, though, no question. Well,
I'd figure something out. Now, it was finally time to celebrate, not mull
over credit limits. But no sooner than I was heading out the door for a
drink and a bite to eat I received a couple of e-mails. One Birkin sold!
The second e-mail was from Grace.

From: "GraceoftheGarden" <graceofthegarden@yahoo.com>
To: "Michael" <armoire_auctions@yahoo.com>

Hi Michael, wow! You are really on a roll. What's your secret, who are you sleeping with? Teehee. More importantly, where have you been (other than Hermès, I mean)? Grace

From: "Michael" <armoire_auctions@yahoo.com>
To: "GraceoftheGarden" <graceofthegarden@yahoo.com>

grace, sorry, i've been a little delinquent in filling you in. i've been on somewhat of a Birkin buying binge. i figured out a new shopping method, i call it "the formula" (it doesn't involve sleeping with anyone) and so far i'm 3 for 3 today. (3 Hermès shops, 3 birkins). I figured out if I pile up about $1000 in merchandise, then pop the Birkin question, they're happy to sell me one. MUCH more on all of this later. i'm starving and was just about to head out to dinner.

michael

p.s. i'm in aix-en-provence heading for cannes tomorrow . . . then on to st. tropez and monte carlo, will write more from there. mt

That night, when I returned from a delicious dinner at Le Clos de la Violette (lamb with garlic cream and a half bottle of Saint-Emilion), I was ready for a good night's sleep. I loved leaving my windows wide open when I stayed in Provence, so that lavender-scented air would waft through my room—and my dreams—all night long. But I couldn't resist checking my e-mail one last time. Bingo—Birkin #2 had a buyer. I snuggled down under the duvet. Sweet dreams indeed, one of which came true . . . when I checked my e-mails in the morning, the last of the purses had sold.

There were six little Birkins, all in a row, snug in the trunk of my car as I headed back to Barcelona a few days later. There was also about

$5 of spending limit left on each of my credit cards. If I played my cards right, I would have plenty of money for food and fuel on the ride back. Okay, so this was going to be an issue. I needed to start my creative juices flowing about this conundrum of cost versus credit limit, that's for sure. Because Birkins weren't about to get any cheaper, I knew there was only one solution . . . more credit for *moi*. I wondered—could you take out Hermès handbag equity loans?

16

How Do I Buy These? ...
Let Me Count the Ways ...

Okay, so it took me a really short time to get the Birkins, at least compared with the average bear, but it took an even shorter time to sell them. All six went bye-bye-Birkin in a matter of hours to various private clients, netting over $20,000 in the process. I didn't even need to auction, because sending those bulk e-mails to previous Hermès eBay customers worked like a charm. This venture was clearly going to be all about my capital. Thanking my lucky stars that I had cleaned up my credit many moons ago, I immediately started filling out credit card applications as a hobby. I also tried to think of ways I could get Birkins without leaving the comfort of my home. I did dearly love Barcelona and my cozy pad, but it was mostly a business issue. The less money I spent to get the Birkins, the better my bottom line would be. This kind of work was pretty much all about controlling the expenses, and since I *was* about 90 percent of the expenses, it made sense to explore other ways of buying. One thing I had going for me: I was damn sure that I didn't need to pull together an advertising budget. Thanks, Hermès, you guys really had my back on this one.

I knew the stores didn't take credit cards over the phone (charge-sends), but one store employee had mentioned the possibility of a bank wire transfer. Allowing transfers in lieu of charge-sends served two purposes. Besides preventing some pickpocket from ordering off some poor schmuck's stolen cards, it also eliminated the chance of someone doing a chargeback after receiving thousands of dollars of merchandise. It was logical fraud protection on their part, given the price points involved. This was fine by me, since I had no intention of committing fraud of any kind. I just needed more stuff to sell—I would have paid in crocks of cheese if that was their preferred currency.

I pulled out *Le Monde d'Hermès* and looked first at the French stores, trying to find one that I hadn't been to in the last few weeks. Deauville popped out at me for a couple of reasons. First, I knew it was a rich seaside town, along the lines of Newport, Rhode Island, or Carmel-by-the-Sea, California, so the Birkins-per-capita ratio could be good. Second, it was such a pain to get to, about two hours outside of Paris, that the likelihood of me going there in the flesh was pretty slim, so I had nothing to lose. My main concern now was about using the formula over the phone. I wasn't sure how to go about it, exactly, especially with my beginning Berlitz French language skills. But when I called and asked for an English-speaking salesperson, I was informed by the woman who answered that she knew a "leetle English if you speak slow, sir, please." My wish list was too daunting, apparently, given our language issues, and she requested that I fax it instead. Even though I didn't have a fax machine, I quickly agreed. What the hell, I had all that advertising budget money free, I might as well up my technology spending. I ran out, bought a nice machine, and couldn't unpack and set it up fast enough. Hey, if this fax method worked, I might be telecommuting all the time. My half-hermit heart hammered in my chest at the very idea. I faxed the list, which included the usual batch of scarves, a Ulysse notebook thrown in for good measure, and at the very bottom, a Birkin. I hoped it went without saying that I would take any flavor of Birkin.

The fax machine had barely stopped making noises when the phone rang. It was my saleswoman. Fingers crossed.

"Mr. Tonello, this ees Dominique, from Hermès. We have everything you wanted, sir. The Birkin is a 35cm blue jean with palladium lock. Ees that okay?" That little accent still, but her English was markedly better now that I was spending a boatload.

"Yes, yes, that will be fine, thank you for all your trouble." I was elated. Formula by fax—this was beyond amazing.

"No, no . . . thank *you*, sir. And so when can we expect you to be by the store, Mr. Tonello?"

Uh-oh. This was the only hurdle left to handbag hog heaven.

"Well, actually, Dominique, I won't be able to come in to pick them up. I wish to have the items shipped to my home here in Barcelona." Authority with just the right amount of affability, or so I hoped.

"Sir, Hermès does not do charge ships, I am sorry." Dominique sounded slightly horrified I would even ask.

"No, no, I am sorry, of course not . . . I meant to say, I can arrange a bank wire transfer . . . is that an acceptable sort of payment?" Improvising as I went along.

"Well, yes. That would be acceptable." Her voice had gone from superfreeze to warm and cozy in world-record time. We got down to business and sealed the deal to our mutual satisfaction. Another Birkin was coming my way—and oh yeah, some scarves and a Ulysse—items that I had begun to think of as the Birkin bait.

So that was easy. Expensive, of course, but easy. I was *very* glad I had bought the fax machine, and as it turned out, it was a savvy move indeed. Because it ended up that Dominique and I would have a long, glorious relationship of the purse-based sort. Over the next two years, Hermès via Deauville via Dominique would provide me with more than twenty Birkins, all ordered over the phone. To this day, I've never crossed its threshold, but I traveled via phone line so often it remains one of my very favorite Hermès stores.

When the blue jean Birkin arrived, I pondered what to do with it. I knew for sure that I could e-mail everyone in my Hermès inner circle with the delectable details and watch as they all fell over each other like bridesmaids after the bouquet. The sales method I had been using *did* work without fail. But an entrepreneur has to be open to risk and willing to embrace change, or at least that's what I had read in *Business for Dummies*. So, I decided to put it up on eBay instead, with a "Buy It Now" for considerably more than I had been getting. I hemmed and hawed over how long I should make the auction, and after much hand-wringing, I went with a seven-day listing. What a waste of my time and energy all that internal drama was, since five minutes after I posted the listing, someone with the user name "DeluxeDiva" snatched it out of cyberspace, using the "Buy It Now" feature of the auction. I got an e-mail a moment later, almost frightening in its intensity.

From: DeluxeDivaMe@yahoo.com
Subject: eBay Auction
To: armoire_auctions@yahoo.com

Michael—I am thrilled with my purchase. I will send a bank wire transfer to you upon receipt of your details. And, going forward, I would gladly buy from you all Birkins you can get, at a price fair to both of us. I think we could both benefit from such a relationship. Let me know your thoughts.

Cordially,
Sarah

This woman meant business. I wondered if she realized what she could be in for. If I kept going gangbusters like this past week, as I was determined I would, she would be buying two or three purses a week, minimum. California Closets would have to hire a whole design team to meet this particular lady's storage needs if her pace matched mine. So, I needed to clear things up, but nicely.

From: Armoire_Auctions@yahoo.com
To: DeluxeDivaMe@yahoo.com

sarah, yes, bank transfer is of course fine. (if it's good enough for
Hermès, it's good enough for me.) but as to the second part of your
email: as I have not listed any birkins on eBay before, you may not
realize what you are asking. i am buying and selling several birkins
a week to private clients, so I am not sure if you truly want every
single one that I manage to procure. let me know . . . michael

Less than two minutes later:

From: DeluxeDivaMe@yahoo.com
To: Armoire_Auctions@yahoo.com

Michael, I have an insatiable love for these purses, and it would be
great to get at least first refusal on any you get. I guarantee I will be
a great client. (And I would love to know your secret to getting so
many bags!) But seriously, I have a feeling we are going to get along
just fine. Thanks loads and be in touch. Sarah

Well, well, well, wasn't that interesting. What would she do with
all those bags? But really, did I care? She could use them as planters
for all the difference it really made to me. No harm in giving her first
refusal—after all, she *had* paid top dollar.

I decided not to write back again until I had another Birkin to hawk,
and then we would see how that went. I had met people obsessed with
Birkins, but Sarah's obsession touched on the surreal. What if she re-
ally wasn't an overly wealthy socialite but something more insidious?
I had a brief vision of Sarah knocking on my door in jackboots and a
leather overcoat, and behind her, the Hermès Death Squad. Dangling
from her outstretched arms would be polished crocodile skin and glint-
ing palladium—hard evidence of my reselling hijinks. Okay, I was truly
deep in the Hermès Fun House now, where people's personal realities

(including mine) were as distorted as a reflection in one of those wavy mirrors. I needed to come back down to earth, where purses were in the two- and three-figure range, so I called Mom.

"Hi, honey, I was going to call you if I didn't hear from you soon. I assume things are good in Spain?" Her voice, as always, sounded like home to me.

"Yeah, things are good, really good. I'm doing well with the Birkin thing, but I think I might need to move closer to the post office."

She laughed. Thinking my stupid jokes were funny was one of her finest qualities. Then it suddenly dawned on me—I hadn't called to make her laugh, but because I needed to tell her something that I was pretty serious about. I hadn't fully realized it before dialing, but I knew now without question—it was time to spill the beans.

"Mom, remember how I've been mentioning Juan, and how great he is, and all that?" I didn't give her a chance to answer my rhetorical question. I talked about Juan enough recently that the only way she wouldn't have remembered him was if she had undergone a full-frontal lobotomy since the last time we talked. "So, anyway, I wanted to tell you something because I know I've thought I was happy before with other people and all that . . . but I want to tell you first . . . and, well, I think he is my soul mate, you know, like, The One."

I waited, surprised at what I'd said. Juan and I had started saying "I love you" a few weeks before, so I knew he and I were at least feeling the same things, or similar things, but still—I had never said the word "soul mate" before, about him or anyone else. It had jumped out of my mouth of its own accord.

"Oh, Michael, I'm so happy for you. That's so wonderful." Her voice held real emotion. For no reason at all, I was on the verge of tears. Well, the verge of the verge, actually.

"Yeah, Mom, I'm really happy, too. Really, really happy. Took long enough, right?" And I realized I *was* really happy, too, ecstatic even, though seconds ago I had been battling for control of my tear ducts. Up and down, up and down, that's how powerful this whole thing with

Juan was. And the more I thought the word "soul mate" to myself, the more right it sounded. Clearly, I was a wreck.

I half listened to my mom talk for a few more minutes, simply enjoying the sound of her voice, pleased to hear how much both she and my father loved their retirement lifestyle. After I got off the phone, while getting ready for my dinner with Mr. Soul Mate later that evening, I couldn't stop thinking about my subconscious revelation. I wondered what *else* I was going to say unexpectedly. I'd better not get drunk tonight, that's for sure. I would probably start reciting Elizabeth Barrett Browning or something—Jesus. I needed to get a grip. I needed to pull it together. I needed . . . well, something. Or maybe, this time, it was someone I needed.

Juan was, as usual, excellent company that evening. I was quieter than normal. I began wondering what our future held. "Our" future . . . had I just thought that? That was one heavy thought. I was keeping it light tonight, remember, brain? Enough schmaltzy soul-mate stuff for today. I distracted myself from myself by admiring the restaurant he had picked for the evening, a place called Botafumeiro. It epitomized Old World Spain, with autographed photographs adorning the walls, a brass-accented interior, and a handsome suit-clad waitstaff. They squeezed by the tables, arms straining under plates of amazing Galician seafood, some of it looking like the best of what you can find in Barcelona (and that was saying something). The place felt cozy, but Juan had mentioned the seating capacity was much larger than it looked, each room opening off the other, creating a labyrinth of dining. I craned my neck, trying to get a better look down the hallway at the cavernous opening of the next room, but soon gave up. I could explore later, on a trip to the men's room.

Snug on my seat at the enormous horseshoe-shaped mahogany bar, I realized this was a place Juan knew I would love, and that he had really taken care to ensure the perfect evening. I had no doubt he had reserved this seating specifically so we could sit side by side, and he had even remembered I didn't like *cava*, the local sparkling wine. I drank

only French Champagne, and I always ordered it despite the prevailing sentiment that the local "champagne" was superior. (I had finally learned to stoically endure the raised eyebrows of my Spanish waiters.) I had also told Juan all about my days back in Ptown, when I used to order a case of Bollinger to kick off the summer. The green bottle sitting atop the cracked ice in the large hotel-plate urn in front of us was none other than that exact brand. He must have phoned ahead to ensure they would have it already chilled for us—they never kept anything but *cava* on ice. I smiled over at him, thinking flowery thoughts again, and took a gorgeously Gallic sip. A few seconds later, I busted him staring at me over the top of his champagne flute.

"Yes? Can I help you?" I cheerily inquired. I always took refuge in humor.

"No, I'm okay." He smiled back.

Juan was more literal than I. I attributed this idiosyncrasy to his job teaching English at a private high school. In that business, you'd better say exactly what you mean. He also spoke half a dozen languages, give or take, which might have something to do with his "dictionary definition only" approach to conversation. I could live with it. Which made me wonder . . . could I live with him . . . period? I was starting to think I'd like to share a home with him, but I wasn't sure where he was on the subject. Which, I guess, is a timeless problem. Adam probably felt awkward about broaching the subject of garden cohabitation with Eve, or, in this case, Steve. Either way, I had no intention of bringing it up tonight.

"Juan . . . I've been thinking . . . well, I . . . wanted to know if you maybe wanted to move in with me." What!?! What did I just say? I *meant* to mention that I talked to my mom today about us, or to say that I really did care about him, or to emphasize that I meant it whenever I said "I love you." I certainly hadn't meant to ask him to move in, right then, there, in the restaurant, before we even got the olives and bread. I glared accusingly at my glass of Champagne. Foiled myself again.

"Michael, I . . . have you thought this through?" His brown eyes searched mine. I hoped he couldn't see that I was panicking, and then, suddenly, I wasn't panicking at all.

"Yes, Juan . . . I have." My voice was confident. What's a white lie between soul mates?

"Then, yes . . . I will . . . I would love to, actually." He smiled.

"It will save you on your commute, and you're at my place most nights anyway, and our cell phone bills are atrocious, and . . ." I have no idea why I was still talking. Neither did Juan. He laid a hand over mine, in that gentle way he had, and I stopped midsentence.

"I said yes, Michael, okay? You don't need to convince me. This is right, between you and me . . . don't you think?" His voice was soft, but it carried. It carried more than any expensive bag could. Juan's voice carried love, and it went right to my heart.

17

Knight in Shining Croc

Juan and I spent the next couple of weeks settling into our new life together, which mostly consisted of playing armoire arrangement acrobatics—thankfully, his wardrobe was of a much more reasonable size than mine, so we finally succeeded, albeit snugly. It was then time to tackle the guest room, since my mom and dad were finally making good on their promise to visit. I was really excited, not only for them to see Barcelona but also for them to meet Juan. He seemed a little nervous about it, but he had definitely been given more time to prepare for their visit than the scant warning I had received before that first Sunday lunch at his parents' (although I have to admit, the Sunday afternoon feast was now a highlight of my week). Anyway, I knew as soon as the three of them were in a room together, it would all be fine. I had given up trying to reassure Juan of this, though—it definitely fell on deaf ears.

When the doorbell buzzed downstairs on that long-awaited afternoon, announcing their arrival, I was as excited as a little kid on Christmas morning. Juan and I both went down to the lobby to help with their luggage, and I enthusiastically hugged them both and then introduced

them to Juan, who was awkwardly standing a little apart. My dad shook his hand, formal for once, and then my mother grabbed my boyfriend into a big hug. They had some small whispered exchange during the embrace, and both emerged slightly wet-eyed and bashful; but after that, you could barely get them away from each other. They sat next to each other on the couch all afternoon, giggling and chatting, and Juan won her over even further by always remembering to serve her beer to her in a frosty cold mug (you had to give her a new one with each new beer too . . . it was quite a process, and I was glad Juan had taken charge of it). So, she was obviously smitten. My father pretty much always followed her lead, and this day was no exception; once he started talking to Juan about the Red Sox and how the two of us would have to visit the States next summer so we could all catch a game together, I knew Juan was already part of the family. Later that night, after dinner at the apartment, my parents crashed early, worn out from their flight, and I asked Juan what he and my mother had said to each other in the lobby. He tried to act innocent, but I wasn't buying it.

"Come on, I know you said something . . . I saw the whole thing, you both said something, come on, just tell me . . ." I had to know.

"All right, all right . . . fine. Well, first she thanked me for making you so happy . . ."

"Oh, so sweet . . . and what did *you* say?"

"If you have to know . . . and I know you do, Mikey, you always have to know everything"—he rolled his eyes a little, but smiled too—"then I thanked *her*, for making you, well, you." He looked down at his feet as he spoke this last, and I was glad he did, because now I was the one with wet eyes to hide.

I spent the next ten days playing tour guide, with the aid of Juan's insider tips. With a true local's touch, he crafted us daily itineraries that had a good blend of relaxation and sightseeing. Instead of being footsore and tired at the end of each day, as many tourists are, my parents and I were really able to *enjoy* the city. For example, a strenuous late-morning hike up to Park Güell (Gaudí's masterpiece of public

space set high on a hill) ended with us sitting around for a couple of hours at the café at the top, enjoying our lunch while overlooking the city. At night, we would go to one or another of Juan's and my favorite haunts, or I would cook for us. Sunday, of course, brought us all to Juan's parents' house, and by the time we left *there*, the two older couples had started planning a trip to Seville for the following winter. (It was amazing how people who didn't even speak the same language could get that far in a single afternoon, but I guess there really *is* an international language—it's called *cava sangria*.) Overall, I was pleased to see how much they loved "my" city, and I loved showing them the best of it. We even took a side trip to Sitges, a coastal town about thirty minutes out of Barcelona by train. We spent a lazy day on the beach there, did a little shopping, and got personalized service at Al Fresco, an extraordinarily good restaurant where I was well acquainted with the owners, a husband-and-wife team. My mom got a real kick out of it when the wife/chef came out of the kitchen to chat, and laughed even more when she discovered the two of them shared their first name—Marilyn. After the restaurant closed, Marilyn and her husband, Xavi, could both abandon their posts (while she cooked, he served as both sommelier and maître d') and they joined us for some wine and conversation. Once my parents and I finally got ready to leave a couple of bottles of red later, the two women were fast friends, and couldn't get enough of saying "Bye, Marilyn!" and "Nice meeting you, Marilyn," amusing themselves—and my father—ad infinitum. As I dragged my parents out the restaurant door, I concluded that Sitges, and Al Fresco, were definitely a hit.

Of course, the ten days went much too fast, and I was slightly forlorn when it came time to say good-bye. Packed and suntanned, the two of them sat in my living room for the last time that week, waiting for the cabdriver to arrive and start them on their journey home. They both told me a dozen times to thank Juan again for them when he got home from work, and then we sat there in silence for a moment, all a little lost in thought.

"Well, Mike, it certainly has been a great trip. Nice place to live, I'll give you that." My dad leaned forward as he spoke, and patted me on my knee, smiling. I could tell he was happy for me.

"I'd say it's better than nice, John, really. *Much* better than nice. It's *wonderful*, is what it is. What a life you and Juan have." She smiled as she spoke, but her voice sounded emotional. I knew it was hard on her sometimes, me living so far away, but finally I knew my mom was happy for me too. I started to say something, probably something sentimental, but just then the cabdriver buzzed the downstairs bell. I walked them down to the lobby, where I let my fierce hugs do the talking. Maybe, on second thought, there are a *few* international languages.

I sort of slumped around for the weekend, feeling homesick for the first time in ages, but once Monday rolled around, I had to collect myself. My parents' visit, great as it was, was now only a very fond memory. It was time to put my nose back to the Hermès (presumably, gold-plated) grindstone. After all, work was definitely going well, well enough that I had taken almost two weeks off, no problem. So I decided, in my overly confident state, that it was time to go for the Hermès jugular—I was going to breach the walls of the Faubourg flagship fortress.

If there was a secret Birkin bunker anywhere, this was the store. It was enormous, an imposing multistoried limestone building. (I had tried to figure out which floors held what while lurking inconspicuously on the sidewalk on my last trip, feeling like a fifteen-year-old

casing a theater that showed X-rated movies.) I knew not all the floors were devoted to merchandise (and I assumed there was at least one floor devoted to housing the Oompa-Loompas). Well, I'd soon find out, I guess. I booked a plane ticket for the upcoming weekend, and dropped Grace an e-mail, maybe hoping for some last-minute advice.

From: "Michael" <armoire_auctions@yahoo.com>
To: "GraceoftheGarden" <graceofthegarden@yahoo.com>

hi grace, i'm off to paris this coming sunday to work "the formula" at Hermès faubourg (and the other two shops too!) my guess is that if the smaller shops have birkins then the faubourg must be like federal reserve birkin bank. any thoughts or suggestions or do you have the name of a salesperson there? michael

From: "GraceoftheGarden" <GraceoftheGarden@yahoo.com>
To: "Michael" <Armoire_Auctions@yahoo.com>

Michael, in days gone by (too many to even remember) I had a wonderful salesperson at the Faubourg whom I'm not certain would still be working there nor do I remember her name. You seem to have a high batting average so I'd stick with your formula. Any plans to attend the Hermès vintage auction while you are in Paris? I assume you planned this trip around the auction? You might also consider paying a visit to some dépôt-ventes (French consignment stores) for some older scarves. Just a random thought. Grace

Fuck Heloise, I'd take Hints From Grace over her tired tips any day of the week. Come on, anyone can tell you how to get a stain out of an Hermès scarf, but it is a rare woman that can tell you where that scarf was made, when it was made, and what it is worth. She never ceased to amaze me with her expertise. A lot of the time, the house of Hermès

felt like one of those giant Birkin boxes, with never-ending layers of tissue you had to sift through to get to the goods. I was sure glad I had Grace on hand to help me dig.

From: "Michael" <armoire_auctions@yahoo.com>
To: "GraceoftheGarden" <graceofthegarden@yahoo.com>

grace, first off, what Hermès vintage auction? more info s'il vous plaît. i DO of course know of the depot-ventes but never actually thought of them as a source for Hermès scarves . . . do you really think it's worthwhile? m~

From: "GraceoftheGarden" <GraceoftheGarden@yahoo.com>
To: "Michael" <Armoire_Auctions@yahoo.com>

Michael, Artcurial—one of the large Paris auction houses—has a 2-day Hermès vintage auction which is this week. The auction (600+ lots) draws hundreds of collectors and resellers from the world over. I can assure you that there will be numerous unusual and rare items there—which is exactly why the Hermès museum curator is often in attendance (oddly enough, they are famously cheap.)

Bidding can be fierce among the serious collectors, and last year several highly sought-after scarves sold in excess of $700. If nothing else, it will be a good learning experience (take notes!) How lucky your timing is!

As for the depot-ventes, yes, they always have a selection of Hermès scarves although you must be careful regarding condition (lipstick, pulls, etc) but keep in mind that you can bargain at a depot-vente. Grace

It looked like I had more than my Faubourg fish to fry while in France: Hermès-hunting at an auction, courtesy of my fortuitous timing, plus the

dépôts-ventes sounded like scarf heaven. Thank God I was in peak packing form to meet the challenges of Paris. With all the past month's clothing rearranging, I was confident I could now fold a scarf (or anything else) smaller than any Hermès (or even Gap) employee could. I hoped this peculiar ability—and my already formidable skills in the art of suitcase stuffing—would prove handy for my return flight. I wanted to be bringing back to Barcelona a jumbo that would be so heavy with Hermès merchandise that the airline reps would crack "dead body" jokes.

That next Sunday was a drizzly and chilly early-spring day, not the soft-aired example of "April in Paris" I had longed for, but I was still content to be there, gawking out the cab window. I love Paris. I love every silly tourist trap that the city has to offer. I love the monuments that inspire the souvenir stands: the Eiffel Tower, the Arc de Triomphe, the Notre Dame cathedral. I love the clichèd "only in Paris" experiences—drinking wine in the sidewalk cafés, riding in the *bateaux mouches* that operate on the Seine, buying crêpes instead of hot dogs from sidewalk vendors. I pretend to be worldly sometimes, and often succeed, but something about Paris makes me want to buy crappy T-shirts with Mona Lisa on them, and key chains in the shape of Jim Morrison's gravestone. In short, Paris makes me stupidly happy.

I was hoping that I could overcome my giddiness long enough to appear as blasé as a typical Birkin-buying millionaire. Maybe I should have donned a blindfold right at Charles de Gaulle, as soon as I got in the cab, and ridden to the store first thing. God knows I was always world-weary when I got off a plane, and cranky, and starving, which would make me an Hermès customer prototype. But on second thought, I probably couldn't lug in the suitcase. Kinda tacky. Good thing I had told the cabbie to drive me to the Hotel Mansart.

I checked in and prepped for my mission. I always dressed to the nines for these outings, for obvious reasons, and I had agonized about the choice for today, wanting it to be perfect. I had finally packed Jil Sander charcoal trousers and a dark lime green cashmere turtleneck, with a pair of *tabac* matte crocodile Bottega Veneta brogues. I had also

recently decided that I should always wear a touch of Hermès. The typical choice for men is a tie, but I'm not really a tie guy. And I wasn't about to wear a scarf. So instead I had decided to keep one of the Birkin-bait items—a man's *chaîne d'ancre* bracelet, made of sterling silver, in the *très grand modele*, which meant it had the largest links possible. I had to admit I liked the heavy weight of it on my wrist, the divided-oval design, and the artistically oversized toggle closure, although I couldn't imagine how they charged $1,000 for it. Yes, I had bought it, but I had more than its elegance in mind. For me, it was a business expense, so I guess I did have an advertising budget after all. Because, in a way, I was both the author of the advertisement and the advertisement itself. I was selling me, so that they would sell *to* me. But hey, as long as I didn't have to sleep with anyone.

I wanted to be strolling down the street, confidently, but instead I was shivering down the street. So when I got to the corner, instead of going left, toward Hermès, I went right, to Galeries Lafayette. There I could buy my tea, for later, once the hypothermia had set in. My tea was Mariage Frères Earl Grey French Blue, so it wasn't exactly Lipton, and I knew that store was one of only two places in Paris that sold it. Galeries Lafayette is a kind of outsized French Bloomingdale's, spread out over three separate buildings, and one building, the Lafayette Maison, is dedicated entirely to housewares. The basement of the Maison is devoted to teas, spices, and coffee, and every imaginable accoutrement thereof. Once there, I tried to justify buying myself a treat—hey, who *doesn't* want a 24-karat-gold-plated tea ball?—but in the end bought 300 grams of my tea instead. To celebrate my uncharacteristic self-control, I immediately went across the street to the building that housed the men's department. The third floor featured mini-boutiques of several designers I liked. Well, I could use a jacket . . .

It was made by Dsquared2: chocolate brown leather, form-fitting, with oversized pockets, gusseted sleeves, and a half-belt in the back. It was car-coat length, it was a runway piece, it was . . . going home with me. I strolled out of there a half hour later, snug against the sprinkling

sky in my new purchase, somehow feeling richer, although I definitely was poorer. (I always figured money is neither created nor destroyed when you buy high-end—there was always eBay if circumstances got desperate.) It was a suit of armor, to match my enchanted bracelet, and I was off to rescue the Birkin, cruelly imprisoned in the dungeon. And *I* was . . . someone who had seen *The Princess Bride* too many times. Either way, no more procrastinating, it was time to go to work.

I walked into the Hermès Faubourg with utmost confidence, at least as far as how I looked. Now, I needed to watch how I acted. I immediately drew some attention from a salesman hovering among the handbags, or, more likely, my jacket did. He came over to my area quite quickly, and I ignored him for a while, taking my time before overtly noticing him, staying just out of the natural range of a hello. I sized him up a little—dishwater-colored hair, slim, well-dressed in an Hermès-regulation outfit, around my height. I perused the bags and finally let him get close enough to greet me.

"Good afternoon . . . Are you looking for something special, perhaps?" His near-perfect English was delivered with a French accent so thick it was almost a caricature. I immediately thought of Pepe Le Pew, only this man's voice lacked that skunk's suaveness; due to its high register, it almost sounded squeaky. Turning to speak with him, I caught his casual glance at my croc brogues. Money well spent, judging from the appreciative look that sprang into his eyes.

"Aren't we all?" I said, smiling. I wasn't playing any of my cards this early.

He looked at me, almost oddly serious. "I have something very special to show you . . . Please wait here, I will be right back with it." With that, he turned on his heel and then stopped. He turned back to me and said, "My name is Serge." He then left me alone with the displays of purses. None of which were Birkins, naturally.

I puttered around, then I meandered around, then I wandered around, and still he wasn't back. I was about to start lolling around when I saw a bit of an informal salesperson gathering at a glass dis-

play, with Serge at its center. He gestured me over. The three sales-women around him looked nonplussed, as though they had been dragged away from their shifts of shredding the Birkin waiting list in the backroom. That all changed as soon as he pulled a black bag from out of the tissue.

It sure as hell wasn't a Birkin. It actually looked like a genetic ex-periment where a purse and a briefcase were mated, with outstanding results. It was oblong, about 40cm, with three zippered pockets on the sides, a handle situated on the top, and a flap that closed with a Kelly-like clasp. The material of the top, bottom, and sides was black leather, the pockets were toile (canvas), the hardware was palladium, and the overall look was amazing. And it actually looked practical, unlike the burdensome Birkin, which was largely nonutilitarian.

Now, I didn't know what this bag was, but I realized that the sales-women clearly did, since they looked like kids on Christmas morning. I didn't say a word but eavesdropped on their French, which was pep-pered with *"Quelle surprise"* and *"C'est très beau."* Serge obviously had their attention, and mine. He knew it too—he made a big show of pulling out the two-inch-wide toile-and-leather shoulder strap, and at-taching it to the shiny clips. This new addition further cemented the bag's gender-neutral appearance.

"You have to try it on," he insisted, already putting the bag over the top of my arm. He busied himself adjusting the strap so it fell over my shoulder and the bag rested comfortably behind my midsection, its tri-angular shape molding perfectly to the curve of my back. I peered over my shoulder to peek down at it, and Serge smiled and wordlessly led me to a mirror. Here I turned back and forth, looking at my reflection, until I realized I was preening a little.

"I haven't seen this before." I knew the right thing to say: my rudi-mentary French had already helped me find out that much.

"No, you wouldn't have. This is an incredibly rare bag." Serge said this with no small amount of pride in his voice. When he paused dramatically, I noticed that we—or, more accurately, the bag—had drawn a crowd.

The onlookers were other shoppers, and I saw in their eyes nakedly raw Hermès hunger for the item on my back. I realized also that if I didn't buy it, this store was going to degenerate into an atmosphere akin to the annual wedding-gown sale at Filene's Basement. I would have to toss the bag at our spectators, wedding bouquet–style, and run for the door. Serge's next sentence reinforced this.

"This is a Kelly Lakis bag, created for Hermès by a man named Lakis Gavalas, a highly respected Greek designer. It is for either men or women, as you can see"—this, with a smile—"it is well suited to you." I smiled back, slightly embarrassed he had noticed my vanity. Sharp guy. He continued smoothly. "This is only the second one to come from the workshop. The first one, this same bag in red, was purchased by Jean-Louis Dumas-Hermès, a Christmas gift for his wife." His voice was both matter-of-fact and conspiratorial. It managed to convey a confidence in me, in my ability to see the common sense in purchasing this bag, the foolishness of leaving without it. The ultimate salesman, in other words. I glanced at the other listeners around us, and a couple of the women were nearly panting. Serge had a way with words, all right. But he could have stopped talking a while back. There was only one word necessary to sell me *completely* on the Kelly Lakis, and he had invoked it right out of the gate. Ever since I had started this whole Hermès gig, it was undoubtedly my favorite four-letter word—R-A-R-E. Like my steaks, I took my Hermès handbags as rare as I could get them.

18

Ping-Pong I'll Play,
but Purse Penelope?
No Way!

I was very pleased with my first Faubourg foray until about twenty
minutes after leaving the store, when I remembered that the shoulder
bag inside my shopping bag was not a Birkin. It was like one of those
times you go to the store for bread and come home with chocolate chip
ice cream, but no bread. Whoops. Well, I would just have to go back
tomorrow. I was sure my new buddy Serge would be happy to see me,
and hopefully happy to sell to me. For now, I had a pressing engage-
ment—today was the auction.

I had been to a couple of art auctions before, so I wasn't exactly Joe
Clueless, but those hadn't been in France, at a venue on the Champs-
Élysées. And my attendance at this auction was far less casual than
my browsing and drowsing appearance at the other two—this was all
about the money, honey. I was there strictly to score some little trin-
kets that would make my eBay clients' hearts beat faster. But it *would*

be a lie if I said I wasn't damn curious to check out the crowd at this soiree. I'd bet a Birkin there would be some expensive designer outfits on display, and shitloads of bling. And, naturally, copious amounts of Hermès neckties . . . and scarves . . . and purses. This was a golden opportunity to see the different kinds of people that collect Hermès. Plus, I couldn't *wait* to bear witness to the ludicrous overbidding Grace had mentioned in her e-mail. Nothing more fun than watching some zealous completist collectors go at it. I had seen it on eBay, but as with rock concerts or parades or fireworks or sporting events, I had a feeling the experience might be better live.

I had worried about finding the Artcurial building, but that didn't prove to be a problem. It was a Beaux-Arts building that straddled an entire corner, resplendent in all its neoclassic glory, ornately dormered and amply befriezed. It was nothing if not conspicuous, even for the Champs-Élysées. It looked like some old French mini-palace that had been painstakingly renovated, which made sense, since, as it turned out, that was exactly what it was. (Although I would later learn the pre-ferred term is *petit palais*.) I noticed a couple things about the vestibule right off the bat. Number 1: There was a thug in a cheap suit over on my right, aka the security guard, who was trying very unsuccessfully to blend in. (Funny.) Number 2: There was an information desk over to my left, where I could potentially find out where I had to go in this monster of a building. (Useful.) I walked right up and, lo and behold, got the information I needed. Truth in advertising is hard to come by, and you have to appreciate the informative information desk when you actually run across one—it's particularly rare in airports. So, now, armed with knowledge and the catalog for the Hermès auction, I was ready to rumble. Or, more accurately, bid on vintage luxury items. I winked at the security guard—he blinked in confusion—and ambled into the main hallway.

Frankly, I didn't see anything *petit or* mini about the place; in fact, I felt dwarfed. There were paintings and sculptures everywhere, and tons of doors leading off the main hallway, some open, some closed.

Beyond each of the open doors was a room set up as a gallery, to pro-
mote an upcoming auction and display the items to be sold. Behind the
closed doors were the auctions currently in progress—you could faintly
hear the auctioneers' quick-paced patter as you walked by. To help with
navigation, each room was marked by one of those signs you see in
funeral homes. (You know, the black ones with the removable white
letters, the ones that inspire harmless vandalism in a magnetic-poetry-
on-a-friend's-fridge sort of way.) I wandered around awhile, and then
headed upstairs to get a good seat.

I finally spotted the magnetic sign that read HERMÈS VINTAGE AUC-
TION. I was momentarily overwhelmed by the wide spectrum of po-
etic possibilities in those white magnetic letters, were I allowed just
a few minutes alone with them. (For starters, there was: *A cute sage
movin' her tin.* Or: *Her? Me?—Nice vino, stat!* Or: *Go crave thin mints.* I
could have stood there composing half-assed anagrams all afternoon.)
I moved quickly through the door. The place was dotted with little
clusters of fellow attendees, maybe twenty or so people in total. Since
that would only fill around 10 percent of the folding chairs, I was defi-
nitely early. There were the requisite high-heeled Hermès handbag
holders, accompanied by their preemptively bored boyfriends or hus-
bands. (Apparently not all those Kelly and Birkin bags had wallets in
them; hence, the menfolk.) Then there were the dowager types, with
their rarer-than-average scarves tied around their necks to help hide
their age. Neck wattle or no, I instinctively knew *any* of those women
could buy and sell me, and if it could help get them an item currently
missing in their collection, they wouldn't hesitate to do just that. I
couldn't wait to see a couple of these ladies fighting it out for some rare
piece of Hermès history.

I must admit, so far I was feeling pretty cocky about my deductive
reasoning on Hermès types. Without ever having laid eyes on most of
my clients, I had formed a mental picture of these women, and now I
had confirmation that I had them pegged to a T. This auction's cross
section of Hermès couture culture was eclectic in style and age, but

there was nothing about their appearance that surprised me. I had expected it all—the tailored suits, the discreet pearls, the conservative hemlines, the salon-fresh hair, the Chanel No. 5. Then, as my eyes roved the room, I saw a type I hadn't expected, a type I could only describe as "frumpy French farmer." This was, in all honesty, an Hermès fan base I hadn't anticipated, *couldn't* have anticipated, really. But there they were. Dowdy and underdressed, three or four couples all stood together, talking loudly in a hybrid of Hermès-speak and roughneck French—I overheard plenty of scarf design nomenclature, a debate on the condition of various "lots" at the auction, and a heated discussion of the failing health of Monsieur Hermès. You would think the two men involved in that argument were that gentleman's long-lost brothers or, at the very least, his ex-lovers. Such was the level of emotion and implied intimacy. Seeing them grow red-faced as they argued, I was grateful they had left the truffle-hunting hounds at home—things could have *really* gotten ugly.

I had seen this type in the stores, but I didn't know they actually bought anything—I figured they were gawking, or that maybe Hermès hired them to make the store look fuller. And land alive, there they were, here at this auction—a luxury-collecting subclass that lived (and dressed) on the down-low. Why weren't they at least *wearing* the stuff? But wait, on closer inspection, they *were*, or at least the wives were. Each woman had an Hermès scarf on, an item worth easily what the rest of her outfit cost. I had missed that detail at first, briefly blinded by the seedy condition of their ratty cashmere twinsets and ancient tweed skirts. Oh, and over there . . . I spotted a couple of soiled Hermès ties tucked into the well-worn, moth-eaten cardigans of the men. Weirder and weirder. I wonder what a sociologist would make of it. I wondered what *I* made of it. Oh, Grace, where art thou? She, of anyone, must know what the story was with this group . . . why hadn't she mentioned it? (I later found out she sort of had—in a roundabout way. It turned out these "French farmers" were the people who ran the *dépôt-ventes*.) I left my philosophical meanderings alone for now, though, because

it was time to find a seat. Even though the room was still somewhat empty, I wanted to stake my claim. Actually, that did end up being the correct verbiage, because, about ten minutes later, France's answer to the Gold Rush of '49 hit the room, with two hundred or more Hermès hunters flooding through the door. Literally, within two or three minutes, it was standing room only for almost half the crowd. I snuggled a little deeper into my chair and got ready for the show.

The auctioneer moved to the front, and we were off. Whoa, this guy was talking way faster in French than I expected . . . hey, that's already sold and I didn't even see what it was. I picked up my catalog and tried to scan ahead, but it was like an algebra test you hadn't studied for, there was no hope . . . I would take it as it came. *Oh, I like that pocket watch up there, oh wow, it's a jump-hour watch, those are so cool, and superunusual, and with the Hermès logo, I could sell that for a bundle, hey, my hand just shot up, so I'm bidding, I guess, okay . . . no, I want it, Mr. Guy-that's-three-rows-away, put your hand down already, and by the way, that brown suit is SO last year . . . okay, I'll pay more than you, fine, have it that way, I want the watch, dammit, I'm raising my hand again . . . damn you, brown suit guy, put your hand down . . . Mine is up, see Mr. Auctioneer, notice me, notice me . . . And look, how sad, brown suit's hand has temporary paralysis, I guess, by the way it's slowly swinging down at his side . . . hey, Mr. Auctioneer is pointing at me . . .*

Oh my God, I had won my very first item. An Hermès jump-hour watch for the bargain price of $1,700. Seemed about right—I could almost definitely sell it for more, but I didn't even care at that moment. I had beaten Mr. Brown Suit, and that was all that mattered. Take that, buddy. Whew . . . I was drained already, and it was only one item. I guess this is why the barter system has fallen out of favor—too emotionally exhausting.

An official-looking man came by, collected a credit card from me (for identifi-

cation purposes), and handed me a paddle—and the adrenaline surged again. Now if I bid, it would be as if I was an overaggressive Ping-Pong player, rather than an elementary school boy who had to take a whiz. Definitely *much* cooler. I twirled the paddle between my knees and waited for the next match—er, auction lot. The rest of the afternoon was a blur. I bid, I bid, I bid, I won, I won, I won. Sure, I had sucked at Ping-Pong as a kid, but if they ever made auction bidding part of the Olympics, I was gold medal material. I fumbled only once—meaning to grab my paddle to bid, I got my umbrella instead. The bidding was heated, no time to switch, so I swung that umbrella around until all the paddle-holders surrendered in confusion. The auctioneer banged the gavel and announced that the lot would go to the man with the *parapluie*. This drew a big laugh, and naturally, everyone craned every which way to get a better look at me. I waved to them with my umbrella, and rather sheepishly picked up my paddle. At least I had won.

At the end, I had three clocks—the aforementioned pocket watch, a clock for travel, and a crocodile-sheathed purse timepiece—plus a cashmere blanket, a leather cigarette box, and a desk lamp. Back in the vestibule, I waited to pay behind all the other buyers and half listened to the conversations around me. In a twist of fate, Mr. Brown Suit was standing right in front of me. However, I was fast realizing that Mr. Popularity would have suited him better as a nickname, judging from the number of people greeting him in obsequious tones. As one couple walked away, I heard the husband mutter something to his wife about the *"conservateur de musée Hermès."* So Mr. Brown Suit was the curator Grace had mentioned—the guy who bought items for the Hermès museum at the Faubourg but didn't like paying auction-inflated prices. Imagine, a company with Hermès's money pinching pennies at the expense of preserving their history. No wonder I had won that watch—I was bidding against one of the only frugal men in French fashion.

When I finally got to the front, it turned out I was not quite so frugal as my brown-suited buddy. I had burned through money at an alarming, bachelor-party-in-Vegas rate—more than $12,000 in under

five hours—and I hadn't gotten so much as a lap dance. The tab was somewhat shocking to me (I had been a wee bi' caught up in the moment, you see), but I reminded myself that I had chosen exactly the kind of Hermès bric-a-brac that I could sell easily on eBay for a tidy profit. There was nothing to do but sigh and hand over my credit card. I needed a drink. Well, the Ritz *was* right down the street . . .

I hit the Hemingway bar a few minutes later, stashing my Artcurial bags under my table with a sigh of relief. I decided a glass of Champagne was the logical end-of-this-workday drink (after all, it *is* favored by bachelor parties the whole world over). I was trying to make the painful decision about which kind I wanted when I noticed someone repeatedly turning around in his barstool and blatantly staring at me. A very, *very* good-looking someone, I realized once I finally became aggravated enough to stare back at him. He was a young, dusky-skinned Adonis with jet black hair, a very expensive Christian Dior shirt, and no noticeable physical flaws of any kind. I always hated it when someone called a man "beautiful," but he really was beautiful, breathtakingly so, a male specimen straight out of a Calvin Klein magazine spread. I felt flattered by his too-obvious attention, but it was typical of my life—why *is* it that as soon as you are in a committed relationship, gorgeous men appear out of the woodwork? Although it was puzzling that he would be this infatuated without even talking to me first (usually it's my razor-sharp wit that gets them). His evident interest wouldn't remain a mystery long, though, because right after my glass of Billecart-Salmon Rosé appeared at the table, so did he. I gestured casually at the chair across from me. He sat down, extended a hand for me to shake, smiled a quick yet devastating smile, and introduced himself in an ever-so-faintly-French accent.

"Hi . . . I'm Luc." And so, with those three seemingly innocuous words, began the most unusual, lucrative, and tumultuous partnership of my whole Hermès venture. But I didn't know that yet.

Although he was certainly gay, Luc was after business, not pleasure. He wasn't looking for romance with yours truly, a reality that

triggered feelings of both relief and wounded vanity. Mostly relief—I didn't want to have to mess with those armoires ever again, and oh yeah, there *was* that Juan guy I liked too. At any rate, Luc had been at the Hermès auction and had been swiveling and staring simply because he was making sure that *I* was *me* before he ventured over to say hello. How *I* had missed *him*, I had no idea; possibly he had been dressed as a French farmer. Or sitting behind me, that was more likely, I guess. Either way, he had an interesting tale to tell—albeit a long-winded and self-congratulatory tale. (It ended up that, as with many other strikingly good-looking people before him, Luc was a hell of a lot more attractive before you actually conversed with him.)

Luc lived in Paris and had recently found himself quite the Hermès connection. One of the Faubourg store's salesmen was reportedly "so in luuve . . . he will do anything for me, Michael. Philippe will sell me purses whenever I want, he just luuuuves me." I had a twinge of pity for poor Philippe. Since he couldn't afford to buy the purses outright, Luc had taken to attending the Hermès auctions in search of someone to bankroll the Birkin buying—and, naturally, pay him a nice commission on any purses he squeezed out of his lovesick "bagboy." Noticing all my bidding at the auction, he took a leap of faith that I was a reseller. Which I was, actually, for those of you who just tuned in. Luc had laid his cards right on the marble tabletop, and it was up to me whether I took the deal. Very tempting, since I would love to have a Paris connection and save myself the airfare; but very scary, since I barely knew this man. One thing was certain—I sure as hell wasn't about to hand a relative stranger seven grand and sit in the hotel like some purse Penelope, praying not to get scammed. I was in the habit of playing the Ulysses part in my Hermès heroic quests. After I made that crystal clear to Luc, we bandied possible plans back and forth. Eventually we worked out an arrangement we could both live with. Understandably, Luc was still a bit pouty at my lack of complete and innate trust in him, given the almost-hour we had known each other . . . he was *some* piece of work, this one.

Our Top Secret Shopper Birkin-Buying Script ran thus: At nine, I would meet Luc at a café called the Ladurée, right down the street from the Faubourg. I would walk him to Hermès, as far as the door, and hand him the cash. Then we would see what he walked out with. If he indeed got a Birkin, he got 500 euros—roughly a 10 percent commission for ten minutes of shopping. I got the Birkin. Everyone's happy.

Our negotiations at a close, we shook hands. Luc hinted at a hot date for the evening and departed, drawing appreciative looks from almost everyone he walked by on his way out of the Hemingway. I wanted to do a PSA for all of Paris, to inform the general public that, much like a big jungle cat, Luc was best viewed at a safe distance. Oh well, can't save the world. And on second thought, I wasn't in a position to save *anything* today, especially money. I had spent almost $20,000 before dinner—and I still didn't have a Birkin. It sure would be nice to have a Birkin from Serge, a Birkin from Philippe, the Kelly Lakis bag, and the auction goodies. The purses were the most important, though . . . too bad I couldn't summon *those* up with a Ping-Pong paddle. Or an umbrella.

Parisian Purse Pipeline

I got to the Ladurée a few minutes before nine the next morning, still sleepy, and somewhat doubtful whether I should have bothered showing up at all. I seriously questioned if Luc's dog-and-pony act at the Hemingway was exactly that—an act. I sat down with my trusty Earl Grey, prepared to wait in vain. Then it was nine, then it was nine fifteen, and then it was half past, and it seemed like my suspicions were well-founded. I thumbed through my *International Herald Tribune*, searching for anything good I missed the first three times I went through it, when I heard a couple of appreciative murmurs from the trio of young Frenchwomen sitting to my right. Hmmm . . . I wonder . . . I raised my eyes and there Luc was, dressed to the hilt, lounging in the doorframe and scanning the room languorously. He acted like he didn't notice the attention his pose was getting, but I knew better—his "type" needs attention like heroin addicts need their smack. Although I had to admit, he *did* look amazing. Between the suit and the sunglasses, since our meeting last night he had graduated from a CK model to a Prada billboard boy. I almost waved, and then decided against it—there was no way he hadn't seen me already in this small café. He was definitely

milking the moment, but who was I to deprive his onlookers? He finally "spotted me" over the tops of his shades, and started making his way over.

"Michael, hello . . . Do you have the money?" So much for pleasantries.

"Good morning . . . Yes, I do, I have what you need for the Birkin," I said, tapping my shirt pocket.

"And money for me?" He smiled coquettishly as he said this, but I could sense the neediness lurking beneath his "casual" tone. I found it irritating that he was so gauche as to immediately bring up money, especially on the heels of his late arrival and abrupt greeting. I bit my tongue, however; mainly because it wasn't worth showing him that I was annoyed. All I needed was for him to throw a hissy fit and demand a bigger cut, or walk away altogether. The funny part is, I had the distinct impression he thought I found him utterly charming.

"Yes, of course. That too, right here," I said, tapping my other shirt pocket. I was nothing if not organized. "I have to fly home later today, so we should head out." This was not, in fact, true, but I did want to do things today that would occur outside of the Café Ladurée, and I had a feeling Luc might order the menu if he got a chance. I was likely right, judging from his pout. But all was not lost for him, moochwise—he still managed to steer us near enough to the counter on the way out for him to order a macaroon. Happily munching, Luc was uncharacteristically quiet on the walk to Hermès, which was nice. Meanwhile, I seesawed between my nagging doubts about Luc's character and my growing excitement at the prospect of having a "shopper" who could get bags for me at will. I looked at him, searching for any visible clues that he was planning a heist against me, but like children who are asleep, Luc looked particularly angelic while eating. And, now that we were walking next to each other, I realized he wasn't any bigger than I was—I could take him, if need be. That sealed it. A "safe" distance away from the Hermès store entrance, I stopped and handed him the "Birkin money" envelope.

"Okay, Luc, good luck." I smiled, and quashed my worries.

"I do not need any, I tell you, Philippe luuuvs me. We will have no problems." He opened his suit coat wide, pointed at the Valentino label to make sure I saw it, and slipped the envelope into his inside pocket. I tried not to look disgusted at his show-and-tell. This was his big moment, after all. He smiled again, and headed across the street. I watched until he disappeared through the giant glass doors, and then I had nothing to do but wait. God knows how long Luc would stand around flirting with Philippe, I thought with a sinking feeling. I still wanted to hit those *dépôts-ventes* later today, and the morning was half over. My jaw dropped when Luc walked out a scant fifteen minutes later, practically waving his orange prize. He jogged lightly across the street, already opening his mouth to say something, but before he could ask for his money, it was in his hand.

"Michael, thank you . . . and it is a black 35cm with gold . . . That is okay, right—one of the ones you said you wanted?" He started to hand me the shopping bag, but I shook my head. I didn't want to take a chance on anyone seeing our handbag handoff. Luc seemed to understand, and gestured for me to follow him, mumbling something about his car being down the nearby alley. I simply followed the orange—it wasn't going to be out of my sight for a minute.

We stopped in front of a beat-up VW Golf—apparently Luc's acute style sense didn't extend to his automotive choices. He leaned against its dented hood while he searched his pockets, and at long last pulled out a crumpled store receipt. I scanned it quickly, it had today's date, and the Birkin purchase was there in black and white. Now if the item in the bag matched the receipt, I was good to go. When I peeked inside, the box looked authentic and the ribbon was tied perfectly. Luc handed the bag to me, and I swung it by its handles, testing the weight. Felt right. Well, at some point I had to trust I hadn't been scammed. Luc was not so trusting and was making a show of counting his bills. I decided to have a last chat with him, as a final effort in fraud detection, before he scooted off in his crappy car. (Who the hell drives in Paris, anyway?)

"Luc, this is great! We should do this again . . . Let me get your number?" I gauged the expression on his face as I made this suggestion, but I saw nothing resembling panic. I was now relatively sure I hadn't been scammed, unless he was an actor on a par with Sidney Poitier.

"Yes, we should . . . I can get these whenever you want, and it's good for both of us, no?" He was already eagerly digging in his satchel for his cell phone. After we swapped info, we stood there a little awkwardly.

"This really is good for both of us, like you said. So I'll talk to you once I get back to Spain. And meanwhile, make sure you stay on Philippe's good side!" I jokingly wagged a finger, but I wasn't really kidding. This could be a huge "in," if Luc didn't screw things up with this salesman.

"No, no, Michael, he luuuvs me . . ." Oh Jesus, not again. I cut him off from reciting that speech by pretending to have received an important text message from the cell phone still in my hand. I stared at my address book, making what I hoped looked like an anxious face.

"Oh, sorry, Luc, I have to deal with this . . . All right, then, I'll be in touch!" With that, I turned on my heel and walked away without a single glance back. I made a power exit that I hoped looked a lot more decisive than I felt. Perhaps Luc could learn that he was not the only one who could command the stage.

I scooted back to the Hotel Mansart to drop off the bulky shopping bag and, naturally, sneak a peek at my new Birkin in the process. Everything checked out fine on the bag, and I was ready for phase two. I stopped over at the concierge desk to get the goods on getting the goods. In response to my question about *dépôts-ventes*, he popped over to his *minitel*, this really cool device no self-respecting Parisian concierge would be without. *Minitel* looked like a portable television with a keyboard soldered on, but it could spit out phone numbers, addresses, and business listings, and the concierges used it to check bus timetables, book airline tickets, and make reservations. It was a pre-Internet invention but essentially did much the same work as Google eventually would, only with more of an emphasis on local information.

Immediately, the concierge had the names and addresses of more *dépôts-ventes* than I could visit in a week of afternoons. He quickly scribbled down a list of ten or so, and I was on my way.

The *dépôts-ventes* are essentially consignment stores, but I knew a lot of them were exclusively designer, featuring only one or two of the most expensive brands. They might specialize in Chanel, Goyard, Louis Vuitton, Gucci . . . Hermès. Those higher-end *dépôts-ventes* were the ones I wanted to find, but unfortunately, the list I had in my hand held no clues about which ones those might be. I had to hunt for myself. I decided to let geography dictate, and headed for the closest one. A scant five minutes later, I was standing in front of the store's plate-glass window. It wasn't a fancy display, but it held an assortment of scarves, purses, belts, and so on, with handwritten labels announcing their brand. I spotted a couple scarves labeled Hermès and headed into the store. The store looked as if it had seen better days, as most secondhand stores do, and after wandering around the dusty sales floor for a bit, I saw nothing Hermès outside of what was in the window. In fact, I saw little inside that was of the same caliber of the items they had put in the window, period. Good marketing, but disappointing. I had a salesperson lift the scarves out of the display, and I inspected them carefully. Condition was fine, none of the lipstick stains Grace had warned me against. I couldn't sell them as new, of course, but the designs were both on the rare side, and I was positive they were on someone's wish list. Success, of a sort, I supposed.

I went to five or six more stores that day, but in some of them I found nothing at all. One was really bad—it was a mess of rusted baby carriages, broken toys, stained clothes, and old French romance novels. Even if they had a Birkin hidden somewhere, I don't think I could have stayed there long enough for them to find it. Finally, at what ended up as my last stop, I found a *dépôt-vente* that validated my Hermès-hunting afternoon. It was exactly the kind of store I had been looking for—90 percent luxury goods. It had stacks of Hermès scarves and at least half a dozen Hermès handbags, as well as lots of Hermès jewelry and assorted

leather goods. Jackpot! I quickly spent another ten grand (I was really on a roll this week—Juan was never going to let me go to Paris again). More bags of stuff to traverse the city with.

I had planned on going over to the actual Hermès store to see Serge, but all the walking and cabbing had me less than fresh as a daisy (and when I went a-Birkining, I always went as fresh as possible). So, I decided on a late lunch, instead, somewhere close to the hotel (and a nap might be in order too). As I cabbed back to the Mansart, I decided other than that last one I had gone to, *dépôts-ventes* were for the birds. Too much time spent traveling—time that could be better spent charming an Hermès salesperson out of a high-end bag. And it was completely hit or miss whether they had anything at all that I wanted, so I could waste a whole day and walk away with nothing. The *dépôts-ventes* might be good for the collectors, like Grace, but they weren't a savvy use of resources for someone like me, who viewed this all as a business. On the whole, though, I was damn pleased with my trip so far. I had lots of treats to put on eBay, and I had also miraculously found a Parisian purse pipeline. If Luc kept up his end of the bargain, my insatiable client Sarah wasn't going to need a new closet for all the Birkins coming her way—she was going to need a whole new house.

20

Devilish Prada Pants and Heavenly Cuisine

I entered Hermès the next morning, ready to cap off my trip with just one last itty-bitty Birkin . . . now that wasn't so much to ask, was it? Serge was engaged with a Japanese woman who looked like the buying type (she was carrying an indigo blue crocodile Kelly bag), so I strolled around his periphery. I wanted to remain on his good side, and interrupting a potential big sale was not the way to do that. After about twenty minutes, he managed to exchange a few words with me on his way to the "handbag vault" downstairs. By then I was sitting at one of the two small wooden desks that the store provided—usually, you sat there to fill out your de-tax papers or CITES (the infamous croc "passport"). I was content people-watching, but Serge looked troubled on my behalf.

"Michael, I am so sorry to keep you waiting. The woman I am with has a lot of requests and questions, plus one of my long-standing clients phoned, and she will be here momentarily. So perhaps later today?" He sounded hopeful, so I knew he had assumed I was there to buy, not browse.

"No problem. I can come back later this afternoon. I need to get my dinner plans settled, and finish packing—I leave tomorrow. Recommendations for dinner? I was considering L'Ambroisie." Worth a shot—I bet Serge knew the reputation of every three-star restaurant in Paris. I had gotten in the habit of using Hermès salespeople as a Zagat guide when I was on my "business trips." None of them had let me down yet.

"Have you been to Pierre Gagnaire?"

I shook my head.

"In my opinion, it is the best restaurant in the city. I think you would find it very interesting." Here he paused, looking a little troubled. "However, on this kind of notice, getting in is impossible . . . Well, you know, let me see what I can do for you, Michael. I do know someone there, and if I dine along with you, we could perhaps get a table?" This last was definitely a question, and there was no way I was going to give the wrong answer.

"Absolutely, I would be happy to have company, and if this restaurant is all you say it is, I wouldn't want to miss out on it." Besides the practical business side of establishing a friendship with Serge, he was likeable enough. Also, with all of my recent traveling, I often felt as though I was the most frequent solo restaurant diner in Europe.

"Great, great, I will give Jacques a call, then, and see what he can do for us. He may come through; I have dined there on any number of occasions with clients. And also, it is where my boyfriend and I always go for our anniversary dinners, so they are guaranteed to see me at least once a year." He smiled as he said this, and I was relieved to hear he was with someone. To paraphrase Meat Loaf, I would do anything for Birkins, but I wouldn't do that.

I spent the afternoon doing a little window-shopping and enjoying a late lunch at Ladurée (no Luc in evidence, thank God). If this place was as good as Serge promised, it was worth killing the afternoon for. I didn't get back till around five, but my timing was good—Serge was free when I walked in, and he greeted me immediately.

"Michael, I got us a table, at eight thirty, you want to do it, right?" He was obviously pleased with himself.

"Yes, of course . . . But wait, I'll need a suit-jacket for this place, won't I?" Panic. I didn't have one. Stupid, stupid. The Dsquared2 bomber was fab, but not exactly finer-dining material. In Paris, you still dressed for dinner. Okay, I had the power to solve this, I would go and buy something. Crisis averted. Deep breath.

"Yes, you would need one, you don't have one?" Serge raised his eyebrows.

"It's fine, it's fine. I'll go and buy one, I can always use another suit jacket." I waited for lightning to strike. "But that means I don't have time to shop here . . ." This was unfortunate, but I did have tomorrow morning free. My flight wasn't until four, so it wasn't a disaster either.

"You can come tomorrow morning, right? I am working then too," Serge said, echoing my thoughts.

"Yes, that's fine. Okay, let me get the address from you for tonight, and I'll meet you there at eight thirty . . . in a jacket." Serge had their business card on the ready—wow, what a Boy Scout. I quickly headed out, determined to find my wardrobe change for the evening. It shouldn't be too hard: I was in Paris, it wasn't like there was any short-age of beautiful clothing. And then, like an answer from above, I spot-ted a Prada store across the street. I like Prada, devil's brand or no.

Prada was a series of good-news/bad-news vignettes. They didn't have a jacket that I liked (bad news). They did have a suit I loved (good news). The jacket fit me perfectly (good news). But the pants were too long (bad news). Looking at myself up and down in the full-length mirror, I decided that I could pin the pants, just for the evening, and get them tailored later—no time now, that's for sure. I reasoned that if I waltzed in wearing a single-breasted, cream-colored, microfiber Prada suit, no one would be looking at my ankles. As I handed over a credit card so new the surface was still gummy from the security sticker, I had a premonition that Juan would definitely never let me come to Paris again—ever. (Al-though I knew he would *love* the suit, you sort of had to.)

I was headed back to the hotel, Prada bag draped over my arm, when it occurred to me that I should get shoes too. I didn't want Serge to think I had only that one pair—and I wasn't sold on how crocodile brogues would look with this suit anyway. At least those were the justifications I went with, but the Armani Black Label store I saw across the street could be what triggered the whole shoe thought in the first place. The mind is a complicated landscape.

More good news/bad news. Armani had a gorgeous pair of black woven leather slip-ons, sleek and tailored, and they had them in my size (good news). It occurred to me I needed a black belt to match them, which was an item I hadn't packed (bad news). They carried belts at Armani, of course (good news). None of them fit my trim little waist, though (bad news). I bought the shoes and headed back to Prada. I had seen a couple of belts in there I liked, but hadn't been thinking I was going to buy new shoes . . . what a comedy of errors. And I only had, let's see, two hours before I would meet Serge. Less than two hours. I was practically jogging, desperate to get back there before the store closed at seven. Thankfully, on my encore visit to Prada, only good news awaited. They were open (barely; I was glad I had hustled) and they had the most fantastic belt I could have pictured to complete my ensemble. The leather was black edged with cream, the exact cream of my suit, *and* it wasn't too big. I realized that if I paired it with the black cashmere turtleneck I had back at the hotel (and my trusty *chaîne d'ancre* bracelet, of course), I was more than ready to take on Pierre Gagnaire—as soon as I fixed the pant legs, that is. What had I gotten myself into? All I wanted was a suit coat, and now look—more business expenses.

Back at the hotel. Showered and coiffed. But after struggling with the suit for twenty minutes, I decided to enlist the hotel staff for help. Ever attempt to safety-pin your own pant hems? I don't recommend it, unless you are into calisthenics. I went down to the lobby and over to the front desk, and explained my situation to the nice lady working. This may have been somewhat unnecessary, as my pant hems were dragging on

the floor in a rather unsubtle manner, and I was walking while trying to hold them up (another possible exercise for the calisthenics fans among us). I said that I had less than an hour till kickoff at Pierre Gagnaire, and the desk clerk immediately got excited for me. She called over the concierge, and he also got excited about my upcoming dining experience. I guess Serge wasn't screwing around with his restaurant choice; everyone was acting like I was presenting at the Oscars. The concierge led me downstairs to some hotel netherworld, like the maids' office or something, and had me stand up on a stool while he pinned the hems. His technique was amazing—he meticulously manipulated ten or so teensy-weensy safety pins to hold the hem on each leg, and you couldn't even see them. Then he had me strip to my skivvies . . . and then he . . . well, he ironed my pants. After a last dash to my room to do a final once-over, I was ready for the ball, without a second to spare. Three or four employees, including the tailor/concierge, saw me off in the lobby, beaming like proud prom parents. I thanked everyone again, tipped everyone accordingly, and silently resolved to always stay at the Mansart whenever I came to Paris. (And since that day, I always have.)

The restaurant was located on Rue Balzac—the neighborhood was an old haunt of its namesake, as well as moments from the Arc de Triomphe. _Très Paree_, in other words. It was inside a hotel (named the Hotel Balzac, not surprisingly), but you entered off the street. Serge wasn't there yet—the afternoon's escapades notwithstanding, I had managed to arrive a few minutes early. The place was very chic, very feng shui, the light-wood tables contrasting with charcoal gray walls and accents, all clean straight lines. There was a little lounge area, and it was there I waited for Serge to arrive, immediately ordering a bottle of Bollinger RD '90. I had already blown my trip budget by about thirty grand, so no amount of penny-pinching on Champagne choices could save me now. Serge breezed in a few minutes later, we transferred ourselves and the Champagne to the dining room, and we settled into our table for the night (and I do mean settled in . . . we were there for almost five hours). Our location in the dining room was great—we were in a loge

area, at one of two tables that overlooked the entire restaurant. No question about it—Serge was a VIP at this place.

Pierre Gagnaire served cutting-edge fusion cuisine, gourmet French dishes with a contemporary twist—or at least that's what Serge told me. All *I* knew was that my first glance at the menu made me worry that my French was rusty. But even after the waiter provided me with a menu in English, I was still perplexed. Toast with woodcock and sardines; carpaccio of fennel warbler; "frozen" bouillabaisse with green pepper; small gray snail étouffée; golden celery with velvety ewe; and a number of other, um, selections. And no hints at all about dessert—under the word DESSERTS appeared simply the words PIERRE GAGNAIRE. I hoped there wasn't some freaky cannibal thing going on here. Luckily, I was saved from menu oblivion by my dining companion. Serge wouldn't hear of us choosing anything other than the gastronomic tasting menu, seeing how it was my first time there. Course after course came, and the food was bizarre, yes, but sublimely so. Everything was delicious, the unique combinations a true delight to the palate. Serge's "in," Jacques, turned out to be the sommelier, and he came over with his personal recommendations on the wines. Naturally, we needed a bottle of white, and of red, what with having both fish and meat. The wine seemed to loosen us both up, considering we were relative strangers.

Serge talked extensively about his clients and his life in general. I was more reticent, obviously—"Oh, well actually, Serge, I sell Hermès items on eBay and have a formula for getting Birkins . . . I'm going to use it on you tomorrow, actually, if I need to . . ." Yeah, that would go over real well. Check, please. I didn't lie, though; I *was* in the import/export business. And it wasn't really difficult to be slightly vague, because Serge, while not in the slightest a bore, had plenty to say. He told me all about some of his famous clients, one of whom, Mrs. Fisher, was of the Gap Fishers. I was like, oh, *that* Mrs. Fisher, right . . . saw her in Capri last week. Oh wait, no I didn't, I was too busy running around the south of France buying handbags. Serge also spoke extensively about Lakis Gavalas, the designer of my new bag, who, I now found out, was a friend

of his. Serge and his boyfriend frequently vacationed with Lakis in the Greek islands, and Lakis even used Serge as a sounding board for new designs. Lakis was an increasingly important Greek designer and self-manufacturer, and also the Mediterranean area retailer/distributor for other high-end fashion brands. He was well-known to the style world of Europe for his socializing, his eccentric style, and the decadent late-summer parties at his home in Mykonos. And he had what very well might be the largest personal collections of Hermès bags in the world, at two hundred plus and counting. I tried to imagine why a man, even a gay man, would need that many purses, and I couldn't answer the question. I didn't have any purses (at least for personal use), and I wasn't feeling some big chasm in my soul or anything. I wondered what Serge thought of Lakis's collection, deep down, but knew I couldn't ask—he would never be indiscreet enough to comment. I reflected that discreet was probably a way of life for him now; even here, he was running into clients. First, a Frenchwoman approached to chitchat, and then later, an American woman. These women didn't look merely well-off—they dripped money, with their Van Cleef jewelry, croc clutches, and haute couture ensembles. Seeing their obvious affection for Serge, I fully appreciated what a unique position he occupied within the orbits of the elite. This man saw more black AmEx cards in a week than most people would see in a lifetime. He specialized in handbags at the Hermès flagship location; thus, he had met thousands of the wealthiest people on the planet, many of whom he now called friends.

When the bill came, I whisked it off the table and wouldn't hear of letting Serge chip in. He had gotten us the reservation, after all. And in all honesty, I did want to keep up the pretense of committed Hermès customer, and committed Hermès customers had money to burn. I also never mind paying $800 tabs if the food and drink are of the caliber we had just enjoyed. The wine probably made it an easier blow to take, as well. It was really good wine.

Serge and I said our good-byes, and swayed off in opposite directions. I couldn't believe he had to open the store tomorrow morning.

Of course, I had to work too, but not at eight. I was thinking eleven sounded about right. It sure was nice to get to make your own schedule, especially on the morning after you had split three bottles of high-end libations. Poor Serge.

I wasn't quite so fresh as usual when I got to Hermès the next day, but I was fairly certain that Serge wouldn't notice my hangover through the haze of his own. Once again, he was with a customer when I arrived, looking a little miserable but gamely trying to hide it. He quickly excused himself for a moment as soon as he saw me (I think my customer stock index had improved overnight).

"Michael, I need to finish up with her; we are almost done. Let me have one of the girls get you something while you wait. Coffee, or tea, perhaps?"

I tried to refuse, but ended up succumbing when he revealed they had Earl Grey. I went back to my new favorite perch at the desk, and awaited my tea like a good little Birkin buyer. It arrived momentarily, on a silver platter, in an Hermès Toucan teapot and matching cup. This was great. I decided I would try to get here at an inconvenient time every time. Before I could get bored, Serge appeared, warmly greeting me. I was at a crucial point here. Did I need the formula? Or could I go full steam ahead, and try for the Birkin right off? I decided nothing ventured, nothing gained. (And thanks to Luc, I did have one Birkin already.)

"Serge, I want something for my mom's birthday—I actually meant to get it the other day when you distracted me with that bag, and then yesterday when you distracted me with that dinner" (here we shared a laugh). "I really want to get her a Birkin." I waited with bated breath (and crossed fingers, because my mom would rather be shot than spend that kind of money on a purse, but I couldn't very well say it was for me—I was no Lakis Gavalas, and Serge knew it).

"Let me go see if there is anything available. I will be right back," he said, already heading for the Birkin basement. He emerged with a stack of three boxes, doing the Christmas-gift goose walk over to the

table. I bought just one; I thought more than one would be greedy (and the one I took was a beaut—an *étrusque*-colored ostrich 35cm Birkin, very desirable).

Serge gave me a kiss on each cheek, we said our farewells, and that was that. Now I had two Birkins, and I hadn't had to buy a single scarf to get them. On this trip I had found both an effective "shopper" and an effusive salesman—what else could a boy want? I had a hunch that in my future dealings with the Faubourg, the only thing I would have to wait for would be my tea.

21

Chilean Charades
and Buenos Birkins

Back in Barcy, I made it my first priority to get money into my bank account, and stat—partly to ensure Juan didn't realize the full extent of my expenditures. I didn't know if I could explain the whole spending-money-to-make-money ideology to a Catalan man. His culture tended to be . . . um . . . frugal. Plus, I knew Juan would be shocked by the sheer sums I was dealing with. It *was* a bit scary the first time you saw a $50,000 AmEx statement, although eventually you did get used to it (especially since I knew I was going to make all the money back, with profit). But I still felt it was best to ease Juan into it slowly. So, in the interest of saving time, I offered both Birkins to Sarah right off. She responded within an hour.

From: "Sarah" <DeluxeDivaMe@yahoo.com>
To: "Michael" <Armoire_Auctions@yahoo.com>

Michael—Fantastic, I will take both of them. I will bank wire payment tomorrow.

Also, I got a really interesting tip recently that I thought I would share with you. My friend Shannon is a flight attendant, and a big Hermès fan, and she recently discovered you can get Birkins a lot more easily in South America. The two stores she had luck with were Buenos Aires and Santiago. Might be a thought for you.

From: "michael" <armoire_auctions@yahoo.com>
To: "Sarah" <DeluxeDivaMe@yahoo.com>

Sarah—thank Shannon for the tip. I am surfing airline websites as I type this. be in touch - mt

I found a flight into Buenos Aires, and realized that with all my recent credit card purchases, I wouldn't be paying a dime for the tickets—my miles count was through the roof. I would have to tell Juan—he loved nothing more than getting something for free. I booked myself a plane ticket for the weekend after next. I was eager, but not eager enough to miss out on lazing around the house for another few days before climbing on a fourteen-hour transatlantic flight. I also didn't want to miss seeing what kind of bidding wars my Artcurial goodies would incite—I planned on sitting back with a bowl of popcorn for *that* show. I also figured I could make a quick trip to Andorra (still in operation at this point, the axe hadn't fallen yet), and maybe one of the Barcelona stores as well.

I had fewer end-of-auctions that Sunday than I had expected—but that was because people had leaped at what I had considered rather ambitiously priced "Buy It Now"s. So that was fine. And I had made my little side trips, and got some eBay Hermès trinkets, plus a Birkin in Barcelona (formula back in operation). As planned, I also sat around a lot, drinking Earl Grey. So by the time the trip came, I was rested and raring to go. I was excited about South America, since I had never been south of Cancún.

Santiago was my first destination. I had never really considered going to Chile, and once I got there, I wondered how I had made such an oversight. The city was bustling, larger than I expected, and reminded

me a lot of Barcelona. Fewer high-rises, definitely, but the same sort of small-town-disguised-as-a-city feel. The Hermès was right near the Hyatt I was staying at; I was getting pretty expert at booking hotels, locationwise. The store was fairly good-sized, with huge windows along the lines of the Faubourg store. More important, the formula worked like a charm, and they coughed up two Birkins for me to choose from. Not sure which one I should take, I had a moment of inspiration. A new formula, of sorts.

"Do you mind if I make a quick call? I'm just going to call my mom and ask her what she wants me to do, she's the big Hermès fan in the family." With that, I took out my cell phone and called my own voice mail.

"Hi, Mom, I'm here at the Hermès store in Santiago . . . Flight was fine . . . Yup, I'm here already . . . It's great, they had everything you wanted, and I'm looking at two Birkins now. Yeah, they have a 35cm blue jean, and they have one in gold. Oh, okay." I paused here. "Yes, well, I can ask, hold on." I turned and addressed the saleswoman, my hand over the mouthpiece of my phone (which was playing my saved messages ad infinitum).

"Is there any way I could get both? My mother wants the blue jean, but she also wants to buy the gold, as a present for my sister." The saleswoman was a little hesitant.

"Well, sir, Paris does not really like it if we sell two bags to one individual." Here she paused, looking at the stack of merchandise I had at the register. "I suppose, though, that if you paid with a card today, you could get the other perhaps tomorrow, with cash. That way we wouldn't get in any trouble."

"Oh, that's no problem at all. I fully understand. Let me tell Mom, she'll be thrilled." I finished up my fake conversation, and that was that. One Birkin in my hands, and another to pick up tomorrow in the A.M. Perfecto.

Ironically, my phone rang almost immediately when I left the store, and I half expected it to be my mom; she was spookily psychic like that sometimes. But, no, it was a different leading lady in my life.

"Hello, Michael here," I said crisply, as I concentrated on dodging the throngs of pedestrians crowding the hot sidewalk.

"Hey, stranger," Kate's low voice responded, in a tone much more mellow than mine. I immediately looked for somewhere I could sit, spotted a little bench, and plopped myself down on it, safely out of the way of the madding crowd.

"Kate, oh my God, it's so good to hear from you, you will *never* believe where I am right now," I said, watching Santiago's shopping district bustle around me, cars whizzing by and the sound of Spanish filling the air. I nostalgically pictured Kate at our old kitchen table back in Ptown, sipping her coffee and gazing out the window at the dinghies floating in the bay.

"Nothing surprises me with you, Michael, you know that. So where are you? You aren't in Barcelona, I assume?" Kate's voice was dry, but I could hear her smile through the phone line.

"Nope. I'm in South America—Santiago, Chile, to be exact, buying Birkins."

"Wow, that's a long flight for a handbag purchase. I can't believe you're making a living with that Hermès thing, it's too funny." Kate and I talked on the phone once a month or so, and when we did, it was usually for at least an hour. But since she had never owned a computer, it was difficult for me to explain my eBay venture to her—especially the part about how it had snowballed and become my career. Although I had told her about my Birkin business success, I think she still assumed it was something of a lark. And I secretly suspected she found it all kind of boring. She had never even owned a purse, preferring to carry her cash and license tucked in her coat pocket. So we chatted about other things: Juan, some of my recent travels, Kate's new job at a flower shop, the newest exploits of the old Ptown gang. We were starting to wrap things up when she remembered why she had called in the first place.

"Oh, that reminds me, Michael . . . I was actually calling to tell you that Ward phoned me yesterday, looking for your new cell phone number. I gave it to him, I hope that's fine." That was a blast from

the past—Ward was my erstwhile almost–business partner, who had planned to set me up as a jewelry guy in Barcelona and then dropped the idea. There were definitely no hard feelings, and I'd e-mailed with him a few times, but we hadn't spoken in ages.

"Absolutely, of course. I'd love to hear from him. Well, this is costing you a fortune . . . talk soon?" Kate and I said our good-byes, but I had barely hung up before the phone rang again. It was, in a remarkable feat of timing, none other than Ward. That wasn't even the weird part, though, because it turned out that Ward had a really good friend who lived in Santiago, mere blocks from where I now stood. She was a young woman named Pime, and he insisted on calling her on my behalf.

That night I was unexpectedly treated to a home-cooked Chilean feast, courtesy of the hospitable and lovely Pime, who became immediately fascinated by my Hermès adventures. She also proposed us going into the Birkin business together: an arrangement similar to what I had with Luc. She said she would buy for me in both Santiago and Buenos Aires, as long as I took care of the initial travel arrangements and paid a suitable commission. Oh, boy, a South American connection for the "designer drug." What could be better? Ward really hooked it up for me, however accidentally.

Off to Buenos Aires, two bags in tow. (I had snagged the other one that morning, as planned.) But as I juggled them on my way down the plane aisle, I decided I needed to find a better way. I wasn't willing to go to the three-Birkin mark and risk the wrath of the flight attendants, nor was a $7,000-plus handbag check-in material. There had to be a solution. I could ship them back to my house in Barcelona, of course, but then they were traveling over the ocean twice (since most of my Birkin buyers were from the States). I also didn't want to take a chance on nobody being home when they arrived at the house—it wasn't like Juan sat around in the kitchen drinking tea all day, like yours truly. As I sat in the cab on the way to Caesar Park, my hotel in Buenos Aires, the criteria for a middleman were clear-cut enough, if somewhat peculiar. Who did I know who didn't have a real work schedule, lived in

the States, had my implicit trust to the tune of thousands, and was nice enough to make multiple trips to Mailboxes Etc. for me, with little or no recompense for her trouble?

"Hi, Mom, it's Michael . . . I wanted to ask a favor . . ." I began.

Thankfully, my mother agreed to help me. I think she somehow thought it would be exciting, although why, I wasn't sure. The travel part was a little exciting, yes, but the purses themselves were boring to me now, about as exciting as a Whopper to a BK franchiser. But whatever made her happy was fine by me, and this would make my life a ton easier. Those Birkins were a lot heavier than they looked, and the orange was too conspicuous for my taste. Sure, the Hermès logo got a lot of innocent gawking at the check-in counter, and envious looks at the gates, but it also got some speculative looks, and I wasn't about to hire a bodyguard. Not just yet.

Buenos Aires was way bigger than I thought it would be, making Santiago appear provincial. It simultaneously looked nothing like I had expected, and exactly the way a South American city should look. It had a stylish, fashionable vibe, like Paris, but the salsa beats and passionate personality of the Latino culture. I also loved the Hermès store, seeing how I was able to use the "formula" to get three bags in two days. Similar to the store in Santiago, they had me spread out the purchases timewise, because of possible "detection" from the Hermès headquarters. I still found it very odd that a store couldn't freely sell merchandise as they saw fit, to customers willing to pay for it. I didn't know why the home office wouldn't be thrilled they had sold such extravagantly priced merchandise, period. It wasn't like I planned on undercutting their prices, that's for sure.

It was time to head out of South America, although I wasn't sure I had drunk my lion's share of the Malbec yet (Malbec was a wonderful local red wine that was like an excellent cabernet sauvignon crossed with one of my beloved Catalan Rioja wines). I found out that even if you could find Malbec out of the region, it wasn't going to be of an older vintage. Much like the Spanish, the South Americans hoarded

all the best of their libations for their natives. Curses to such hedonis-
tic nationalism—curses, I say. But they didn't care what I said, and I
was stuck buying a case with the rest of the tourists. I also called and
warned my mother to be on the lookout for incoming purses, and Fed-
Exed all five of the Birkins bye-bye. My flight back to Barcelona was
via Paris, with a six-hour layover. I found out that they didn't always
give you the best flights when your ticket was free, a fact I would be
reminded of again and again in the upcoming years. But I decided to
make the most of it. Going back to the Faubourg so soon was out of the
question, but there was George-V and the Hilton Hermès store, and I
thought I might as well give it a try.

I ended up juggling two Birkins down that plane aisle after all, plus
the bag of "ingredients" I had used to conjure up the two purses. I had
hit a new record—seven Birkins in five days. I wasn't looking for a men-
tion in the Guinness Book, but it was certainly a far cry from where I
had started. Which reminded me, what about all those waiting lists in
the south of France—why hadn't I heard back yet? Oh, silly me, that's
right—it takes two years to get a Birkin, and I had been on those lists
for only one year. As I sipped my Champagne in first class (having de-
cided that seven purses = upgrade), I figured it was just as well. I mean,
everyone needs something to look forward to . . .

22

Blueberries and BlackBerries

I sent out a killer e-mail the next day to Sarah, wondering what she would say to a laundry list of seven bags. Certainly she wouldn't want all seven. *Nobody* would buy seven Birkins all at once. Her response to my e-mail was short and sweet.

From: "Sarah" <DeluxeDivaMe@yahoo.com>
To: "Michael" <Armoire_Auctions@yahoo.com>

Michael,

I think we should talk on the phone . . . do you want to call me or send me your number and I will call you? It's up to you.

From: "michael" <armoire_auctions@yahoo.com>
To: "Sarah" <DeluxeDivaMe@yahoo.com>

Sarah,

it's fine, I will give you my number if that's ok, spain has a phone monopoly and it is outrageous to call from here. it's xxx-xxx-xxxx. talk to you soon. mt

So I guess Sarah had different feelings about phone time than Grace. That wasn't the only difference between them, as I would soon find out. The phone rang not five minutes after I sent her the number.

"Hi, this is Michael." I wanted to put her at ease. People could be weird with overseas calls—they always thought they might have screwed up the number somehow.

"Michael, hi, it's Sarah."

"Hi, Sarah, it's great to actually talk with you finally." I barely got the words out of my mouth when she started spouting rapid-fire:

"Yeah, it's great to talk to you too . . . Michael, how the fuck did you get seven Birkins? I know you went to South America, but seven? That's fucking outrageous. I'm sorry, I know I have the biggest potty mouth, but I cannot fucking believe you got seven bags!" Her voice sounded husky but young, and with definite class lurking underneath the crass. I pictured some beautiful thirtysomething, lounging by a pool, smoking a cigarette, and impatiently waiting till noon to have her first martini. The effect was charming, and I immediately liked her.

"Well, I went to Paris too . . ." I felt oddly flattered by her reaction. Although why anyone should feel proud about his ability to walk in a store and buy a handbag—well, that was another story for another day, I guess.

"Yeah, whatever . . . but seven bags is totally outrageous, never mind that two of them are fucking croc! That's so over the top. Where have you been all my life?"

"Well, um, thanks, I guess. What one, or ones, do you want?" I had two repeats on the leather ones, meaning I'd gotten the same exact bag twice, so the most she could *possibly* want was five.

"I want five. One of each of the different ones . . ." She acted like I should have assumed as much. She was right, I suppose. But I guess I had thought spending over seventy grand in one week for handbags was out of the question. How plebeian of me.

"All right, sounds great. Two will be coming from here, and . . ." Once again I was taken down midsentence.

"Why aren't they all coming from there? And you still haven't told me how you get them . . ." She laughed as she said this, but there was an edge there, albeit a friendly one.

"Oh, because my mom is doing some of the shipping for me, since lugging them around in airports is a drag. I ship 'em to her in Florida instead, makes life easier. Sarah, I have a deal for you . . ." I paused dramatically.

"Yeah, what?" I could tell from Sarah's voice she had no clue what was coming.

"If you tell me what you do with all these bags, I will tell you how I get them!"

By the sound of her laughter—she had one of those great, full-throttle, I-don't-give-a-shit-what-anyone-thinks laughs—I could tell I hadn't offended her.

"All right, all right . . . I was just curious but okay . . . I'll let you keep your trade secrets. I guess as long as you can get them I shouldn't complain, right?" She went on without waiting for an answer. "But I

have a favor to ask. I know you must know some of those salespeople pretty well, like in Barcelona?"

"Well, yeah, the ones in Barcelona, definitely . . ." I wondered where this was going.

"Do they like you? I mean, really like you a lot?" Her voice was insistent again. This was not a woman to be jerked around.

"I don't really think about it that way . . . but, yeah, they like me." It wasn't as if I'd taken a survey, but I thought they did. Especially since I had brought them my homemade "Grandma Johnson's recipe" banana bread last Christmas, back in my scarf heyday. That had gone over pretty big. I make a kick-ass banana bread.

"Okay, there's a bag I really want, but the problem is, it doesn't exist."

"That might be hard even if they do like me, Sarah." I wasn't getting this at all. But again, I got to hear that great laugh of hers.

"You're a riot, oh my God, too funny. Yeah, but Michael, my point is, what kind of money have you dropped there? A shitload, right?" That was a good question. I didn't even have a guess, except I knew it was in the tens of thousands. I figured that probably equaled a shitload.

"Well, yeah, a lot of money, I guess."

"Okay, so they aren't going to want to say no to you? Right?" Another question I knew the answer to.

"No, I guess not." I had heard of custom-ordering bags before, but I didn't really have too much interest. I could get bags tomorrow, so why would I bother ordering them? It also seemed like something that would garner unnecessary attention from the powers that be. The last thing I needed was the name exposure at the home office. But Sarah was, well, she was Sarah, and she was dropping that proverbial shitload with me. So rather than explain how impossible this idea was, I decided to look at Sarah's request as a step in a new direction—custom-buying. I couldn't do it a lot, certainly, but I might as well try and keep her happy. (I did end up growing bolder about ordering as time went on—but overall the slow turnaround was less than appealing.)

"*Guess* not? Michael, they aren't going to fuck with one of their best customers. I really, really think you can do this, and I know I can't get it without ordering it. And I know they won't order for me at the store here, they have to know you, like superwell, and I just get my bags from you, you know. So anyway, my point: there is this *perfect* shade of pink that I totally *need* to have a Birkin in."

"Well, I've seen pink bags before . . ." I don't know why I said that.

"Michael, no shit, but not this fucking color pink, trust me, not the color I want. I went on Wikipedia today and looked at the 'Pink' page, okay, like I knew what I wanted but not what to call it. And the color I want is French Rose. French Rose—isn't that fucking perfect? And that is the exact pink I want, okay? In crocodile, you know, of course." That was a given. I knew that she always preferred the crocodile bags, although she "settled" for the leather ones. I preferred crocodile too, since I generally used a percentage markup to calculate my profit. It was like the difference between selling scarves and selling Birkins—I got a lot more money for my effort if I got a croc bag instead of a leather one. Hence, I was currently trying to figure out how to get crocodile bags more often. Hey, if you aren't growing your business, you might as well assume it's going to fail.

"Okay, Sarah, let me see what I can do. I'll get the color info and then it's up to my salesperson, I guess. No harm in asking." I wasn't making any promises.

"Please please please! I really want this fucking bag, it would be so over-the-top to have a one-of-a-kind Birkin, I have this killer dress that color and I can carry a black Birkin with it, but that's so, you know, boring, and this would be so so amazing, I will love you if you can get this for me. I know it's going to take for fucking ever, like a goddamn year or something, whatever, good things come to those who wait, right?"

Yeah, like a chance for me to get a word in edgewise. She was hilarious. I really would do my best to get her this bag. It would be worth it just to get to watch her reaction.

"Okay, I promise to do my best." There, I came up with something I could promise. "So I have to get going, but you want those others, right? Send them? When should I look for the money so I can get them shipped and everything?" My poor mother. See how exciting it is, Mom? Yeah, FedEx offices are riveting, let me tell ya.

"Yeah, yeah, I'll take care of the payment stuff later today. And tell me as soon as you know if you can get the bag ordered. And, Michael— one last thing?"

"Yes?" I hoped she could hear the smile in my voice.

"However you are fucking getting these bags, keep 'em coming!" And with that, she hung up, still laughing.

I should have known I wouldn't have the last word. And what had I agreed to? To order a bag in a color that Hermès doesn't even make? Time to bust out Grandma Johnson's recipe again—maybe I would bring some muffins too. Blueberry ones—with fresh blueberries. I couldn't believe I was going to use baked goods in order to bribe an Hermès salesperson to allow me to order a bag that would cost more than a car. I decided next week sounded like a good time to deal with all that. I had other business to attend to—plus, it takes a week to get the bananas ripe anyway.

I sent out an e-mail to my other "clients" who might be interested in the remaining two purses. I now had many people I considered "Birkin" people. These women weren't buying bags at the Sarah rate, but they had bought one (or more) from me already. I had started keeping a list of who wanted what so that if given a choice in the store, I could go with a preferred color that someone had requested. But I was realizing that no matter what "flavor" I got, these handbags didn't have a long shelf life. And once again, less than two days later, I was Birkinless.

Like last time, I kicked around the house for a little while, but now when I was at home I felt like I should be on the road. Then, when I was on the road, I was worrying about monitoring my auctions and feedback and e-mails, not to mention Juan. (My cell phone bills were going through the roof again.) I still had a pretty steady sideline going with

the scarves and Hermès miscellany, and an e-mail I failed to respond to promptly could result in bad feedback (an eBay PowerSeller's worst nightmare). I had a laptop, but there were times you couldn't just whip out a computer: "Hey, can I move the salt and pepper shakers for a second? Grab your wineglass too; I don't want it getting tangled in the cord . . ." I decided it was time to go to the next level—take the plunge—bite the bullet—and get a BlackBerry. I had told everyone I abhorred them ("Come on, who needs to be *that* available all the time?"), but I had lied. I wanted one. I like new toys. The bananas were ready too, so I guessed today was the day for heading over to the Hermès store and trying my luck in ordering that bag. From baking muffins to mastering cutting-edge technology—I was fast realizing that if I wanted to be the "It boy" of the "It bag," I sure as hell needed to be well-rounded.

23

A Roster of Reservations

I got that pink handbag ordered for Sarah ("No problem, Mr. Tonello") and had my requisite downtime at home, and I was ready to hit the road again. My job was lucrative, yes, but also had a lot of expenses involved, and some of those bills didn't roll in until after you had kind of forgotten about them. I probably maybe also occasionally had been known to be a tiny bit self-indulgent in matters relating to food/drink/clothing/lodging . . . And as much as Juan loved having me home, he knew as long as I was home, I wasn't really working. Plus, he had raised his eyebrows at the BlackBerry purchase, so I felt I had better start using it ASAP.

I decided that I wanted to break new ground in terms of stores— fresh Birkin blood (so to speak). I decided on a tour of Germany, a place I hadn't been since I did a road trip with my parents the year the Wall came down. For the hell of it, I decided to do Luxembourg and Belgium too. I always liked the way Luxembourg looked on maps—such a small country having such a long name seemed ballsy to me somehow, and Brussels was so darn close by then you might as well go there too. By renting a car and hitting a new Hermès each day, à la south of

France, I could potentially net six Birkins. So, Nuremberg first, then Frankfurt, then Hamburg, and on to Cologne. Then to the city of Luxembourg (same name as the country, and not too much smaller) and Brussels. Whew. Screw *Road Rules*, they should do a reality show based on my one-man *Birkin Brigades*.

I was still scarf shopping with my wish lists, although there was an increasing number of stores that I had already milked dry. I had long ago bought out every scarf of value in the Barcelona stores, and now the south of France stores were getting a little weak on inventory too. For me to profit on a scarf, it had to be an older design, on the rare side, and it wasn't like they were going to magically materialize in the stores I had already cleaned out. (Hermès saved *that* kind of trick for its handbags.) So I had branched out. Now I bought shawls, Ulysses (the notebooks), jewelry, whatever was available, whatever would get me to that magic $1,000 mark I needed to ensure a shot at a Birkin purchase. I didn't usually profit on the other bric-a-brac, but I generally broke even. The Ulysses and *chaîne d'ancre* bracelets (like the one I had) always sold in practically moments, so I was partial to those. However, I was hopeful of running across a couple of scarf treasures, since these stores hadn't played the role of "wish list wells" yet.

Nuremberg was a rather attractive place, with old castles looming around the perimeter of the walled-off city center. It also had the requisite bevy of gothic churches, plus the added charm of many cobblestoned streets. *And* I had no problem getting a bag, which always makes me consider a city in a favorable light.

Frankfurt was more industrial, less of a tourist destination, but I have nothing but glowing recommendations of the Hermès store there. Two for two. Both leather, though, which wasn't optimal.

So, when I walked up to the front of store number three in Hamburg, I was delighted to see a *rouge Hermès* (or Hermès red) 35cm crocodile Birkin. But, as I got closer, I saw a tiny brass sign holder propped up next to it, displaying an ivory placard with one word

printed in elegant black script—*RESERVIERT*. Now, what the hell did that mean? How could anyone be expected to believe that there was a two-year wait for these bags, and a constantly growing waiting list, but when the bag finally came in, the customer just let it hang out a while longer with a RESERVED sign on it? That made no sense at all. And in any case, why would Hermès let $30,000 worth of bag languish in their window? Wouldn't it be more of a "here it is, come and get it, and now" scenario? Did they have some kind of layaway program I wasn't aware of? I could only imagine *that* conversation: "Oh, yeah, the croc Birkin, right, great. But I only have half the money now—repairs on the yacht this week, you know how it is . . . don't sell it, just put in the window, pop a RESERVED sign on it or something. I'll send the chauffeur by with the other half by next Sunday at the latest . . . Great, great. You guys are the best." I mean, really, WTF? I didn't believe it for a second. I knew that Birkin was for sale, to the right person—namely, me. I almost tapped on the glass and cooed at it like a puppy you're going to buy at the pet store—Don't worry, little guy, you get to go home today.

The saleswoman in the store was on the older side, and this further bolstered my confidence. Having a kindly older woman running the show is the best of all possible Birkin worlds. With them, I barely even thought consciously about the formula—I'd just play a little parlor trick. Approaching the display case where the scarves were neatly layered, one atop the other, with only a hint of design and color showing, I'd casually identify several by name. All it took was "Ah, Brides de Gala, still selling as well as always, I'm sure" and "Oh, you have a Pierres d'Orient, that's a favorite of mine," and a woman like this would be swooning, as proud of my Hermès knowledge as she presumably was about her grandchildren's finger painting. The only issue could be a language barrier, but Hannah (that was her name) spoke excellent English, so no problems there. I piled up a few scarves and some Ulysses, and then decided I needed to up the ante for the croc with a RESERVED sign. I selected a *chaîne d'ancre*

too, so that I had almost three grand worth of merchandise. Then it was time.

"Hannah, this is great, my mother is going to be so thrilled. And that lovely red bag in the window . . . it's a crocodile, right? That's exactly what she has been looking for, so this is perfect, you have everything right here."

"Oh, sir, that bag is reserved, didn't you see the sign?" Hannah sounded caught off guard.

"No, I didn't . . . Oh no . . . It's really what caught my eye to come in. Do you know who it's reserved for? Or for how long?" I wondered how this part would work—this whole reserved thing added a twist.

"Well, let me go talk to my manager, maybe he has more information . . ." She scurried off to the back room. She came back almost immediately, looking disappointed. "Sir, I am so sorry but the bag is reserved, as it says on the sign. My hands are tied."

I didn't have to think twice about what to do; I sure wasn't dropping three grand and not getting a Birkin.

"Hannah, let me give my mother a call . . . see what she wants me to do. Just a second." I dialed my voice mail and walked away so I didn't really have to feign much of a conversation. A couple minutes later, I strolled back over, having "hung up" with my mom.

"Well, she says she really wants a Birkin, and I'm heading to Paris in a few days, so I'll just do one-stop shopping and get everything there . . ." I tried to keep a poker face. I had to gamble that there was no way Hannah wanted to lose this sale. "So, thank you so much, it was nice talking with you. You've been very helpful."

I started heading out. I pushed open the door, my heart already sinking, but then I felt a hand fall gently on my upper arm.

"Wait, wait one second . . . Maybe something can be done . . . Let me speak with my manager again," she pleaded.

"Well, if it's reserved I don't see what your manager can do . . ." I let my sentence trail off. I figured if I pitched a slow one, Hannah might hit it out of the park for me.

"Let me just ask again, maybe we can call the customer . . ." Batter up!

"Okay, if you think there's a chance, I would love to be able to do everything here, especially after you have been so helpful." This much was true, at least. Hannah disappeared and returned with a big smile on her face.

"Sir, my manager called the customer, who said she had decided against it. So you want it, then?" She was obviously pleased to have saved the sale.

"Yes, yes, oh, this is wonderful." And it was. Home run.

Over the next few years, I ran into RESERVED signs on a regular basis. If they ended up selling the "reserved" Birkin to me, as they did 90 percent of the time, they gave a number of different explanations. There was the "reservation cancelled" script, as in Hamburg. Sometimes they claimed they had been trying to reach the customer, but two weeks had passed, so they were now willing to sell me the bag. Often salespeople would show me the "reserved" bag, acting as though it was for sale, and when I actually went to buy it, they would panic and act flustered, running for the manager to find out their next step. I never believed any of those bags were on hold for anyone, even on the rare occasions when they didn't choose to sell to me. Usually when that happened, they explained that their manager wasn't in the store, and that I should come back. I believed that part, and I hoped for their sake they never told their managers they dropped a $3,000 B.B. (before Birkin) sale to honor a RESERVED sign for an imaginary third party. Because, obviously, when I got refused a bag, I didn't buy a thing from the store. It was like buying a car—you can't be afraid to walk. Most times, I got stopped before I really left, like in Hamburg; and on a couple of memorable occasions I was even "chased" down the street by my salesperson, so they could tell me they had somehow managed to finagle me the bag. Eventually, I realized the RESERVED signs *were* real—the Birkins they labeled were reserved for the next person who walked in and dropped a few thousand on other,

non-Birkin Hermès items. In other words, what a RESERVED sign on a croc bag in the window told me was (a) they definitely had a Birkin and (b) I needed to add about a grand to the formula to ensure they would crack and sell it to me. Pretty convenient, when you really thought about it—a visual clue. Took out a lot of the guesswork.

Cologne and Luxembourg were "normal" Hermès experiences; I worked my magic and got a leather Birkin at each. I did find out why Luxembourg was so cocky with that oversized name—that country's namesake capital city was loaded. The first four letters weren't any coincidence, either. Everywhere I looked there were gigantic steel-doored investment banks and high-end boutiques, and I'd swear about every fifth car was a Bentley or an old Rolls-Royce.

Then it was on to Belgium, where I did hit pay dirt of a kind (although not the crocodile kind I was hoping for). Though, at first, things didn't go that smooth in the Brussels Hermès. This was because the first person waiting on me was a young girl who was totally baffled by my scarf requests. She fetched another salesperson, an unpleasant-looking woman who had kind of a nasty attitude until I revealed my scarf "expertise." She warmed up to me after I inquired about a few rarer items, and indicated for me to wait where I was. She returned from the attic or wherever she had gone with a box o' treasure of the scarf persuasion: old designs I had given up on finding, even ones I had on wish lists but had never managed to track down. I took ten of them, quickly launching myself into Birkin-worthy territory. Plus, it added a little bit extra to the bottom line—these beauties would get top dollar at auction. All around, success.

I was getting back to my hotel after an early dinner, comfortably full on the Belgian specialty of *pommes frites* and mussels, and happy to be starting my journey back to Barcelona tomorrow. I checked my BlackBerry in the elevator and got an e-mail that brought me down a little. It was from Pime, who was "on the job" for me this weekend in Buenos Aires. She had taken Thursday off too so she could make the most of her time in the city.

From: "Pime" <PimeX123@yahoo.com>
To: "Michael" <Armoire_Auctions@yahoo.com>

Michael, I don't think I can do Birkin thing like you. I went to Hermès in Buenos Aires in afternoon yesterday and there was a woman who was so mean, and ugly too, I hate her, no I didn't but I didn't like at all and she say no Birkins, barely let me talk and do formula. Then this morning I go back and she not there, but girl I get doesn't know scarfs from list of wishes and I feel dumb like I am saying wrong or something . . . and no birkin again. So I will pay back for ticket and I am so sorry. Pime

Oh, no. This was not good. I headed down the hall to my room, BlackBerry limply dangling from my hand. South America was a sea of unbought Birkins, and I knew Pime could do it, she just needed practice. Tomorrow was Saturday, her (and my) last shot for the week, since Hermès was closed on Sunday. I needed to show her the ropes; I mean, that woman today hated me at first, but at the end she was eating out of my hand. But exactly how to demonstrate my technique from thousands of miles away was another thing. I wish I had some kind of Hermès handbook I could ship off to her . . . Wait a minute, what if I made one? I wasn't doing anything tonight but lounging around—I had already eaten. And it would cheer her up—I didn't have to work to make this material funny; it already was. I thought about the "types" I dealt with in the stores and decided that I could give her the rundown on them, since that was really the main thing. As every good salesman knows, you need to tailor your approach on a case-by-case basis. Of course, we were technically buying, not selling, but the principle remained the same.

So that night I sat in my room, sipped wine, and typed up something I later came to call the Hermès Store Employee Roster. I even formatted it so it looked kind of real, bullet points and all. (And from then on, whenever I got a new shopper, which I did about ten more times, I sent

them a copy. It also served the purpose of making sure they had a sense of humor.) A couple hours later I sent her the e-mail:

From: "michael" <armoire_auctions@yahoo.com>
To: "Pime" <PimeX123@yahoo.com>

Pime, i got your message, but i think i can help, if you are willing to give it another shot. some of the Hermès people were mean to me too (remind me to tell you about marseilles). but what i have learned is that i just had to use different approaches with different salespeople. but what makes it easier is that there are definitely a few distinct "types" that you find working in stores over and over again. some are combinations of a couple types, so that can be tricky, but you can do this, i know you can. i am attaching something i wrote for you, it sort of gives a rundown. AND don't worry about the plane ticket, it's on me, either way, you tried!

mt~

ps you dealt with a farmer on fri, and then an ingénue today . . . if you go back, look for a grandmother ☺

Attch.

HERMÈS STORE EMPLOYEE ROSTER

The Incurable Romantic

- **GENDER:** male

- **SEXUAL PREFERENCE:** queer as a three-dollar bill

- **AGE:** 21–60

- **HAIR:** very Vidal Sassoon

- **TEETH:** highway reflective strip white

- **MOTTO:** "Appearance is everything"

- **PERCENTAGE IN HERMÈS CAPTIVITY:** 10–15%

- **LIKELIHOOD OF BIRKIN PURCHASE:** almost 100%

- **PREVIOUS JOB:** Gucci

- **THE LOWDOWN:** this employee outwardly pretends to enjoy his job but is really just hoping to meet Mr. Right (a knight in a shining Hermès croc bomber jacket) and be saved from salesperson serfdom forever

- **MALE APPROACH:** flirtatious without blowing kisses, create false sense of dating potential. Flash croc agenda book (more subtle than flashing black AmEx card) early in encounter to activate his innate gold-digging instincts. In cases of extreme desperation (yours, not his), bait him with promise of after-work martinis at local Grand Hotel

- **FEMALE APPROACH:** flirt a little too, but better off to compliment his acute style sense, and talk about some hot guy in the store. Also insinuate you have a rich gay cousin you can set him up with.

The Farmer

- **GENDER:** female

- **SEXUAL PREFERENCE:** what? Are you kidding?

- **AGE:** 50–70 (but looks and acts not a day over 90)

- **HAIR:** gray with highlights of chicken-piss yellow

- **TEETH:** possibly

- **MOTTO:** "You'll never see a Birkin in this lifetime"

- **PERCENTAGE IN HERMÈS CAPTIVITY:** 5–10%

- **LIKELIHOOD OF BIRKIN PURCHASE:** see Motto

- **PREVIOUS JOB:** meatpacking plant foreman

- **THE LOWDOWN:** this woman was born into a farming family from the hinterlands, raised on a diet of condensed milk and cattle by-products. She hates money and anyone who has it. The idea of a handbag that costs more than her car awakens both loathing and confusion in her soul. One can only wonder why she is inevitably store manager; perhaps some strange work release program of the fifties

- **APPROACH:** avoid at all costs due to potential for catching any number of agrarian-related illnesses. If interaction is inevitable, compliment her fake pearl studs. Brace yourself for rejection coupled with overwhelming waft of clinical halitosis.

The Grandmother

- **GENDER:** female

- **SEXUAL PREFERENCE:** not these days

- **AGE:** 60+

- **HAIR:** frosted, gray or white, roller-set

- **TEETH:** yes

- **MOTTO:** "Aren't *you* adorable?"

- **PERCENTAGE IN HERMÈS CAPTIVITY:** 15–20% (wish they would breed more)

- **LIKELIHOOD OF BIRKIN PURCHASE:** very high

- **PREVIOUS JOB:** nurturer, cookie maker, boo-boo kisser

- **THE LOWDOWN:** this woman does not need the job. Her husband recently passed away so she likes getting out of the house and being paid to play with pretty things all day. Secretly hates the Farmer, although would never verbalize this feeling even when talking to herself. After several years still has yet to realize the Incurable Romantic is gay and keeps trying to set him up with her granddaughter and/or niece

- **APPROACH:** approach without fear. Think of this woman as your grandmother for one hour. Really, it's *that* good!

The Nazi

- **GENDER:** either

- **SEXUAL PREFERENCE:** overridden by career ambitions

- **AGE:** 25-60

- **HAIR:** severe

- **TEETH:** gnashed

- **MOTTO:** "Refer to Employee Handbook"

- **PERCENTAGE IN HERMÈS CAPTIVITY:** 30-45%

- **LIKELIHOOD OF BIRKIN PURCHASE:** extremely high if you stick with "the formula"

- **PREVIOUS JOB:** mall security guard/hall monitor

- **THE LOWDOWN:** determined to be store manager. Cutthroat and totally by the book. Detests the Farmer but secretly longs to have her position. Bulldozes over the Grandmother, ignores the Incurable Romantic. Career-driven pathological liar. Recognizable by the glint of desperation in his/her eyes

- **APPROACH:** tread cautiously . . . this is the employee that perpetuated the need for "the formula." Dollars count! Since they don't know diddly squat about Hermès history or merchandise from previous collections (remember they only care about $$$), use your knowledge to impress/disarm and go for the croc Birkin. All bets are off—keep your cool, and they will crumble like the Germans at the Nuremberg trials.

The Ingénue

- **GENDER:** female

- **SEXUAL PREFERENCE:** whoever's paying

- **AGE:** 20–25

- **HAIR:** shiny

- **TEETH:** perfect and framed by Botox-enhanced lips

- **MOTTO:** "Let me ask"

- **PERCENTAGE IN HERMÈS CAPTIVITY:** 15–20%

- **LIKELIHOOD OF BIRKIN PURCHASE:** what's a Birkin?

- **PREVIOUS JOB:** kegger

- **THE LOWDOWN:** this employee, although willing, is anything but ready-and-able. Apparently hired yesterday and has yet to go through any sort of formal training. Quick to get help from either the Incurable Romantic, Farmer, Nazi, or Grandmother . . . just hope that it's not the Farmer you end up with!

- **APPROACH:** immediately ask if the Grandmother is working today.

I got an e-mail back late the next afternoon, right before I got on the plane for home.

From: "Pime" <PimeX123@yahoo.com>
To: "Michael" <Armoire_Auctions@yahoo.com>

Michael-

I laugh so hard I cry . . . I had to try again for bag, you are so funny and nice to try and cheer me up . . . so I went again in, and guess what? I got a grandmother this time, and a Birkin. Tell me where to send, and all. Pime

I couldn't help feeling proud of myself for this one. After my Birkin 101 course, Pime was ready for anything Hermès could throw at her. Well, except maybe a Farmer/Nazi with a croc and a RESERVED sign . . . that could spell doom for anyone.

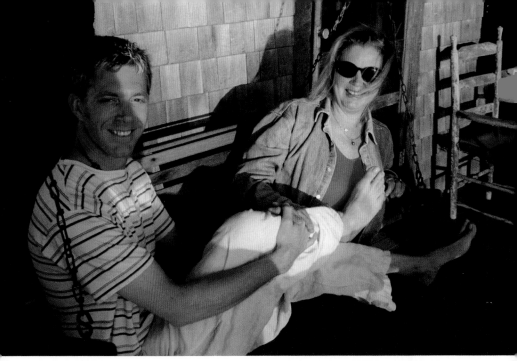

With my friend Kate at the Corn Hill house near Provincetown, Massachusetts. We often gave big, elaborate dinner parties there. I'd grill lobsters while we watched the sunset, sipping Kate's famous margaritas.

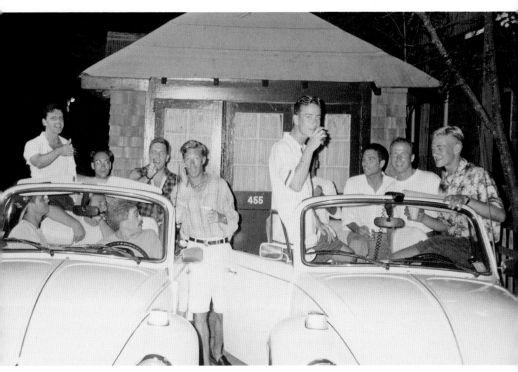

With friends in front of my boathouse cottage. The first summer I moved to Provincetown is a time I'll fondly remember, or, more accurately, wish I could.

I wore the iconic Hermès chaîne d'ancre bracelet whenever I went Birkin buying . . . It was my good-luck charm. Along the way I bought dozens of these bracelets in the process of using the "Formula," and they sold like hotcakes on eBay.

A page from my Hermès Ulysse notebook with a list of Birkins I purchased in October 2005. I have to laugh when I read articles that claim Hermès produces "about 100 Birkins per year." If that were truly the case it would mean that I bought the entire annual production that year—and then some!

Another of my Ulysse notebooks, in which I kept the address and phone number of every Hermès store in existence (as well as salespeople's names and numbers).

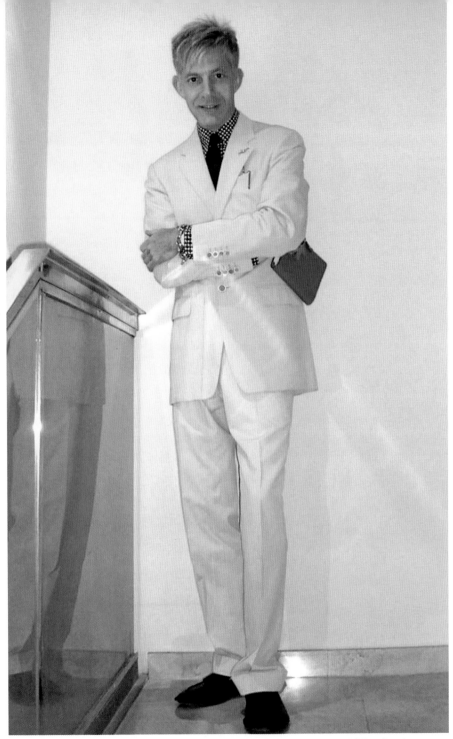

My Birkin-buying uniform: Prada suit, Hermès shirt, Hermès vest, Jil Sander tie, Hermès cashmere socks, Giorgio Armani shoes, Hermès chaîne d'ancre bracelet, Polo Ralph Lauren sterling watch fob (worn through the lapel buttonhole), S. T. Dupont "Medici" fountain pen (tucked inside the breast pocket), Hermès crocodile agenda (inside breast pocket), orange Hermès Ulysse notebook.

A 35cm fuchsia crocodile Birkin. It's a rare color, so finding one of these is like winning in Vegas . . . the odds are stacked against you, but it's sensational when it happens! Victoria Beckham (Posh Spice) has an ostrich Birkin in this color.

This Kelly Lakis was my first bag purchase at the flagship Hermès store in Faubourg Saint-Honoré in Paris. I like to think of it as my qualifying purchase: it opened the door for many future Birkins.

An Hermès Kelly Pouchette (designed by Jean Paul Gaultier), one of four (each in a different color) that a client purchased for about $3,500 each.

A basic 35cm leather Birkin. Aficionados consider this the "starter Birkin." At about $8,000, some would call it cheap (compared with $30,000 for the same bag in crocodile).

This blue crocodile Birkin was the subject of an international "hostage" situation and a square-off with one of my "shoppers." I'm happy to report that the bag is now safe and living in a good home.

Birkins can be as collectible as rare stamps or old coins. I bought, sold, and resold this Birkin several times.

Pime is a friend from Santiago, Chile, whom I trained in the fine art of Birkin buying. After a false start or two, she really learned how to bring home the Birkins.

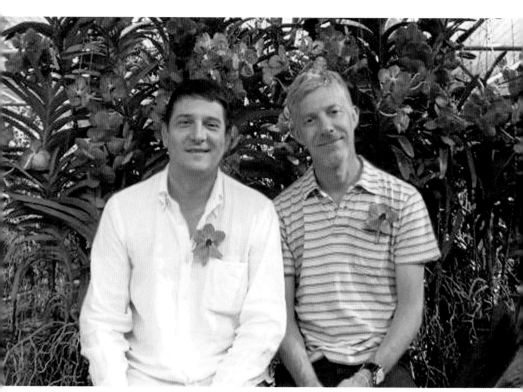

After moving the three thousand miles to Barcelona I found my soul mate, Juan. Here we are in Chiang Mai, Thailand, beflowered at an orchid and butterfly farm.

A Polaroid of Mom, with my high-school graduation portrait in the background.

Juan and I first met at the Ritz-Carlton Hotel Arts in Barcelona. It was kismet, and we felt it most appropriate for our parents' first meeting to take place there. Here Juan and I are with (left to right) Juan Sr., Mom, Carmen, and Dad.

With my family on a Caribbean cruise: my sister, Dorothy; Juan; my niece, Riane; Mom; and Dad. (My brother-in-law, Edward, was unable to come.)

I have fond memories of Capri: the spectacular stairs at the Hotel Villa Brunella, and the breathtaking via Camerelle with perhaps the tiniest Hermès store on the planet. One day I hope to return . . .

24

A Yen for Hermès

Four or five months of madness whipped by—lots of tea drinking and eBay auction gawking and passport stamps and hotel directions lying in the passenger seat of my rental car. I had gone through all the bags from the Germany trip, naturally. I had also made another round of the south of France, looped Spain and Portugal a few times, dropped in at Serge at the Faubourg, and had the odd bag rolling in from Dominique (my Deauville connection), Pime, and Luc. I had fifty or more auctions running on eBay at all times, on the items that "financed" the Birkin purchases. I closed on half of them each weekend, and Monday was now shipping day. I scanned/responded to/refreshed my e-mail inbox a lot. I cherished the friendly, obscenity-laden updates from Sarah and Hermès hotline posts from Grace, which arrived nestled amid the monotonous stream of customer queries.

I read a lot of e-mails. I wrote a lot of e-mails. More e-mails than I personally believe a person should read or write. Especially if that person is me. Rather than seeing my BlackBerry as a shiny toy, I now viewed it as an electronic ankle bracelet for Hermès stores in Europe— I had to constantly be around one or risk a chance of missing a croc

Birkin for some wealthy woman who really wanted one. I had lovely clients—and clients the sight of whose return e-mail address I winced at. I progressed to form e-mail, making e-mail templates that answered the top ten repeat-offender questions. I stopped short of making FAQ to mail out; there was too much chance of a homophobic typo appearing in the subject line of a customer's angry reply. Not that they were angry often, but I did deal with the public, albeit chiefly through cyber-means. And I was in the service industry—it has its moments, as any waiter can tell you. I bought Birkins. I sold Birkins. I worked on specializing in the croc bags, and it was coming along nicely. Business as usual.

I could tell it was taking its toll on my home life, as well as on me. I wanted to enjoy the money I was making, not just spend it on hotels in cities I barely even got to see when I was there. And while Juan didn't begrudge me my nomadic life, he didn't adore being my Hermès golf widow. Plus, Christmas was fast approaching, along with Juan's three-week break from teaching. It was obvious: we needed a vacation. We had to make up our minds where, although I was willing to bend to whatever Juan wanted, since I was always traveling. What was funny was that whenever we discussed going somewhere I knew there was an Hermès store, I couldn't help calculating how much of the trip's cost could be defrayed if I got one good croc bag. It didn't really matter much in the choosing process, though—a vast majority of the world's most desirable locations have an Hermès store. Unless we settled on Calcutta for our romantic getaway, I could at least do a croc drive-by regardless of where we went. Fortunately, we went with two major cities neither of us had been to—a quick weekend in Moscow and then Tokyo for ten days.

I spent the first morning in Moscow sightseeing with Juan, taken off guard by both the bitter cold and the haphazard class distinctions among the people. After living in a Spanish city where both the thermometer and the socioeconomic ladder lacked such extremes, my system definitely felt the shock. Christian Dior, Dolce & Gabbana,

Cartier, and Louis Vuitton all had multiple store locations, but parked on the same street were fifty-year-old cars rotting from rust. And the landscape was dominated by gray—gray skies, gray streets, gray faces. It's not that I didn't think it was beautiful . . . I did. Red Square, the Kremlin, St. Basil's Cathedral—how could you feel anything but awe when you looked at the onion domes? Plus, Juan and I had a gorgeous room at the Park Hyatt, a luxury hotel in a central location. It was really that Moscow fell squarely into the same category as Vegas—great place to visit, but you wouldn't want to live there.

Hermès was no issue, at least. It was relatively easy for me to get a leather Birkin from the youngish "grandmother" working there, although there was a panicky moment when I found out that they didn't take American Express. I ran to an ATM to fetch some rubles, and the crisis was averted. (Side note: My banker in Barcelona had been very understanding a few months prior to this, when I had mentioned the issues that having a "maximum withdraw" limit on my ATM card could cause for me. As a result of her kindness, I now had twelve ATM cards. You do not want to be in line behind me when I have to get Birkin money—it's not pretty.) So, the Park Hyatt now paid for by Hermès clients, it was time to head for the exotic Orient.

Tokyo was a complete mind-fuck, even for a seasoned traveler like myself. First off, Juan and I had booked at Hotel Okura, and it blew us away. Our suite had a commanding view of both a traditional Japanese garden and the skyscrapers that crowded every inch of the city's horizon. However, I think Juan and I were more entranced by the little remote control next to our bed, which ran everything. All the lighting in the suite, the television, the drapes, the electronic do-not-disturb message—you could deal with all of it while in a reclining position. Apparently this was nothing special for Japan, but to us it was technology on a *Jetsons* level. Possibly even cooler was this silent printer/fax we didn't even really notice until we called the concierge to request that he make our dinner reservations. Five minutes later, a piece of paper spouted out of the aforementioned machine with the confirmation of

our plans, the restaurant info, and the directions for the cabbie printed out in Japanese. Very spiffy.

The day after we arrived was Christmas Eve, and we were unexpectedly given a fantastic present. My mother had called ahead and made us reservations at La Belle Époque, selecting it out of the nine restaurants in the hotel. She also made arrangements that she would take care of the bill. There were only a few entrées to choose from, as it was a prix fixe menu for the holiday. We settled on Kobe beef—a tenderloin dusted with truffles, wrapped in pastry, and finished with a truffle demi-glace. The waiter actually rolled out a cart bearing the entire tenderloin, accompanied by the chef, who then carved pieces from it in front of us. Since there were no prices listed, Juan and I had no idea of the cost of our meal until my mom told me two months later that a $1,000 charge from Tokyo had appeared on her Visa bill. She hadn't realized what she had gotten herself into either—whoops. (Good thing she and my dad had inherited a sizable amount of money, which meant she was laughing, not crying, as she told me what had happened.) But anyway, that night, blissfully ignorant, we ate Kobe beef until the chef's arm must have been ready to fall off. Hey, at least they hadn't been charging by the pound . . . then we *really* would have been in trouble.

The Hermès in Tokyo makes the Faubourg look like a mall kiosk. Renzo Piano designed the twelve-story building, which is constructed completely of glass boxes about a foot square. Now, that sounds very cool, but it doesn't sound close to as cool as it actually is in person, seeing this mammoth translucent building glowing with an ethereal white light. What was funny was that it is often described as architecturally understated, which I guess it could be mistaken for if compared with the other consumer temples of the Ginza shopping district. Chanel, for example, had the front of its building made as a gigantic LED board, upon which they change the "fabric," making the entire façade shift between plaid, polka dots, paisley, or whatever else they can dream up. The Dior building has two layers to its exterior walls, the smallish holes punched in the steel of the outer layer allowing the light of

the fiber optics housed beneath to peek through. (Think really, really big Lite-Brite.) The Sony building right next door to Hermès has a brightly colored mural stretching eight stories, plus the added bonus of free PlayStation on the sixth floor. Shiseido cosmetics made its building look like one of its trademark maroon glass bottles, either that or a light stick for the world's largest raver. But, as visually appealing as they all were, none of them sold my merchandise, so I started my day at the Hermès store. However, I didn't end up getting "the usual" that day. The pricing in the Tokyo location, including that of the Birkins (amazingly enough, they actually keep them out where you can see them), was prohibitive to really aggressive formula enactment. So I went with a black crocodile Kelly bag that was prominently displayed in the store, and then sent Juan in to get "his Kelly" in brown. That worked. I could bear to sacrifice some Birkins, as long as there was a little bit of crocodile skin coming home with me.

Juan and I did the typical tourist stuff: the Kabuki theater, the Imperial Palace, and, most memorably, a two-day sojourn near Hakone National Park. We went there to enjoy the *onsen*, the hot restorative springs that have made the region famous. Our *senshin-tei*, or traditional Japanese room, was a *hanare*—a completely separate building where we were attended to by a personal geisha of sorts . . . no makeup or any funny stuff, of course. She did make us our meals of sushi, prepare our beds, provide us with traditional dress, and, most important, bring us copious amounts of sake. Our lodging was complete with its own private *rotenburo*, a natural hot-spring Jacuzzi tucked in a bamboo hut. The 108-degree water was piped directly in from a natural hot spring, and never recycled. This spring was one of the many near Mount Fuji, whose looming presence was mirrored in the nearby Lake Ashi. Overall, I felt enchanted, like Ralph Macchio in the second *Karate Kid* movie (minus the peach fuzz and the guy who wanted to fight me). Juan was so relaxed by our days in the spa that he never even mentioned the price, which normally would have caused him to faint and drown in the waters of the *onsen*. In other words, our stay was a rousing success.

We rounded out our culinary adventures on our vacation in Tokyo with one more notable meal. On New Year's Eve we ate at the Park Hyatt building, in a place called the New York Grill. The restaurant was on the fifty-second floor, reached after a ride up to the fifty-first and a short walk through a massive library on whose shelves intermingled books and objets d'art. The view was obviously surreal, as was the theme for the night: fire and ice. When we sat down, we were each presented with an ice block a foot square (like a temporary brick of that Hermès store) with two tubes protruding from it—one filled with caviar, one with Champagne. Ice. All night, there were copious flambé dishes and flamenco dancers wielding flaming batons. Fire. The meal needed no theming, as it was pretty much anything you wanted, from lobster to more of that Kobe beef we had gorged on a week earlier. Between Surf & Turf and Fire & Ice, Juan & I were deliciously Dazed & Confused by our environment (and the two bottles of Champagne we drank). We were there till well after the new year had rolled in, relishing the bizarre opulence of the place.

Oddly enough, we got to revisit our evening unexpectedly a year or so hence, when we rented *Lost in Translation*, set almost in its entirety at the Park Hyatt. All the "bar scenes" from that excellent movie were filmed in the bar attached to the New York Grill. I always thought it was a shame that it hadn't been Fire & Ice night in one of the scenes set there—it would have added a whole new level to the Bill Murray character's cultural confusion.

I also found out some valuable information about "my" company while I was on vacation in Japan. Tokyo had a fetish for the Hermès brand that exceeded anything I had heretofore seen. In addition to the gigantic glass building I had gone to, which was obviously the mack daddy of them all, there were eleven other stores spread throughout the city. Intrigued by this, when I got home, I pulled out my *Le Monde d'Hermès* and counted the stores in Asia. Roughly a hundred Hermès stores made their home in the Orient. Even given the population distribution on the planet, that was a whole lot of people sporting the H logo in one form or another.

I wasn't really sure why this was, and when I asked Grace about it in an e-mail, she confirmed that the Asian market was booming, but didn't really know why either. I knew from my experience in Japan that virtually everyone there loved branded items, and my hypothesis was that Hermès had built the "brand to end all brands." And it wasn't an easy brand to afford, which always adds to the cachet. The handbags I had seen in that mammoth solar panel of a store were priced as though they already had a Tonello markup. I mused idly over whether I could justify going back with European-bought handbags and hosting some kind of Hermès purse Tupperware party. The practical concerns overwhelmed me, though, and I decided I had to wait on it. At least until I figured out how to hack into Tokyo's five-star hotel computers and send my invitations through all their directions printout systems.

25

Shop 'Til You Drop

When we first got back from vacation, I was more relaxed than I had been in a while. Juan and I were definitely solid again too. But after two more months of weeklong bag-buying quests, and trips to *correos*, and constant BlackBerry messages, it was as if we'd never even taken a vacation (except for the photo on the fridge, of us in front of the Imperial Palace). I started feeling sort of logy, blaming it on "the grind," and I took another mini-vacation in the early spring. I puttered around the house for two weeks, back in my pajamas, as in those good ol' scarf days, getting the odd Birkin here and there from my "shoppers." Two weeks was a long break from airports for me at this point, but as much as I self-medicated with Earl Grey, my fatigue didn't seem to be going away. I decided I had to pull out of my funk and take another journey. There was no reason for me to feel fatigued after two weeks of nothingness. Presumably, I was just bored.

I flew to Geneva and was feeling a little energized by the mid-May mountain air. I was always partial to May, since in New England it was the first month it was safe to bet that you weren't going to get any more snow that winter. It could happen, but the odds were at least stacked in

your favor. I was further energized by the Hermès store, which sold me a 30cm fuchsia crocodile Birkin after I dropped about three grand on shawls and scarves.

Then I rented a car and headed to Lyon. On the highway, I gradually realized I wasn't feeling all that great. The hour and a half in the driver's seat dragged by, and I breathed a sigh of relief when I got to my destination. I went into Hermès Lyon and continued my lucky streak—they sold me another 30cm croc bag, this time a matte barenia. That would fetch a pretty penny. However, even with the excitement I felt at this, I felt my exhaustion more. Something was definitely not right; maybe a bug? I also had a pounding headache—unusual for me. Well, my cranial pain system was making up for lost opportunities, because it was a goddamn doozy this time. I wandered weak-kneed back to the hotel, showered, took some aspirin, and lay on my back, staring at the ceiling and wanting to die. I decided I needed to drink some water before I expired, though—my throat was the fucking Sahara. I guzzled two bottles of water and passed out around four in the afternoon. Two things to note here: I don't drink water, and I don't pass out in the afternoon. So I was sick. Away from home, and sick. To quote someone or other: "To those who understand, no explanation is necessary, to those who don't, none is possible." In short, my situation was misery on a stick. I was awakened a couple of hours later by my cell phone ringing, a sound that was so painful to me that I considered jamming a hotel pen in my eye, ending my misery. I answered the phone instead. Juan. Somehow he convinced me to try to go eat something, and I was too weak to form a coherent argument.

Mission failure. I had choked down one or two bites of dinner and then motioned for the check. The waiter seemed relieved; I think he was sick of refilling my water glass. I staggered back to the hotel (the front desk clerk likely thought I was wasted) and fell back into bed. Chugged more water, used it to wash down three more aspirin, and passed out.

I awoke the next day still exhausted. I was in a true dilemma—should I stay here until I felt well enough to travel, or suffer through a daylong

journey and sleep in my own bed tonight? My itinerary wasn't an easy one—I had to drive four hours to Perpignan to return the car, and then take a train home. Basically, for someone in my current condition, those two tasks were on a par with running the Iditarod. But my homebody tendencies carried the day—I could bear anything if it meant I could go be sick in the privacy of my own apartment.

The drive from Lyon to the train station took far more than four hours, since I stopped multiple times to get water and Gatorade at gas stations. Then I had to park in Zimbabwe (well, nearly) and drag the two Birkins and my suitcase into the station to hand the car keys to the Hertz guy. Even the weather was conspiring against me, although the fever I suspected I was now running was likely adding to my paranoia. Either way, it was an unseasonable eighty degrees, and that wasn't helping matters. But there was nothing to be done—I got in line behind a dozen or so people (thanks again, cruel universe, for the lengthy line) to buy my train ticket. Almost done. I stood there, shifting my weight between my feet, so miserable and hot and headachy and fatigued I could barely stand. And just like that, I wasn't standing anymore. Nor was I conscious.

When I came to after my faint, I was lying on the pavement of the sidewalk, with most of the "line people" peering down at me anxiously. There were also a couple of policemen there, both looking at me rather grimly. When they realized I wasn't drunk or high, they looked even grimmer, and argued vehemently with me in broken English about my stubborn resolve to travel. I think they wanted to handcuff me and put me in an ambulance themselves, which was actually the only way they could have kept me in France at this point. I hadn't got this far to turn back now. And I didn't seem to have any broken bones, so I thought I would just go to the doctor in Spain. One little old Spanish lady took pity on me, and once the officers finally left, she propped me on a bench next to my Birkins and bought my ticket for me.

The train ride was a fucking nightmare. I definitely had a fever, and all of a sudden I became chilled from the air-conditioning. I was

Greg Brady trapped in the meat locker at Sam's butcher shop. I drifted in and out of consciousness, and when the train mercifully got to my stop, I mustered my final bit of energy to drag my bags and my body into a cab.

Once I was home, Juan took one look at me and immediately ordered me to bed. He fiddled around the kitchen, making me soup and muttering in Catalan, while I gratefully climbed into my pj's and into bed. Darkness. Fourteen hours later I awakened to Juan's stormy but concerned countenance next to the bed.

"Michael, you must get up. You must shower. And then we will see, we maybe should go to the clinic." His tone was not the one that I customarily argued with.

After the shower, my head still pounded, and I wanted to go to bed again. Instead, I was dragged to the clinic around the corner by an unrelenting Juan. As soon as the nurse saw my pallor, she grabbed a doctor, who, upon hearing my symptoms, pronounced me severely anemic. He ordered us to get a cab and go to the hospital immediately, or he would put me in an ambulance himself. I had been in the clinic all of two minutes at this point, and I already felt as though I had been there for hours; the agony of the fluorescents was unreal. We called a cab. Less than ten minutes after getting to that hospital, I was hooked to an IV and being wheeled to a room.

In the end, I was laid up for almost two weeks. My anemia at the time had progressed to a level so severe that I was asked whether I had received an organ transplant in the last year. (What? Not that I remember!) The hospital I was in was amazing, though. Always half-full, that glass, always. I was on the same strip of beach as the Hotel Arts, and from the tenth floor, where I was, the view was spectacular. It didn't hurt that I knew all the care I received was free, either. After my experience those two weeks, I had a hard time listening to people who spouted the "cons" of Spain's socialized medical system. If I had been in the States, I would have either been sent home earlier or up to my ears with "nonapproved" service charges that insurance wouldn't cover.

The funniest part, maybe, was that the list of items I had Juan bring from home included not just my pajamas and my toothbrush, but my BlackBerry. While I languished and had iron fed to me through tubes, I sent my shoppers to work. I even had Luc enlist his sister as a secondary Paris connection. The first week I was laid up, I got four Birkins. Not bad for a sick guy, huh? In the United States, that alone would have proved I didn't need to be in the hospital. (I could just picture myself hiding the BlackBerry under the sheets every time a nurse came in.) *¡Viva la España!* And to the little old lady from the Perpignan train station, just in case I forgot at the time . . . *gracias.*

26

Capricious Life

It had been scary, that whole collapsing episode. My doctor had said that if I had waited even another day to seek care, I could have died. And, although no one told me this right away, apparently the first twenty-four hours I had been in the hospital were touch and go. But the show must go on, as they say, and my show was a traveling one. I decided that I needed to visit a new place, somewhere I could get a couple bags along the way, but that I would essentially be enjoying myself as I "worked." No south of France road trip, in other words. It also might have been a simple human reaction to a close call like mine, but I really wanted to go somewhere that I had always wanted to go, and hadn't gone.

The Isle of Capri—I didn't know when I had first heard that name. (I did find out I had probably heard it pronounced wrong, since everyone wants to pronounce it like the name of the pants, Ca-PREE. It's not. It's CAP-ree. Who knew?) It was part of the lexicon of my thwarted travel; the places I've never been, the landscapes I've longed for but upon which my feet had never trod. The ones that make me pick up *Condé Nast Traveler* and lose twenty minutes in a bookstore as I mentally place myself into the frame of each photograph. Its mere invocation at a

dinner party summoned up the dream-fed scraps of my yearning: lemons gleaming the only true shade of yellow there is, the Mediterranean lapping on the shore, the sun deliciously too strong on my back, a silk shirt's caress on that sunburn later. Beautiful islands have always held this kind of sway over me—maybe because they are islands, and maybe because they are beautiful. And, of course, there is an Hermès there. Because, first if not foremost, Capri is the playground of the rich. Capri is the glint of priceless jewels worn with a cotton sundress, a meticulously kept lap pool overlooking an unswimmable rocky coast, a sweating crystal glass pressed against the tanned neck of an heiress. It was all this to me, and I hadn't even gone. Time to change that.

I spent one night in Naples, since there was also an Hermès there. Got a leather Birkin for my trouble, even though I had spent a little more money than average, crossing my fingers for a croc. I thought maybe there was something I was missing with the formula in Italy, some part of the script I didn't know. The salesmen always seemed to be wise to me somehow; they eyed me up and down, and looked at me suspiciously through their designer wire-rimmed glasses. I wondered if it was part of the Italian business culture—this assumption of dishonesty. Could be, since Italy remains the only country I've ever visited where I have to pay for my sandwich before they make it for me. I was likely being too sensitive. Still, I hoped for a more exotic bag in Capri; I hated to come out of a vacation behind.

The ferry ride from Naples to Capri was a little rough, but any feelings of discomfort quickly disappeared as we pulled up to the dock. The brightly colored boats and buildings of the harbor silently campaigned against one another for the title of most picturesque. (I was voting for the bright red fishing boat draped with nets; it made me reach for my camera immediately.) Behind and beyond the village right in front of me, sheer rock loomed, cliffs stretching up thousands of feet, interspersed here and there by stalwart vestiges of green and sprinklings of white houses. I refused to push and shove to get off the boat with the rest of the lemmings, so I waited and drank in the view and

riffled through my guidebook. Apparently, my next step was getting tickets for some kind of funicular. Oh boy. What about my Birkin and my suitcase? They would be a real pain in the ass. I scanned a few more pages to see how I could avoid carrying a huge orange bag on a funicular, and found a footnote about porter service up to my hotel for 40 euros. Works for me.

Bag-free, having handed my goods over to a hopefully honest porter (he didn't look like the Hermès type), I got in line for the funicular. I waited about ten minutes and then found out they didn't sell the tickets at the place you boarded. (That would make too much sense.) Went to a different building up the street, waited another twenty minutes, got my ticket, and I was good to go. The ride in the funicular was like Big Thunder Mountain crossed with a monorail crossed with a quad ski lift. It rode steadily up and up at a forty-five-degree angle, allowing a rather dizzying view downward at the harbor and the ocean. When I disembarked, I was in another town, this one the real center of life on Capri. There was another settlement—Anacapri—but that area was famed for its solitude and distance from hobnobbing masses of the island. Not really a tourist mecca, in other words. Not like the place where I stood right now, surrounded by restaurants, shops, inns, and my fellow travelers.

I decided to go straight to the hotel to get settled, then I could explore at leisure. I started in the general direction of downtown, which meant I basically followed the crowd. The people around me were mostly gawking day-trippers. I assumed when the last ferry left, it would clear out the island quite a bit, like it did on Nantucket. That would be good, because it was a bit claustrophobic downtown at present. There were hordes of people seated at the tables in the Piazzetta, although why you would spend your day sitting and drinking at a hot, crowded town square was beyond me. Stucco and stone buildings crowded together and formed charming little alleys and walkways, even more winding and narrow than average, because there are no cars on this part of Capri. Between the labyrinthine paths of whitewashed

buildings, the scent of flowers filling my every breath, and the sun beating down out of a crystalline blue sky, I was thoroughly disoriented in the most pleasant way imaginable. I spotted a white and blue tile—the Capri version of a street sign—with an arrow pointing me to Via Tragara, where my hotel was. I was staying at Villa Brunella, and I had that familiar nervousness that you get after having picked your lodging out of a guidebook. Hey, I was on Capri, how bad could it be? Likely not bad at all, judging by what I was seeing on my stroll. Now the highest of the high-end boutiques lined the paved walkway, all clad in matching white awnings. I mentally tipped my cap as I walked by Hermès, which was on tomorrow's itinerary.

As I got farther out of town, now on the Via Tragara proper, the atmosphere softened. On both sides of the walkway were wrought-iron gates, beyond which I could see courtyards overflowing with flowers; most were rendered romantically complete by stone steps winding up or down to hidden homes. The houses I *could* see were of more diverse architecture and color than in town, although I already knew any one of them would have suited me fine. I was thoroughly hooked. Bougainvillea draped purple over the stone wall to my left, and my walk was intermittently shaded by the oak and pine trees that hovered protectively above the path. All I could smell was flowers. The vegetation was Garden of Eden–style, lush and brightly colored and biblically dotted with both lemon and olive trees. Then the path widened up into a "scenic" area, and I really saw what Capri was. To my right was a largely unobstructed view of half of the island, the houses so far down and across from my vantage point they looked like toys scattered across a boulder. And across from me, rearing higher and higher so that it appeared to loom over all, was more of the sheer rock I had seen from the harbor, the vegetation scarce enough to appear as a transgression against the craggy sculpture of limestone that is Capri. I could see hollows in the rock the size of skyscrapers, playgrounds for the birds flying in and out, tiny white dots wheeling against the grayish brown. But it was the sea itself that was the most mesmerizing, the Mediterranean glinting im-

possible shades of green and blue, alternately concealing and revealing the forbidding edges of the coastline as it eased in and out with the tide. I continued along, and moments later the words VILLA BRUNELLA appeared on a tile in the wall of the building on my right. I had arrived.

The hotel was unconventional by necessity, five levels of rooms built into the side of the hill, connected by a stairwell that looked impossibly long. The place had no elevator either. (On a subsequent trip, I was grateful they had mercifully added one—it sure was a bitch if you forgot your camera in your room.) However, I was dazzled by Villa Brunella and didn't care at the moment how my calves might feel in a couple of days. It was a multileveled garden palace, the terra-cotta terraces projecting their flower-bedecked surfaces further outward with each level. The pool beckoned on the third terrace down, a perfect square of water, surrounded by blue-and-white-striped chairs in militaristic rows that belied their decadent sun-worshipping purpose. I also learned from the desk clerk that the floor above me housed a restaurant with a wall of windows. I assumed almost anything would taste good if eaten overlooking this panorama, so I made a dinner reservation.

My suite was fanciful, as though an imaginative six-year-old girl had been put in charge of designing a hotel room, and her stylish mother had modified it ever so subtly, to accommodate even the most discerning of visitors. Pink-and-green-flowered tiles accented the mostly white floor, with the same floral design mirrored in the quilt. The pair of overstuffed chairs and couch were all pink to match, and my masculinity was momentarily threatened until I remembered I was gay. My Y chromosome was further comforted by the dark mahogany furniture and ceiling fans, as well as the gender-neutral white walls. Not to mention the private terrace that I spent a quiet afternoon lounging on, sunbathing while I calculated how much money I needed to save in order to move here for the rest of my life. And also, how many stairs I would have climbed by the time the week was out.

I never left the hotel that day at all. When I finally made the uphill journey to the restaurant for my nine thirty P.M. reservation, it was

full-on dark. I blinked at the entrance, catching my breath and liking what I saw. The dining room was dimly lit, with white linen tablecloths made luminescent by the candles flickering throughout the long room. Through the glass of the far wall, the distant lights of the homes of Capri twinkled, as though the dark earth were reflecting the star-filled sky. And on the most important note, the wine list immediately assured me this was a top-rate dining establishment. I settled on a bottle of Masi Amarone. Amarone wine has its origin in a winemaking technique dating from the fourth century—and they definitely have it down pat. Unfortunately, you could barely find it outside of Italy, another freaking Malbec situation. Well, I could have a bottle tonight, no point in crying into my wineglass for Amarone-less evenings yet to come. When the waiter delivered the wine, he also brought me a chunk of cheese, which he informed me was a pecorino, a Parmesan-like dry, hard cheese made from sheep's milk, a serving suggestion from the vineyard itself. I agreed with the pairing. Mmmarone.

As an appetizer, I had a seafood salad, whose simple name belied its profusion of top-grade shellfish and fish, nary a vegetable or a dollop of mayonnaise in sight. For those who are concerned, I did order a glass of Ruinart rosé to wash down the seafood, no red wine with seafood . . . of course. And this dish, nearly a meal in itself, was merely a tasty prelude to the traditional two-main-course Italian dining experience. First I had the ravioli Brunella, as I have found going with a house specialty is rarely wrong. It wasn't wrong this time, as the tangy tomato sauce, fresh cheese, and homemade shells alone would have been sufficient, never mind the sumptuous lobster they cushioned. I went with veal Lombatine for my meat course, immediately pleased by the native white asparagus, but then even more by the tender meat it accompanied (not always the easiest thing to find in Europe). I themed dessert—*limoncello* cake with *limoncello* on the side. Limoncello is the region's alcoholic claim to fame, a chilled lemon liqueur served in tiny frosty glasses—made from lemon rinds and sugar but with no actual lemon juice that could sourly tint the citrusy sweetness. Villa Brunella

claimed theirs was made fresh on the premises, from the very lemon trees that shaded "my" patio, and two glasses later, I was more than willing to agree that it was likely the best *limoncello* I had ever had. Of course, between those two glasses of ambrosia, the flute of Champagne, and the bottle of wine, I also would have agreed to go skinny-dipping in the pool if the right person had asked me. Oh boy. Time for bed.

I awoke to the scent of oleander drifting through my slightly ajar patio door, and the bright sunlight that peeked through the corners of the drapery. You can't block sun like Capri's; a force of nature of that magnitude finds its way in. First stop of the day—Hermès. I wanted to get my business over and done with, so I could get back to pleasure. It was unseemly to even think of money in this kind of environment. I didn't want to play a purse pauper among the kings, that was certain. I got dressed, donned the *chaîne d'ancre*, and checked my pockets twenty times for my wallet and key so that there was no chance I would have to climb the stairs a second time. I walked the incredibly painless mile or so into town, and did my "thang" at Hermès, wooing the woman working into forking over a coveted croc Birkin, this one a particularly tasty 35cm *gris* pale. (Nice, although the name always struck me as a little spooky—*gris* pale. It means "pale gray," but the *"gris"* sounded grisly, "pale" always made me think of sickly, and gray wasn't the happiest color anyway. Still, these are not my problems, I suppose. I just sold the things.) So anyway, my work in Capri was done. Not my play, though, not by a long shot.

I drifted through the rest of the week, more and more enamored of the island by the day. The only thought that kept me from dropping everything and convincing Juan to move here was a short story by Somerset Maugham I had read, about a guy who did exactly that. (It's called "The Lotus Eater," and the guy lives on Capri till his pension runs out, and he goes broke, and once that happens things don't go so well . . . it's a cautionary tale for sure.) But I was still infatuated. I adored the Arco Natural, an improbably huge rock formation whose arc framed the ocean sparkling hundreds of feet below, its half-moon of limestone

seemingly defying every law of physics in the process. I was suitably awed by the Blue Grotto—the color inside the ocean-bottomed cave a shade of blue I had never seen, and likely would never see again (unless I braved the queue of boats bobbing endlessly and waiting their turn for a *second* time, which I wasn't 100 percent sold on. Once really did the trick, I think). I was entranced by the I Faraglioni, limestone stacks rising right off the coast, soaring to hundreds of feet, one of them the exclusive home of a blue lizard. How could you resist a place with *blue* lizards that make their home on one particular gigantic rock? Huh? You can't, that's how. You succumb. And succumb I did, reveling even more in every aspect of Capri. I loved the downtown area as well, and made it my habit to walk to town around seven every evening and have a glass of Krug Champagne at the Quisisana, a venerable old hotel. The Quisisana was an island legend, its patio both the best vantage point to see and the best venue in which to be seen. Seven P.M. was the hour of reckoning—after the last ferry but before dinner—and it was then that I could best survey the boutiques' wares parading by on tanned bodies. It was like watching *Lifestyles of the Rich and Famous* in real time—cheap voyeuristic thrills. I amused myself further by counting the Hermès items that made the scene.

Inevitably, my reverie and revelry on Capri came to an end, and I miserably packed on my eighth morning, vowing to come back as soon as possible. I sent my luggage down the hill with another transport team of one, but decided to carry the two Hermès shopping bags myself. Better safe than sorry. As I walked the Via Tragara for one last time that week, my mind was on nothing at all but the journey ahead of me, and the week behind me. I hit the outskirts of town, hardly breaking stride. Then, as I rounded the last curve into the white-awninged boutique runway, I spotted a familiar face that had no place in my farewell moments. It was, improbably as could be, the salesman from the Naples Hermès, standing under the awning of the Capri Hermès, languidly smoking a cigarette. Huh? I did recover quickly, though, realizing that he must cover the Capri saleswoman's day off, or something

to that effect. And here I was, strolling by bold as a rooster, with two giant Hermès bags. It must be said that the *size* of the bag I had was a dead giveaway—you really only got the giganta-version for Birkins or Kellys. Plus, I had implied strongly I was en route to Florida, with the birthday Birkin for Mom. I was potentially screwed, so I moved fast. Ducking behind a fragrant bush, I stood there sweating and waiting for his eventual retreat into the storefront. I also stacked the bags atop each other best I could, figuring I could carry both on the far side of me as I passed the windows of the store. I couldn't do too much else, except muss my hair a bit and wait for a cluster of people to walk by. Which they did, eventually, long after he had stepped back into his cool, leather-scented cave. I alternately hustled and loitered as I passed the storefronts, trying to keep pace with a window-shopping quartet of British women (no easy task). Apparently, I was successful, because I wasn't halted in my Hermès tracks—not then and not for a long time after, either.

I stood on the ferry, watching the island retreat, feeling then as I always do at such moments—that I was in a movie of my own making, a maudlin scene of which I was the only participant and the only onlooker. The view was legitimately cinematic this time; Capri was nothing if not that. I couldn't help but trace the rises and falls of the landscape with my eyes, willing my mind to capture its every nuance for time immemorial. It had restored me, this place, and I knew that, whatever story my blood test next week would tell. My body had echoed the vitality of the island, I could tell that much without a physician. I could sense it, in my color, my energy, my pulse, myself. Me as me, full-out me again, not a wan or sickly me. The crocodile bag it had yielded paled in comparison to that . . . no pun intended.

27

The Italian Way

I did finally figure out what I was doing "wrong" in Italy, after a few more months of largely unsuccessful Birkin voyages to that country. It all became clear to me after one particular journey to the shop in Rome, and sure enough, once I got the clue there, everything changed for me in Italy, Hermès-wise. I spent two months flying there for three or four days at a shot, and coming back with six or so Birkins each time. Success at last. Of all people, the person I was most excited to tell about my "breakthrough" was my young Italian hairdresser, Simonetta.

For my last haircut, I had been forced to use another of Toni & Guy's salon employees, because Simonetta was on vacation. July was her holiday month, and she had gone home to Sardinia. The haircut had been fine, but you know how it is with hairdressers—you want yours, and only yours. Plus, Simonetta was *so* great, with her long black hair, sultry little body, and hip Italian wardrobe. She and her (also Italian) boyfriend, Piergiacomo, a pastry chef at a five-star hotel in Barcelona, had moved to Spain a couple of years earlier from London, where Simonetta had been working for *that* branch of Toni & Guy. Juan and I had actually met them for a dinner out on a few

occasions, loving their sexy accents and cool-as-can-be clothes. Oh, and they were supernice too.

Simonetta was fascinated by my lifestyle, and always asked lots of questions, especially while she snipped away at my hair. Our conversations at the salon always went more or less like this:

SIMONETTA: "Michael, are you still getting lots of Beerkens?"

MICHAEL: "Yes, I still am."

SIMONETTA: "Only in Paris? I love Paris."

MICHAEL: "No, I buy Birkins all over the place."

SIMONETTA: "In Italy? You buy Beerkens in Italy a lot?"

MICHAEL: "No, not too much . . . only once in a while."

SIMONETTA: "Aaaaah."

This time, reunited at last, my head in the shampoo sink, her capable fingers kneading my scalp, I changed the script. When she asked about Italy, I told her that I went to Italy all the time for Birkins.

"You do . . . really? For Beerkens? All the time? That is new, no?" Her voice was incredulous.

"Well, yeah . . . it's new."

"You must tell me," she said, leading the way to her chair and then rooting around in the drawer for the tools of her trade.

"Do you want the long version or the short version?" I asked with a smile. She smiled back, scissors cocked in her fist.

"I want the forty-five-meenute version, sweetie."

I explained my long history with getting Birkins—or, I should say, *trying* to get Birkins—at Hermès stores in Italy. It was very hit or miss, and when it came to crocodile, forget it. It never seemed to matter how much I spent in a store in Italy, they never produced a crocodile bag for me (except at the rather inconvenient and highly seasonal Capri store,

naturally). Oftentimes I got no Birkin at all. Once during this "dark era" I even bought twelve Hermès scarves in one shop in hopes of getting a crocodile Birkin, but nothing materialized . . . except the scarves. Throughout my story, Simonetta said "mmmmm" and *"dio mio!"* in all the right places, but I got the distinct feeling that my story was unsurprising to her. I continued with my tale anyway, and caught her eye in the mirror to signify the juicy part was coming.

"Well, Simonetta, it all changed last month when I went to Rome for what I had decided might be my last shot at Italian Birkin-buying. I dressed for success, wearing lots of Hermès—I've told you all about that. I picked out some scarves, some jewelry, a shawl, and even a pair of khaki pants for myself, which I never do, I never buy their clothing. But I wasn't holding back, it was all or nothing this time. My pile totaled about $3,000 . . . and then I popped the Birkin question to the salesman I had been working with. This is when it started getting really interesting." I glanced in the mirror again at Simonetta, and I could tell she was listening intently now that things were rolling.

"He shook his head slowly, brow furrowed, but then, like he had made some decision, pulled out his business card, scribbled a number on the back, and handed it to me, telling me I should call him later that evening on his cell phone. I thought this was really weird, especially since he was wearing a wedding ring. But I completed my purchase, just curious enough to go through with it even though I didn't get a Birkin, and left the store with the business card in my wallet."

"No Beerken, then, but he give you number? You call number, though, right?"

"Yes, yes, I was just getting to that. That evening, about nine, I dialed the number on the back of the card. I explained who I was and that I was calling about getting a Birkin. It was definitely the same guy I had met, I could tell by his voice. He then shocked me by asking if I 'only wanted one Birkin, or more than one?' I told him that I would love two, so that I could give them to my mother and sister as presents."

Simonetta cocked an eyebrow at this, and I shrugged.

"I have to tell them something, it's not like they think the bags are for me."

She motioned for me to go on.

"He then started talking about the two-year waiting list and the demand in Italy for these bags, blah blah blah . . . and how he could only do favors for very special customers."

Out of the corner of my eye, I saw Simonetta's mouth quirk to the side.

"I quickly caught on to where this was heading, so I told him that I would take care of him, as a good customer would. I was told to return to the shop tomorrow and ask for a Birkin again. When I got to the store, I spotted 'my guy' and headed off in his direction. We said our hellos, and then I asked him if it were possible to get a Birkin for my mom, and one for my sister. He left and returned with two Birkins for me, one leather and one crocodile. I naturally took both."

"Crocodile? Those are good for you, yes?" Simonetta looked serious again.

"Good, yes, very good. So, then when I got back to the hotel and opened the boxes I discovered his business card, with an address on the back written in pen, and the number 200 written in one corner. In tiny script in the opposite corner were also the words 'American dollars, please.' I wondered if that was the 'total due' or price per bag, but to be on the safe side I wrapped $400 in hotel stationery, and mailed it off to him. Two weeks later I phoned my new Rome Hermès salesperson and was invited to come in for another Birkin at my convenience. And since then, Simonetta, I can get a crocodile Birkin at a lot of Hermès stores in Italy. A lot of them. I go there all the time, like I said." I finished, proud of myself.

Simonetta finished cutting my hair and paused for a moment, so quiet and still I knew to stay silent and wait.

"Michael, it is very simple, not complicated, I knew all along why you didn't get Beerken in Italy. But now you will have no problems." She paused again. Standing directly behind me, she put her hands on

my shoulders and looked at me in the mirror, her brown eyes staring right into my brown eyes, and said, "Now you know the Italian way." She held my gaze, solemn, and then laughed a little at herself, but mostly at me, and the dawning comprehension on my face as her words sunk in. She had known *all along*. And she hadn't said a word. I did sort of wish she had mentioned it to me, before, and saved me some time and energy. But, she *did* give a hell of a haircut, so I forgave her (eventually).

ADDENDUM TO STORE EMPLOYEE ROSTER

The Godfather

- **GENDER:** high-testosterone male

- **SEXUAL PREFERENCE:** yes

- **AGE:** 25+

- **HAIR:** slicked back, highly gelled

- **TEETH:** possibly one is gold or has a diamond in it

- **MOTTO:** "We can't really talk about this here"

- **PERCENTAGE IN HERMÈS CAPTIVITY:** 5%

- **LIKELIHOOD OF BIRKIN PURCHASE:** absolutely!

- **PREVIOUS JOB:** "waste management," broker, maître d'

- **THE LOWDOWN:** this employee has it all figured out and is essentially running his own business. There is no need to even bother with "the formula"; it's as simple as sending some money (aka payola) to this person's home

- **APPROACH:** if offered a business card with a home or cell phone number written on the back, then you know that he is on the take.

28

In Hermès We Trust, Aston We Shall Receive

Sleepily seated at my "desk" (formerly known as my kitchen table) one workaday morning, I scanned some chitchatty e-mails from friends and popped over to my eBay account to check on my pending listings. Six "auction closed" notices? I almost choked—wasn't expecting anything that dramatic this early. Maybe on a *Monday* morning, since Sunday was still my customary end-of-auction day. But today was definitely a *Tuesday.* That meant all six must have ended in a "Buy It Now," which was an odd coincidence, at best. A little leery, I quickly checked the buyer info on each auction. My heart sank as I kept reading the same user ID over and over. Bad doings.

This kind of thing almost inevitably spelled trouble, or had in the past. In its infinite democracy, eBay attracts all sorts of people, some of whom are fictitious. In other words, occasionally the user who "buys" an item is nothing but a recently invented screen name, and about as real as Ebenezer Scrooge (and even less likely to part with money). It was like this bizarre adult online version of "ding-dong ditch." Except instead of running away with peals of adolescent laughter when I an-

swered the virtual door, they merely vanished off the doorstep. Um, can someone please tell me why that would be fun? But, in any case, a new-to-me user who casually dropped four grand overnight on Hermès odds and ends aroused my immediate suspicion.

Now, the only way to validate the buying power of FightingBulldog-Mom was by scoping out her feedback. Minutes later, I was still scrolling through the five-hundred-plus comments and purchases listed under her user ID. Oh, she was real all right, and by the looks of it, I had nothing to worry about. FightingBulldogMom, aka Ellen Yeats, really loved brace-let charms, devotional books by some guy named Phillips Brooks, and, more important, anything and everything with the Hermès logo. I had a visual of a woman, wrists wreathed in silver and gold, praising the heav-ens, surrounded by a sea of orange Hermès boxes. Presumably in some sprawling mansion decorated with bulldog paraphernalia. Hey, if I had her kind of money, I'd be thanking God too. I had nothing to fight about with this particular bulldog mom. High time to drop her a line.

From: "michael" <BirkinBoy1@yahoo.com>
To: FightingBulldogMom@yahoo.com

Ellen,

thanks for your purchases! upon receipt of your payment, I will be shipping the items by registered insured mail. please note that I keep wish lists for clients, so if there is anything Hermès you are specifically looking for, let me know. best regards from Barcelona,

michael

From: "Ellen Yeats" <FightingBulldogMom@yahoo.com>
To: "Michael" <BirkinBoy1@yahoo.com>

Michael—

I have such fond memories of Barcelona. The food, the people, the architecture—it's all so lovely. As you must know already—I am sure you adore it there.

The shipping arrangements sound fine, and I will process everything on my end through my PayPal account. I will also ponder my wish list.

Best,

Ellen

Ah, lovely—shades of Grace, for sure. I couldn't wait to see Ellen's wish list, although I wondered what she might still need after all the Hermès purchases on her feedback. But as I would learn again and again, it wasn't a matter of *need*, it was a matter of *want*. And Ellen still *wanted* plenty.

Well, ask and ye shall receive, at least most of the time; over the next eight months, Ellen became a committed client of mine. I learned she lived chiefly in Wareham, Massachusetts, a Cape Cod town a stone's throw from Osterville, where I had spent my early years. So we were neighbors, in a rather convoluted, non-time-zone-sharing way. Although we never spoke on the phone (more shades of Grace), we had a thoroughly pleasant online rapport. Well, maybe pleasant is too lukewarm a description, since at this point she was spending several thousand dollars a month buying Hermès goodies from me. I liked Ellen, I liked her a lot. She liked me, and she liked Hermès a lot. Our friendship was symbiotic, but sincere nonetheless.

I found out she was a highly successful attorney, with two grown children, neither of whom lived nearby. Her recently jettisoned marriage had been to the CEO of a company that ranked among the top twenty on the Fortune 500—a man who might know business but was clueless in every other imaginable way. This asshole had been busy playing footsie underneath Ellen's presumably lovely dining room table—set with Hermès candlesticks and Wedgwood china—with none other than her very best friend. I respected her utterly for not putting up with that bullshit, and dumping his cheating ass out on the curb where it belonged. Things were equally emotive on my end of our

correspondence. I told her all about Juan and my newly acquired and sometimes temperamental Bengal kitty, the ups and downs of being an expatriate, the nuances of my newly formed coupledom. Another virtual, and virtually flawless, correspondence had been formed.

When it came time for one of my periodic pilgrimages to the States, starting off with a couple nights at Kate's in Ptown and ending at my parents' house in Florida, I offhandedly mentioned my plans in an e-mail. Her response made me do a double take.

From: "Ellen Yeats" <FightingBulldogMom@yahoo.com>
To: "Michael" <BirkinBoy1@yahoo.com>

Michael—

I actually have something of a proposition for you, one that doesn't involve eBay or Hermès (believe it or not). I will soon be heading down to Florida, where I winter at my home in Palm Beach. I had been planning to ship my car, but I had a brainstorm when I saw your US travel plans end at your parents' place in Florida. Would you consider a road trip down South instead of a flight, and drive my car down for me? And since it is only September, the weather will likely be nice. I will understand if not, but I figured there was no harm in asking. Let me know one way or another, and then I can plan accordingly.

blessings,

ey

I couldn't believe this woman would hand over the keys to her car to someone she couldn't pick out of a lineup. Kind of taking a chance, don'tcha think? But since *I* knew I wasn't a criminal, there was really no reason to refuse. Save the airfare, make points with a great client and friend, and further loosen up my already laissez-faire travel itinerary—win-win all the way for yours truly. I tapped out my affirmative reply posthaste.

From: "michael" <BirkinBoy1@yahoo.com>
To: "Ellen Yeats" <FightingBulldogMom@yahoo.com>

Ellen—

Sounds great, where's the catch? Just kidding, I would love to, and since I will be in Ptown right beforehand, Wareham is super convenient for my plans (and lots closer than Logan Airport, that's for sure). And if there is anything you need me to snag . . . shoes, bags, clothes, etc—and shuttle down to PB for you, let me know. I'm certainly familiar with all the joys of airline travel these days—I generally fly barefoot now ;-) But at any rate, your wish is my command.

mt

From: "Ellen Yeats" <FightingBulldogMom@yahoo.com>
To: "Michael" <BirkinBoy1@yahoo.com>

Michael—

Wonderful—consider it a done deal then! I will already be gone by the time you go to the house to pick up the car, but I will leave the keys with my assistant Charlotte. I am so pleased, Michael, this means a lot to me, and I am doubly happy if it helps you in any way. I think I have packed most of what I need for the winter, but if that changes (and knowing me, it may) I will let you know. Thanks again.

blessings,

ey

PS The directions are attached to this email, make sure you read them closely as it can be a little tricky to find the place on your first visit.

Less than a month later, I was reading those directions as closely as a freshman English major navigating Joyce's *Ulysses* for the first time, with about the same amount of comprehension. I peered through the windshield of Kate's car and tried to ignore her frequent bitching about the dirt road and the corresponding lack of pavement. And about how lost we were. And about how her hangover seemed to be worsening the longer we kept hunting for this house. I wisely said as little as possible.

"Well, the directions say it *is* quite a ways down this road. It has to be down here *somewhere*. It's not like Ellen doesn't want me to find it. It's just a little tricky, I think." I tried to sound optimistic.

"Tricky is one way of putting it. Fucking entirely without any kind of landmarks or street signs is maybe another way." Kate's glass was less than half-full this morning, perhaps because every time I looked at it last *night*, it was brimming with Mews' margaritas. Little Miss Cranky-Cranky.

"Wait, wait, that was the house number on that mailbox I think . . . slow down, back up, back up." I prayed I had seen what I thought I had. I had only glimpsed the numbers in the side-view mirror by chance. Pretty goddamn helpful to have them on *that* side of the mailbox, really, since it was the dead-end side. I quashed my sarcasm and crossed my fingers. Please let this nightmare be over. My unwilling driver's dubiousness was palpable, but she sighed and put the car in reverse. Thankfully, the numbers were the same on second glance, and Kate and I were finally headed down Ellen's driveway, our long friendship more or less intact. I reminded myself to give Kate the crumpled directions so she could burn them in effigy. (Once she found her way back out, of course. And took a much-needed nap.)

The house was a rambling Cape, the exterior weathered to that driftwood color that always conjures up New England for me whenever I see it elsewhere. Dormer windows peeked out of the roof, and Ellen had wisely chosen to keep all the woodwork white. I always hated when nouveau riche New Yorkers bought a house down here and immediately executed some harebrained pastel paint job. Pink and green

might fly out there on Martha's Vineyard, but they don't fly here. (Take a note, New York, I'm dead-on right about this.) Fortunately for my peace of mind, this particular house was as authentically Cape Cod color-schemed as they come. And if location is everything—and we all know it is—this house had some serious advantages in that department, despite being a bit off the beaten path. Set comfortably back on a hill dotted with gently swaying wildflowers, overlooking a marshy ocean inlet, it all but dripped seaside hideaway. All you could hear were the gulls; and the tang of salt in the air was so crisp you could taste it. I fully expected a hunting dog to run out of the reeds with a mallard in its mouth, or a lobster boat to round the bend with dinner on deck. Right then, as if on cue, a woman straight out of a Winslow Homer painting emerged from the front door. We parked and I hopped nimbly out of the car to greet her.

"You must be Michael. I hope you didn't have any trouble finding the place." She looked a little tentative, as though she thought I was going to start yelling at her. I was sure that at one point or another some rich Duxbury asshole had torn her a new one because he had gotten lost coming here and missed most of the clambake. Well, that wasn't going to be me (I never miss a clambake), and after the warning look I immediately shot in the direction of the car, it wasn't going to be Kate either.

"No, no problem at all, Ellen's directions were great. This is my friend Kate, and you must be Charlotte." Kate waved wanly but remained right where she was.

"Nice to meet you both, glad you made it in one piece. I got nervous you had some sort of trouble—Ellen already phoned looking for you. She said for you to give her a call once you got here. Something about deciding to have you play Pony Express after all?" Charlotte smiled a little as she said this. I had a feeling she had been working for Ellen for decades.

"Okay, no problem." I motioned to Kate to get out of the car, since I didn't want her to leave until I made sure everything was all set for

my journey south. She pretended to ignore me, but then grudgingly unbuckled herself and lurched out of the car door. With her long blond hair, now starting to streak silver in places, and her brightly colored peasant skirt, Kate added another level of picturesque to the scene. Pretty as a postcard—as long as she wasn't talking, my internal monologue intoned wittily. I abruptly turned away from Kate so she wouldn't ask why I was smirking. By doing so, I caught Charlotte a little off guard, and saw something that I perhaps would have otherwise missed. Ellen's assistant was openly studying Kate, and the emotion written on her face could be only one thing: relief.

It hit me all at once—how utterly nerve-wracking this situation would be for a sixty-year-old woman, alone in this giant house in the middle of nowhere. I was this totally unknown quantity, really. I mean, Ellen wasn't even in the state, and poor Charlotte had to do the initial meet and greet. And if all that wasn't enough, she had to decide whether to entrust a vehicle to my care. Well, what can you do? It's not as if any of this had been my idea. I hoped Kate's Rehab at Sunnybrook Farm routine was enough to ease this woman's mind that I wasn't a serial killer, or maybe all I needed was to have brought a female along with me. Just then, Charlotte caught my eye, smiled, and started leading the way toward the front door, all of which I took as a good sign. Not wishing to press my luck, I tried to look as harmless as Bambi while I followed her across the lawn (well, I do have big brown eyes, at least). Kate was seemingly calmer by the second as the sun and sea soaked into her, and certainly wasn't about to come along.

I followed Charlotte through the massive oak front door (replete with nautically inspired brass doorknocker) and blinked around, sun-blind, in the foyer. I hoped my curious glances around at the first floor wouldn't make this woman think I was casing the joint. I mean, I couldn't really help myself; the inside of this house *was* pretty amazing. Light hardwood floors throughout contrasted with the darker wainscoting, and well-chosen antiques intermingled with cottage chic couches and chairs. It looked comfy, but expensive comfy. And you

could have hosted the Last Supper in the dining room. Although at the *current* moment, that wouldn't really be too feasible, unless the loaves and fishes were going to be served on orange cardboard. Because from where I stood, the dark mahogany tabletop was barely visible under a slew of Hermès boxes.

Now, I had seen some orange boxes in my life, but Ellen's collection, or part of her collection, or whatever I was looking at on that table, was large enough to open a Cape Cod Hermès store—like, tomorrow. I'm talking two, three hundred boxes, easy, all artfully arranged by size. It was mind-blowing to realize how much merchandise this one woman had and how much money it represented. I'm not one to bring up starving orphans—after all, it's not as if they can eat scarves—but this was perhaps a tad excessive. I concentrated on not gawking.

"All right, here's the kitchen. The phone is on the wall." Charlotte looked at me expectantly. I reluctantly ripped my eyes away from the French copper cookware suspended from ceiling hooks, and the matching Pierre Vergnes sink with its exquisitely tiled backsplash.

Oh, no, this was going to be awkward.

"Um, actually, Charlotte, I don't really know her number . . ." My voice trailed off. This was definitely not helping with the whole I-am-a-total-stranger thing. Charlotte dialed the phone for me wordlessly.

It took a good half hour to go through all the purse boxes in that dining room to find the two beauties Ellen had requested I bring down for her. Each time I attacked another box, I hoped against hope to see either bag #1—a cream croc Birkin—or bag #2—a blue jean leather Kelly. Charlotte chattered at me while I untied and retied ribbons, and peered through clouds of tissue. She didn't bring up orphans, thankfully, but I could tell she was slightly horrified at the whole Hermès overkill. I found out that packages arrived with such frequency for Ellen that Charlotte got teased at the post office about them needing to hire someone specifically for the Yeats household. I was also informed that the orange stacks on this table were but a small sliver of Ellen's Hermès pie. I employed with Charlotte the same technique I had used with Kate in the car

this morning—I kept my mouth shut. Eventually, I pulled the designer needles out of the haystack, and it was time to hit the road. Finally. As charming as the place was, I was ready to get going. I had some long driving hours ahead if I was going to make any progress at all today.

I followed Charlotte's Ann Taylor–clad form down the stone steps leading to the garage on the side of the house. Squinting at the bright sunshine and trying gamely to see over two giant purse boxes stacked in my arms, I felt lucky when I reached the bottom without breaking my neck. I snuck a quick glance over at Kate, now back in the car, but couldn't tell if her eyes were open or closed behind her oversized sunglasses. Charlotte hit the remote for the garage door, and I awkwardly juggled the boxes to take the keys she offered me.

Then I nearly shit myself.

Because in that garage was not the Mercedes or the BMW I had half expected. It wasn't even the Jag or the Porsche I had half hoped for. No, no, no, and no, it was none of these. The car that revealed itself as that garage door rose slowly up hadn't made it into even my most fantastical imaginings. The car parked ten feet in front of me . . . the car I was about to climb into . . . the car my client was having me drive all the way to Florida without ever having laid eyes on me . . . was a fucking . . . Aston . . . Martin. A candy apple red convertible one, with bright shiny chrome and beige leather bucket seats. A car worth maybe a quarter of a million dollars. As if through a long tunnel, I could hear Charlotte somewhere far off, saying something about how it was such a waste to even have it, since Ellen had driven it maybe twice, possibly three times at most. I became vaguely, peripherally aware that Kate had emerged from her car and was now standing next to me. I slowly swung my head to the side to get her reaction, and saw a dumbfounded expression on her face that made me feel like I was looking in a mirror.

She murmured to me, "Michael . . . what *is* it? It looks really . . . *fast*. And really . . . really . . . *expensive*."

I wanted to say, Duh, Kate, it's a car, but I went with the day's ongoing theme and said nothing whatsoever.

Instead, I gingerly placed the two boxes on the ground and walked weak-kneed into the cool, air-conditioned climate of the garage. I circled the Aston Martin like a predator closing in for the kill, but I wanted only to worship, not to harm. I briefly worried maybe this whole deal was a setup—maybe Charlotte would call the cops as soon as I left the driveway, or maybe Ellen had cut the brake lines to get the insurance money and buy more Hermès stuff. Then I remembered I sold her most of that stuff, and that would be like shooting your own drug dealer. I relaxed. And mentally prepared for the ride of my life.

After settling my luggage and Ellen's boxes into the trunk, telling Kate that the car was, yes, fast, and yes, expensive, thanking Charlotte effusively, then hugging Kate about twelve times, then thanking Charlotte effusively again, I finally slid behind the wheel. The leather was butter-soft, and the interior left nothing to be desired. And I knew, as soon as I saw the Linn sound system, exactly what my first stop would be—somewhere that sold CDs, preferably loud ones. I started up the engine, which didn't purr, as I'd expected . . . instead, it roared in a whisper. I backed the dream car out of the garage, swung it in a three-point, relishing the uncanny responsiveness, and pulled up to where

the two women stood waiting for a last good-bye. I said one final fare-well, beeped, and was off to the proverbial races.

I couldn't for the life of me wipe the lunatic grin off my face. And once I got off that god-awful endless dirt road, bought me some music, cranked the tunes, and hit the open highway, I couldn't think of a single reason to even *try* to wipe it off. So I wore that grin all the way to Florida. Gawking gas station attendants; rubbernecking travelers the next lane over on the freeway; eager valet drivers at hotels, who wanted to tip *me*—I flashed that same grin at each and every one of them. And for once, the wide smile on my face had nothing to do with the Hermès purses in my trunk.

29

Creamsicles and Moonstones

In the past year or so, I'd bought a leather Birkin and a 35cm croc Kelly—plus several shawls, bracelets, Ulysses, and other small items—at the Hermès shop in Luxembourg, always enjoying the company of the kind store manager. So I was not terribly surprised when I returned home from my Aston Martin adventure in Florida to find an invitation from them to attend the grand reopening of their renovated shop. At first, I blithely tossed the invitation in the trash—why would I want to fly to Luxembourg to drink Champagne at Hermès? Plus, I was much more interested in seeing how big Dali (my new Bengal kitty) had gotten while I was gone, and making sure he remembered me. Then, as Dali purred on my lap and looked adoringly at me with his giant green eyes, I reconsidered. Maybe I was being a bit hasty. It *was* a new store and a gala event, so perhaps they would have some special bags sent in from Paris to make the store look extraordinary. If I could get a croc Birkin that was unusual or rare—well, it would make it well worth the trip to Luxembourg. Crocodile and more crocodile, my life now revolved around crocodile. And Sarah's need for it.

Sarah had recently, and accidentally, "come clean" with me, in a manner of speaking. She had sent me a bank wire transfer for a bag, as usual. However, she had sent it out of an account I hadn't seen before, a business account under the name Créateurs de Luxe, with her name listed as proprietor. Hmm. I Googled. And apparently she had one of the largest Birkin Web sites on the planet. Well, well, well. I called her immediately.

"Sarah, it's Michael."

"Hi, Michael, what's up?"

"How is Créateurs de Luxe going? That *poudre* croc I got in Berlin last month looks great on the site, if I do say so myself." I couldn't help laughing. She started laughing too.

"Oh, you asshole, how did you find out? I was going to fucking tell you, but I didn't know how to after a while, and I'm sorry, I should have . . . you aren't mad, right? Tell me you aren't mad!" Sarah pleaded, serious all of a sudden.

"No, I don't care, I think it's great. And I found out because you paid me with your business account, you idiot!" We giggled together for a little while longer, I assured her a hundred more times that I wasn't mad, and that was that. It really didn't affect our relationship at all. I had always maintained that I didn't care what happened to a bag once it left my hands, so it would have been hypocritical of me to get worked up now. My parents also now had some peace of mind—after my dad had realized he had personally sent her more than fifty bags, I thought his head was going to implode from pure horror at Sarah's excess. But ever the proponent of free trade, now that he knew she resold the bags, he *loved* the whole idea of Sarah and me having such a lucrative supply-and-demand relationship.

This party (and the opportunity to score a special croc Birkin) might be a chance to show Sarah there were truly no hard feelings, so feeling very magnanimous, and just a tad bit avaricious, I retrieved the invite from the trash and booked a flight and hotel. Obviously, this was an occasion to dress for shopping success. I packed an Armani Black Label

suit that I had made to measure at Bergdorf's, along with a blue-black-and-white-checked Hermès shirt and black John Lobb shoes. The icing on the cake: an Hermès pashmina shawl that was tissue-thin and changed color from one end to the other, gradating from chartreuse to lime green. At seven feet long, when rolled and simply tossed around the neck, it really looked like a million bucks (or the $1,100 it cost), and I felt very much the Hermès dandy. Why not? Pavarotti got away with it. I'd just have to be careful not to snag my *chaîne d'ancre* on it—that would definitely be a party foul.

The invitation said seven o'clock at the address of the new shop, and when I arrived at seven fifteen, there were already hundreds of people there. The scene resembled nothing so much as a bizarre debutante ball. In the air was a palpable feeling of people dressing to dazzle, and the undercurrent of fluttery need for peer approval, both of which reeked of Waldorf-Astoria coming-out festivities. It was strangely unsettling to see this in an environment where the median age was eighty-one, not eighteen. The masculine fashions of Kiton, Brioni, and Armani were paired off, Noah's Ark–style, with the best efforts of Valentino, Chanel, and Balenciaga. (It dawned on me that parties like this were what bought brand-name designers their hundred-foot yachts.)

I sallied up to the welcome desk in my shawl, presented my invitation, and a tiny, fashionable woman tied a tiny, fashionable piece of Hermès ribbon around my wrist. I stepped onto a carpeted, awning-covered walkway and I had one of those moments of unreality—how the hell was I at this party? But as I spotted the uniformed waiters carrying trays laden with alcohol, I decided that now was not the time for existential angst. Champagne flute in hand, I followed the carpet to a large open-air courtyard. Here, I was dazzled by the Hermès signature over-the-top opulence. Crystal chandeliers, air-kissing employees, lush flower arrangements, a penguin-suited herd of orchestra musicians—and, needless to say, more Hermès handbags than I had heretofore seen in any one place. Virtually every single woman was wearing some style of Hermès bag, with crocodile Kellys out in full

force. The purse purchases made just by those present were no doubt what had paid for the expensive drink I was sipping (not to mention everything else visibly expensive in the general vicinity, which is to say the party as a whole). I had no urge to talk to any of these people. I doubted any of them would sell me the handbag off their arm, or I would have been shaking hands and kissing babies all over that courtyard. No Birkins to bag here, so I wandered back up the faux–Academy Awards walkway to the store, where I hoped it was hunting season. Inside the store, it was as packed as Bourbon Street at Mardi Gras, although it wasn't as fun—no beads in sight. I made it through the crush gawking near the front to discover that many store employees were hovering about, "hosting" the interested guests around the store. My self-appointed store guide was a salesperson (of moderate Nazi persuasion), and as she blabbered on, I eagerly scanned the merchandise. And there it was, glowing bright pink, a croc Birkin sadly imprisoned in a glass display case. Spurred on by my love of freeing beautiful things, I plunged.

"Oh my God, this bag is stunning, I've never seen this color before," I ventured in a voice I hoped was a velvety blend of wealth and Hermès-inspired awe. The Nazi immediately dropped her voice (as if we were suddenly in a church) and whispered back, "You should come back in the morning and see me, we aren't allowed to take the bags out or show any items this evening." Secretly elated, I gave her a casual nod and asked when the store opened in the morning. Now, mission accomplished, I excused myself after a few minutes and returned outside to toss back another glass of Champagne. I took one final survey of the extravagant and, to me, extravagantly silly reception, and then slipped out quietly, having zero interest in socializing with the self-proclaimed "Luxembourg's finest."

The following morning, dressed in one of my "Hermès shopping uniforms," I was back inside the store seconds after they turned the key and opened the door. My salesperson from last night immediately materialized. I wasted no time before proceeding with the formula.

"Good morning, nice to see you again. I spoke with my mom last night and told her about the pink bag, and she's extremely interested. She wants to know if you have anything else in that color from the clothing or accessories collection, because she doesn't think she has anything to wear with it," I said, knowing full well that they would have any number of fuchsia items. About a half hour later, I left the store with a fuchsia cashmere shawl, a large sterling silver bracelet, a couple other trinkets, and the bright fuchsia croc Birkin, liberated from captivity once and for all. The profit on that bag paid all the Luxembourg expenses, with several thousand left over.

Several months later, I heard through the grapevine that Hermès was opening a shop in Athens in a few weeks. Now possessed of a completely different view of Hermès openings, I immediately picked up the phone and called Paris to try and get a phone number for the Athens shop, and with luck finagle an invitation in the process. No such luck. I racked my brain. Suddenly I remembered Katrin, one of my Birkin clients, who lived in Los Angeles and had a summer home in the Greek islands. I phoned her posthaste, hoping she was in California, praying that she had some specific information on the opening.

"Hi, Katrin, it's Michael . . . in Barcelona."

"Hi, sweetheart, what a surprise. Are you in Barcelona? Oh, you just said that. I just got home from Paris last night, so I'm a little dopey." We moved through some pleasant idle chitchat and discussed the new French collections, which she had just returned from seeing. Katrin never missed a single runway show. Usually, I loved talking with her and listening to her prattle on in her thick, sweet French accent. However, today I had an agenda.

"Katrin, are you going to Athens for the Hermès opening?" I hoped it sounded like I was already going, rather than like I was fishing for an invite.

"I'm going with Constantine, who is from Greece and is only twenty-three but acts like he's thirty-five and has more money than Croesus. His father is a real Greek shipping tycoon . . ." Katrin rambled on and

on, giving me every detail of this Constantine character. While I'm sure normally I'd be riveted (yeah, right), instead I was calculating my next question. When she took a breath, I pounced.

"So where are you staying?" I asked in a tone I hoped was less CIA, more drawing room.

"Oh, the Grande Bretagne, I always stay there. It's right near the best shopping and I don't see any reason *not* . . ." she blathered on. Oh, Lord. Why hadn't I asked *when* instead of *where*? Now I suddenly had Rick Steves on the phone. When she was running out of oxygen again, I rolled the dice.

"I better book soon, or I'm gonna end up in some dump. When is this thing again?" Blissfully unaware of my machinations, Katrin threw me the bone I had been praying for. Since any hopes of an actual invitation had been quashed, I decided to crash the party. I booked a flight and reserved a room at the Grande Bretagne. (Thanks for the tip, Katrin.) I figured what the hell, some Birkin buyer somewhere in this universe was paying, even if they didn't know it.

When I arrived into Athens, it was raining, which was kind of a drag. But then I reminded myself I was here for business, not pleasure. Thus resigned, I checked into the hotel and asked the concierge how long it would take to get to the Hermès shop. Much to my surprise, he told me that it was directly behind the hotel, less than a minute's walk. Fabulous. Armed with a ridiculously giant hotel umbrella, I walked over to check out the windows and see if there were any bags visible. As I rounded the corner behind the hotel, I was immediately confronted with a large orange tent that ran the entire length of the small block. I was accosted with a virtual nuclear explosion of orange: a symphony of orange pillows, orange urns cascading with orange flowers, orange carpets with orange fleurs-de-lis; obviously, some event planner was given a fat budget to really orange it up. I anticipated seeing Champagne flutes with orange juice. There were dozens of people (fortunately, none of them orange) frantically working to get everything in place for this evening, and I tried to remain invisible as I maneuvered

my way to the front of the shop and the mammoth plate-glass windows. I could not believe my eyes: I counted four croc Birkins, the highlight of which was a blue *roi* and a *poudre*. Then I spotted the mother lode: a black matte lizard Birkin, which is so rare as to be nearly mythological. Oh boy, this was going to be fun!

I headed back to the hotel to shower and dress. I donned the chalk-colored Prada suit from my Pierre Gagnaire evening with Serge, now properly tailored. This time I paired it with a baby-pink two-ply cashmere turtleneck from Ralph Lauren Purple Label. Now an expert in shawl/*chaîne d'ancre* interaction, the only adjustment I made to that combo was the shawl color—I went with my new fuchsia one this time. I did one last thing before leaving the hotel room—texted Sarah about possible croc Birkins coming her way. I figured, why not be positive?

It was forty-five minutes after the appointed time when I finally arrived. Feeling like a character from a bad spy film, I had already tied a small piece of Hermès cloth ribbon around my wrist. Since I knew that this company's only bit of creativity went directly into their scarf designs, I figured this would again be the "secret handshake." Their dogged love of tradition would serve as my gilt-edged invitation. My instincts were right. I seamlessly bypassed the "ribbon table" and slipped right into the party. I armed myself with Champagne and disappeared into the haze of orange festivities.

Within moments, I spotted Jean Paul Gaultier, the enfant terrible of Paris fashion and the current creative director of Hermès women's ready-to-wear. With all his white hair in all that Hermès orange, he looked like nothing so much as a Creamsicle, albeit an expensive one. I bet he wasn't wearing an Hermès ribbon on his wrist. No way to find out, though—sycophants were circled around him like wagon trains at dusk. I scanned the rest of the crowd. I thought I recognized a woman across the room but was not certain how I knew her. Having little else to do besides people-watch, after the second glass of Champagne, I pushed through the throng and approached her.

"Excuse me, but you look really familiar," I ventured. Catching me totally off guard, she gave me a hug, like a long-lost friend at a high school reunion. I still had trouble remembering how small this Hermès world really was. It turned out she was the woman who had sold me the "reserved" crocodile at the Hamburg Hermès shop. Lovely Hannah, of course. The original Grandmother.

"I'm the manager *here* now," she said with a big smile. I returned her smile without a bit of faked enthusiasm. I *was* really excited, because I knew Hannah loved me. Visions of croc bags leaving the shop with me danced in my head.

As we spoke, a man sauntered up. He looked like he had looted an Hermès shop and was wearing all the bounty: a bright orange croc H-belt, diamond brooch with rubies and sapphires, diamond-encrusted watch, orange croc shoes, the whole nine yards. As if that gauche display on any one person wasn't garish enough, he was carrying a woman's 40cm orange croc Birkin. What the fuck? Some orange crocodile out there was missing her mother. Hannah evidently knew this apparition and introduced us.

"Michael, I'd like you to meet Lakis Gavalas. Mr. Gavalas designed the Kelly Lakis bag for Hermès."

Oh, wow, here he was—Serge's summer playmate. I hadn't expected him to look like this, but on second thought, how could I have? I decided to show him that he might not know about me, but I sure knew a few things about him.

"Wow, this is really amazing. Serge at the Faubourg sold me a Kelly Lakis a couple of years ago. He told me about your vast collection of Hermès bags, and your fabulous house parties out on Mykonos," I said. I inwardly cringed at how gushy I sounded, but that's why I was there, after all. As much as it pained me, I had to play the game.

At this point, Lakis extended a limp hand. I didn't know whether I was supposed to shake it or kiss it, as if he were some sort of pope of homosexuality. I nearly gagged, and settled on weakly gesturing with my Champagne flute in his general direction. Placated by my

pandering, Lakis then launched into what was less a conversation and more a self-aggrandizing monologue. I found myself mesmerized—not by his inane, solipsistic drone, but rather by his teeth, which had been bleached so many times they were now the color of moonstones. Set off against his George Hamilton über-tan, they honestly made him look Photoshopped. He finally begged off and headed in the direction of the Creamsicle.

Reminded forcibly why I loathed these events, I finished my Champagne and said my good-byes to Hannah, reassuring her that I would see her in the morning. I told her that I had brought a big shopping list from my mother, and she lit up like a Christmas tree and murmured, "We have very unusual things from Paris for the opening."

I wanted to say no shit, that I had seen all the croc in the store, but instead told her I couldn't wait to shop with her tomorrow. I needed to be nice—after all, she *was* a Grandmother.

I walked back to the hotel and, famished from all my fawning, wolfed down a steak in the hotel bistro. I called Sarah and dished on the party, and informed her of my plan to be at the store five minutes before they opened tomorrow morning. (I was feeling cautiously confident that my afternoon phone call would be a success story.) Sarah didn't seem to want to count her crocs before they hatched. Or, I reflected after hanging up, it could have been my fairy tale of Grandmothers, Creamsicles, and Moonstones that accounted for her rather disengaged tone. I didn't care, though, as long as tomorrow brought me my Hermès happily-ever-after.

30

There's More Than One Way to Skin a Crocodile

The next morning, I rounded the corner to the shop and immediately spied a line of about ten people at the front door to Hermès. Easily half of them were Asian men. You see, not surprisingly, I was not the only person who had noticed that Japanese people love Hermès but pay too much for it at the store. Increasingly, I was seeing well-dressed Asian men, often in groups, nary a woman in sight, enacting "the formula" and cruising out with a Birkin apiece. It was apparent to me that they were hosting my longed-for Hermès open-house parties and reselling these bags for a tidy profit in Japan or Korea. Some I *knew* for a fact to be resellers, as Sarah would receive e-mails from them trying to get her to buy the "less desirable" (or sometimes the most desirable) bags, but with a gigantic markup. So, I couldn't prevent my suspicious heart from concluding that a group of Asian men, sans women, in Athens at the opening of an Hermès store, meant one thing: I wasn't the only re-seller there that morning. As soon as they unlocked the door, the four men converged on the handbag department and immediately occupied

the four saleswomen working in the store. This included Hannah, who saw me, smiled, and waved hello—however, as a Grandmother, she was helpless in the grasp of the Asian resellers.

Disconcerted, I wandered around the store aimlessly and thumbed through the racks of clothing. In nightmarishly rapid succession, I saw the four croc Birkins being taken from the display cases. My heart sank to my Gucci loafers. But oddly enough, although there was nary a bag left to be seen, the Asian men all filed out empty-handed. I couldn't believe my eyes. What new sort of formula was this? Did these men know something I didn't? I guessed that they did. First karaoke and karate, now this. Hannah approached me and gave me a hug, but I was completely distracted by what just went down. I decided on a new approach. I told her I wanted the *poudre* croc Birkin that was in the display by the front door (a bag which had now disappeared). Hannah replied with words that filled me with dread: "Michael, unfortunately I don't have *any* croc left." I looked at her dumbly.

"I have several Birkins for you, though, but no croc. There is a blue jean 35cm, a 30 and 35cm black, a *vermillon* . . ." She continued on with a supersized shopping list of bags, but these basic leather Birkins failed to excite me. Having just felt all the croc slip through my grasping fingers, I couldn't even feign interest. Before leaving the store, I had Hannah put aside a couple of shawls for me and some small leather items in hopes of a croc Birkin somehow materializing out of thin air. The store was now full of people, so I told her I was going for an early lunch and would return later, after I spoke with my mom. I was anxious to get out of the store and contemplate my next move. A total conundrum, as Asian resellers beating me at my own game was not covered in the formula. Back to the drawing board.

I was originally supposed to check out of the hotel by noon, so I stopped at the front desk and extended my stay, then went back up to my room and changed my flight. I needed an additional day to work this through. Going home Birkinless was not an option. I was into this trip for the cost of a business-class airline ticket and two nights at the

five-star Bretagne, never mind having to kiss that moron Moonstone's ass last night at the reception.

With the weather now somewhat more amenable, I opted for a walk around the Acropolis in hopes of receiving messages from ancient Greek deities. Anyone but Hermès. While wandering around, I decided that if I wasn't going to get a croc, then I'd push Hannah to sell me *two* leather Birkins. After all, she rattled off a long list of leather bags, so that certainly wouldn't put a dent in her supply. I wasn't completely happy with the solution, but I didn't see any other options. As I walked back down to Syntagma Square, my cell phone rang.

"Hey, what's up? It's Sarah." Before I could tell her anything, she launched into an eye-opening tale.

"I got an e-mail this morning from another seller offering me a blue *roi* croc, a *poudre* croc, a matte black lizard, and a *braise* croc, but the prices are nuts."

Holy shit, she just listed the same four bags that I watched vanish before my eyes in a matter of moments just hours ago. I could barely get the words out intelligibly.

"Those are the exact four bags that are here in Athens. They were in the display case when the store opened this morning, but four Asian resellers snagged them right from under me. Are you gonna buy 'em?"

"Are you nuts? The prices are way out of fucking control!" Sarah said, with her customary reserve.

"This entire *situation* is way out of fucking control. I'll call you later."

So there I was. Sarah had no Birkins, I had no Birkins, and due to their surprise attack, the Asians had all the Birkins. Pearl Harbor all over again.

I decided to return to the store and see if anything had changed. When I entered, the shop was still quite busy and I casually glanced at the display cases to see if anything new had magically appeared or if one of the crocs had crept back home. Their empty glass cages mocked me. When I was finally able to get Hannah aside for a moment, I mumbled some bullshit about my mom and her ongoing round of golf and

headed for the door. On my way out, I spotted a handsome young man (undoubtedly an Incurable Romantic) standing behind the cash desk, talking on the phone. I hadn't seen any men working earlier. The light-bulb over my head finally illuminated. I snagged one of the new copies of *Le Monde d'Hermès* from a stack (for the telephone number of this new Athens shop) and skedaddled.

I positioned myself across the street, where, courtesy of the giant plate-glass windows, I had a perfect view of the Incurable Romantic working at the cash desk. Nothing ventured, nothing gained—I phoned the store, and when he answered, I made the leap.

"Hello, I was in the store earlier this morning and one of those nice salesladies showed me a cream crocodile Birkin for my wife. Just my luck, she already has that color so I won't be buying the bag this time. Would you please tell the lady who put it on hold for me that I don't need it? I don't want you guys left holding the bag, heh-heh." I tried to come off as an obnoxious, dime-a-dozen businessman. (I always saw those jokers in the stores, buying Bolides for their brides and Paris Bombays for their bimbos.) I guess I sounded authentic, because he thanked me for calling and said he would give her the message. Half an hour later, I returned to the store and Hannah rushed to me brimming over with the good news.

"Michael, one of the croc Birkins is available." My ruse had worked (love those Greek gods) and I felt not even a twinge of guilt. In fact, I felt elated—my performance of surprise was truly Oscar-worthy. It wasn't as if those Birkins were "reserved" for some nice woman who had waited two years for one—they were on hold for resellers who were just like me. What really bothered me was that they hadn't even taken the plunge and bought them—they wanted to sell them before ever forking over a dime. No-risk Birkin buying? But that took all the fun out of it, didn't it?

My Birkin lust only partially sated, and my entrepreneurial dander up, I decided to double-dip. I left, but my game was hardly over. Five minutes before the shop closed, I had Mom (always a good sport, that

one) call the store from Florida and cancel "her" hold on the *braise* croc Birkin. Another Birkin was safe until morning. The next day I bought the *braise* croc Birkin "for my sister," along with two more cashmere shawls. Time to get gone from Greece, that was for sure—imagine if one of the "competitors" had walked in.

I tried to come up with a Confucius quote I could throw on my sig file for the victorious e-mail I sent Sarah from the Athens airport, because I knew that would crack her up. I couldn't find one that worked, though, so I went with Virgil: "Fortune favors the bold (Birkin-buyer)."

31

Hermès, We Have a Hostage Situation

After my Broadway performance in Athens, things returned to normal. By normal I mean *my* sense of what had become normal *to me*, not what anyone's mother would ever consider remotely normal (although mine was adjusting). I had turned into an impersonator, auctioneer, currency exchange rate expert, and Birkin mogul, burning through two passports in the process. The only thing missing was a Gulfstream 5, but who the hell can afford the gas for one of those anyway? Buying Birkins by the baker's dozen was now like buying eggs. God knows what my bank thought, with huge sums of money traveling in and out of my account on a weekly basis as I bought, sold, and financed Birkin purchases worldwide. I had two laptops now, two cell phones, and the BlackBerry. On the days I wasn't traveling, Juan would leave in the morning at eight and get home at four, and I would be sitting in exactly the same place, surrounded by my technology. I wasn't complaining, though—Birkins were yielding me a tidy profit. Mom and Dad ran the primary shipping center, with 50 percent or so of the bags I got going to Sarah, and the

rest to my other clients. My shoppers bought, I bought, and even Juan bought. Almost all croc, now, too. And thank God we had the cat—at least I wasn't alone all day anymore. Dali would curl up next to my laptop, climb in and out of the empty Hermès boxes, and generally do cute kitty things, providing a much needed distraction.

Luc remained my best shopper, although thankfully I didn't have to see him much. He was as egotistical a being as I had ever met, and on the rare occasions I saw him in Paris, I always footed the bill for everything. But bags from him showed up like clockwork for a year or so, so the business relationship was nothing to complain about. We did hit a glitch at one point, and I received an e-mail in his rudimentary, grade-school English.

From: "Luc" <LucHermès@yahoo.com>
To: "michael" <BirkinBoy1@YAHOO.COM>

hello

big truble. my banque called and asked me all questions about money transfers from you. I MUST send a letter to my banque telling them what all money is for.

This time we should get me my amex card sweetie cuz my banque is only going to be more truble for us later.

have a good evenning and be sure do do this tommorow

kiss

Lava would have to freeze before I would ever even consider giving this narcissistic knucklehead my AmEx card. However, I opted for a more tactful response:

From: "michael" <BirkinBoy1@YAHOO.COM>
To: "Luc" <LucHermès@yahoo.com>

Luc,

can you phone Hermès in Paris and ask them if they accept Travellers Checks? if they do, i can send you Amex travelers checks and you can pay without involving your bank. i can send the travelers checks to you by federal express in one day. let me know . . .

mt

Luc never wasted time where money was involved:

From: "Luc" <LucHermès@yahoo.com>
To: "michael" <BirkinBoy1@YAHOO.COM>

Hi sweetie

This is perfect, called Hermès and there is no problem for cheques—you are geenyus!!! I can have bag tomorrow so can you send cheques today? More good news I am dating a rich man in USA. CALL ME NOW.

Kiss-

My immediate thought was, Luc must be milking this poor guy dry. I really hated the idea of listening to Luc prattle on like a sixteen-year-old girl about his new squeeze, so I got the AmEx checks and FedExed them right out.

This new arrangement worked like a charm, and we continued like this for the next several months, with Luc getting bags every other week or so. I never asked any questions, but I was quite certain that there was no way for him to be getting all those bags from the Faubourg store. I bet he was peddling his wares at other stores. Busy little pollinating Birkin bee. Frankly, I didn't care if he gave blow jobs from Biarritz to Berlin, as long as the bags kept coming.

One day, when I was in the car, doing yet another road trip of the southern France Hermès shops, Norah Jones cranked up, Luc texted me:

Sweetie I am in nyc now and stan the boyfriend gave me a platinum visa for buying bags and you can wire money to his bank in PA. great news right. Shuld I try for Birkin in nyc?

I immediately texted him back:

Great news about Visa card, this will make it so much easier for you. No, forget about Birkins in NYC, way too expensive!

Luc's heartbroken and writes me:

☹ Going to Bangkok next week will try for bag there. Stan is not going just his Visa you fuck the sugar daddiess but you dont have fun with them ☺

The aptly named Bangkok? Oh my God, poor Stan, this guy was really being taken on some Nantucket sleigh ride. I had no doubt Stan was going to get some crazy Visa bill after Luc "Bangkoked." As it turned out, Stan's Visa wasn't up to single-handedly shouldering the production costs of "Luc Does Thailand": halfway through his trip, I got a frantic call and I (another sleigh ride victim) had to wire him $300.

However, unlike Stan, I was in it for the Birkins, not the booty.

Safely back in Paris (presumable travel itinerary: Charles de Gaulle airport, Bangkok, Charles de Gaulle, free clinic, Luc's apartment), Luc e-mailed me:

From: "Luc" <LucHermès@yahoo.com>
To: "michael" <BirkinBoy1@YAHOO.COM>

Sweetie-

Back in paris now. Spoke with Sonja and there two bags this week and Philippe say blue roi croc will be coming very soon (he thinks I

am reelly beutiful and you know he loves me still) OH my berthday comes in 2 weeks and I want a towel for the beech at Hermès.

Kiss

I bet he *did* want an Hermès beach towel; those suckers cost about $500. I restrained myself from sarcasm (for once).

Wildly excited, Luc called a few weeks later while I was still in my pajamas, making my first cup of Earl Grey. As usual, too cheap to pay for the call, he told me to phone him back immediately.

"Sweetie, I have exciting news, the *bleu roi* is ready! *See*, sweetie, Philippe *loves* me. I told you—I can get anything from him," he bragged. I wondered in the year and a half or so I had known Luc, how many times he had said that exact sentence. I largely ignored his preening and concentrated on the important stuff.

"How much is the bag?" I asked.

"I am reading the letter, oh, here it says $22,000. You should bank wire the money to Stan right away and I will buy the bag tomorrow with the Visa card. Sweetie, how much money we gonna win with this?" I mentally cringed. Any figure I quoted to Luc I knew he would try to hold me to. (As time passed, Luc had grown greedier about his portion of the "proceeds" on our purse sales—he now demanded 50 percent of the profit of every bag he bought with my money.) But just to get him off the phone, I made an educated guess.

"Okay, mmm, probably we'll split about $5,000 profit." I had two clients who had previously asked about a *bleu roi* croc, and they had been willing to pay me well for it at the time. But months had passed. For all I knew they could be having three-ways with Mr. Hermès now, swimming naked every night in a pool of *bleu roi* croc.

"Sweetie, be sure it's five thousand."

I immediately realized my mistake as those words left his mouth. He would probably get a tattoo of that number on his ass. Shit, what had I done? I quickly said good-bye before I could do any more damage. I wasted no time—I sent out several e-mails, offering this bag to

my best clients: Birkin 30cm, porosus crocodile, *bleu roi*, palladium (silver) hardware. I knew the *bleu roi* was highly sought after, so I didn't anticipate any problems.

The next morning, I awoke to the following:

From: "Luc" <LucHermès@yahoo.com>
To: "michael" <BirkinBoy1@YAHOO.com>

sweetie-

I got the bleu roi here now. I need very big faver just this one time sweetie can I keep the hole 5000 for me? I need to have surgery and need more money than the 5000 so if I can keep the hole money we win just this one time pleeze?? Ok, let me know ASAP. Oh do you think we can win more than 5000 that wuld be reely great.

BIG kiss

I could not believe this bullshit. Let me get this straight: Luc buys the bag with *my* money + I sell the bag to *my* client = Luc gets the whole profit? I'm no math major but that particular equation did not add up for me at all. Who did I look like, Father Christmas? If Luc could buy and sell the bags on his own, obviously he wouldn't be in business with me. The whole point was that we needed each other. And now he wanted to cut me out of my own business? Huh? And if that wasn't bad enough, I didn't even like the guy. Every interaction with him made me cringe. Really, only a fool thinks that a person who uses everyone else isn't using him.

So I bit my tongue for what I decided would be the last time. After this, I was done with him. I realized as "harmless" as Luc seemed, he was still too manipulative and greedy for my taste. No amount of crocodile was worth this to me. I decided as a parting gift I would be the bigger person in this whole *bleu roi* situation. Then I could sever all ties with a clear conscience.

From: "michael" <BirkinBoy1@yahoo.com>
To: "Luc" <LucHermès@YAHOO.com>

Luc- I hope that your surgery is nothing serious. Of course you can
have the entire profit from this bag (just this once) but please keep
in mind that I have not sold the bag yet and I cannot absolutely
guarantee the profit will be 5000. but I will sell the bag for the most
I possibly can. Hopefully today I will have more news and will let
you know ASAP.

mt

p.s. 22000 bank wired to Stan yesterday for the bleu roi

I hoped this reply would stave him off for a while and buy me some
time, but no such luck.

From: "Luc" <LucHermès@yahoo.com>
To: "michael" <BirkinBoy1@YAHOO.com>

sweetie-

you PROMUSSED 5000. why is everything differint now? This is not
rite when it is my turn to win the hole 5000 then it is changed. Stan
also sezs you promussed me 5000 so do NOT change this now. Ok,
let me know ASAP.

Kiss

Things were rapidly going from bad to worse. I was horrified that I
had ever mentioned a monetary figure to this jackass. I quickly scanned
through my other e-mails, and guess what? Sarah wanted the bag but
would only pay $3K over cost, which meant I would need to kick in two
grand to France's answer to Henry Kissinger to shut him up. Another
client e-mailed to say that mine was the third offer she had received for
the exact same bag, thanks but no thanks. Great—Hermès had flooded

their market and I was left on a sinking ship with an angry gay Soupy Sales as my mutinous first mate.

I brewed a pot of tea (and briefly thought of hunting down a Valium) before phoning Luc to tell him where things stood. I explained the e-mails I had received as thoroughly as I could. I thought I was fully prepared for anything, but the great negotiator really pulled out all the stops this time.

"NO, NO, NO, you say in the beginning five thousand and now you try to cheat me," Luc shrilled.

"But I don't control the supply and demand—" I tried to interject through his hysterics, but he rolled right over me like a Farmer over a Grandmother.

"No, you say five thousand before and Stan agrees, I told him whole thing. If you want to get the bag then come to Paris with my five thousand."

With that he slammed down the phone. Shell-shocked, I went to look for the Valium. And the wine. Hell, it was five o'clock somewhere . . . It took a while before it actually hit me: my bag was being held hostage. Poor little *bleu roi*, in the fetal position in some corner, duct tape over its clasp, blindfold over its *clochette*.

Okay, no more wine. Time to take some action.

From: "michael" <BirkinBoy1@yahoo.com>
To: "Luc" <LucHermès@YAHOO.com>

Luc, I am deeply disturbed and saddened by our phone conversation of earlier today. It seems you are forgetting the 1500 dollars that I have loaned you and how I wired money to you, no questions asked, whenever you requested. I am always the one who pays for meals, pays for phone calls, pays for bank wire fees, pays for Fedex, and on and on and until now have been happy to do so and have never once asked you for repayment of your debt. you should understand that just because someone offers me (or you) a huge amount of money for a specific bag today, that does not mean

that the offer will still be valid a month from now, perhaps not even tomorrow. this is called supply and demand and it's all a part of doing business. you have suggested to me that your boyfriend Stan is some big time intelligent business man, so why don't you forward this email to him and ask him what he thinks. I have always been more than generous and open with you and cannot believe the position you are putting me in now.

please read this twice, take a deep breath and THINK before you answer me.

cordially,

mt

Not surprisingly, Luc did not think:

From: "Luc" <LucHermès@yahoo.com>
To: "michael" <BirkinBoy1@YAHOO.com>

NO, if I not have my money, 5000, I will never give the bag back. END of story.

-Luc

I bitterly noted the absence of a "Kiss."

32

Mr. Sherlock Hermès

I was fit to be tied (although I never really understood that saying, it described my current emotional state nicely). I mean, an Hermès croc handbag wasn't exactly the Lindbergh baby, but it was my bread and butter. And I still couldn't believe Luc had decided to play Bonnie and Clyde with a Birkin. Was there no end to his lack of self-actualization? Did he not realize how stupid and petty this was? And how, well, how *lame*? I mean, Birkin-napping—can you imagine if Luc went to prison with that on his rap sheet? Not that I was going to call the cops: I couldn't even *imagine* trying to explain this to a Parisian policeman. More than anything, I needed to vent, so I sent Sarah an e-mail, telling her the whole drama. Then I was left alone with my thoughts. I had questions, I needed answers. Jesus, all of a sudden I was thinking like Sam Spade.

Question #1: Did Luc plan this all out in advance?

My immediate paranoid reaction was to assume he had, but then I decided that as manipulative as he was, he wasn't really the planning type. Christ, Luc couldn't even plan a basic breakfast, never mind a complex crime. Which brought me to:

Question #1(a): Did "Stan the Man" plan all this *for* Luc?

Again, it was hard to quiet my suspicious little soul, but if Stan was sleeping with Luc, how smart could he *really* be? He couldn't be the sharpest tool in the shed to put up with Luc always running love trains through the living room. So, no. This whole harebrained scheme was almost certainly an imbecilic impulse of Luc's.

Question #2: Did Luc really have the balls to carry out this idiotic scam?

Unfortunately, the answer was probably yes. I had heard him rant against people who were "mean" or "cheap" enough times to know he was expert in painting himself the victim. And once he had that idea stubbornly planted in his psyche, I became the enemy. He wouldn't re-think his plan now; to do so would be to admit he was the jerk. Which never was going to happen.

Question #3: What should I do now?

Well, this of course was the most important question, and of course the one I didn't have a ready answer to. My choices were:

a. Show up unannounced at his apartment with a can of
 Mace and a baseball bat and rescue my investment.
b. Pay him the five grand and call it an expensive lesson.
c. Wait him out.
d. Kill him.

While I liked both (a) and (d), they really weren't my MO. And there were some other flaws with those two options: first, they were both, strictly speaking, illegal; and second, I didn't even know if the bag was at his apartment. Meaning I could potentially end up imprisoned in the Bastille and *still* not have the Birkin. That would really suck. (I wondered if Hermès made iron masks.) (b) had the most straight-up logic, with the added bonus of ensuring I would never have to deal with Luc-the-megalomaniac again. Plus, I vaguely remembered that on multiple-choice tests, (b) had the best probability of being right. Despite this

ironclad logic, I knew I couldn't pick (b), because I would be giving in utterly, and I wasn't going to let some little French wannabe gangster extort money from me. Fuck that. Obviously, this left (c). (c) appealed to me, since it required nothing, but it sort of niggled at me for the very same reason.

I stopped thinking and checked my e-mail in hopes of receiving Choice (e) from Sarah.

From: DeluxeDivaMe@yahoo.com
To: BirkinBoy1@yahoo.com

OMG>>>out of fucking control. Edward thinks you should just pay him the dough and be done with this prick . . . write it off as a bad experience. Keep me posted.

So it appeared that Sarah and her husband were staunch (b) supporters, but I realized I'd sooner wipe my ass with the money and flush it down the toilet than send it to Luc at this point. The depth of my resolve was surprising me, but I'd definitively settled on choice (c). I decided to ignore Luc for some time, let him stew in his own juices (or, knowing Luc, someone else's). Perhaps he'd come back to me, tail between his legs, with a big kiss(-ass) e-mail. I hoped that if he didn't hear from me for several days, he might turn into a nervous Nelly.

Over the next few days, I concentrated on listing items on eBay to try and keep my mind off the Luc situation. I began to feel like a fourteen-year-old girl suffering her first crush: will he call, when will he call, is he going to call? I jumped every time the phone rang and constantly refreshed my in-box. Much to my despair, no e-mail or phone call ever came—I was Carrie at the prom.

Five days later, I did get an interesting e-mail, although it wasn't from Luc.

From: DeluxeDivaMe@yahoo.com
To: BirkinBoy1@yahoo.com

I got an email from my friend Alana and she was just offered a bleu roi croc from a guy in paris. What size is your bleu roi croc? Hardware? Do you think it could be Luc? Have you heard from him, what's going on with that? Did you already pay for that bag? Sarah

The hair on the back of my neck stood up. I fired off a response:

From: BirkinBoy1@yahoo.com
To: DeluxeDivaMe@yahoo.com

mine is 30cm, palladium, porosus croc. does alana have an email or anything from that guy? i haven't heard shit from Luc for like a week, so i am little nervous, bc yeah, i fronted all the money for the bag and now he is just holding it, like extortion style. keep me posted. mt

I sat hunched over the keyboard now, anxiously awaiting e-mails from anyone, something to distract me. Please, give me something here, even an e-mail about erectile dysfunction would be welcome at this point. Anything arriving in my inbox would give me a lift, no pun intended. The suspense of not knowing whether Alana's seller was Luc was killing me. After a torturous fifteen minutes, salvation arrived.

From: DeluxeDivaMe@yahoo.com
To: BirkinBoy1@yahoo.com

Alana says his phone number is xx xxx xxxxxx. the bag is the same as yours. Oh, and his name is Jérome. She said she was going to meet him in paris to buy the bag, let me ask her if she has an address. BRB

Whew, the phone number doesn't match, name isn't right, so I guess it's not Luc after all. By the time Sarah's next e-mail arrived, my heart rate was almost back to normal.

From: DeluxeDivaMe@yahoo.com
To: BirkinBoy1@yahoo.com

I'm sure it's just an odd coincidence, there are more than one bleu
roi 30cm on the planet right now. Alana is going to paris on Monday
to meet this guy and buy the bag, they have a plan to meet at his
apt, 13 rue manet.

No . . . fucking . . . way. Luc's address—13 rue Manet. I couldn't
believe this. He was really going to sell this bag from under me.

From: "michael" <birkinboy1@yahoo.com>
To: "sarah" <DeluxeDivaMe@yahoo.com>

that's MY fucking bag!! that's Luc's address!! I need to speak with
Alana, is this possible??? HELP!

Sarah, sensing the seriousness of the situation, immediately
e-mailed me back to say that Alana would phone me in fifteen minutes.
When the phone rang, after centuries had passed, I grabbed it like a
free ticket to a Babs concert.

"Hello!?!"

"Hi, this is Alana, is this Michael?"

"Hi Alana, yeah it's me. Tell me about this bag, I'm pretty sure it's
mine."

"Okay, so I got a call from my sales associate at George the Fifth
about a bleu roi that some guy is trying to sell; she says the bag is au-
thentic. I spoke to this guy, his name is Jérôme, and I'm supposed to be
meeting him on Monday in Paris to see the bag and pay him $25,000."

As she was telling me this, I was amused that $25,000 was the exact
price I had quoted Sarah, which represented a $3,000 profit. However,
for Luc, of course, this $25,000 was like a winning lottery ticket show-
ing up in a birthday card. It was all profit, he hadn't paid a damn cent
for it. What a windfall that would be for him.

"So you've actually spoken with Luc?" I asked her.

"Well, his name is Jérôme," she replied.

"Alana—here is the thing. *Your* Jérôme is actually *my* Luc. The address you are supposed to be meeting him at is Luc's apartment. He was one of my shoppers, and I paid for that bag, and he's going to screw me over for all that money." I hoped to God she wasn't still planning to go through with this.

"I don't like the sound of that. At all. I don't think I want anything to do with this Luc or whoever he is. I guess I'll call and cancel." Alana sounded flustered.

"No, wait. Let me think about this, I don't want to lose track of this bag. Do you mind calling him and changing the meeting to another place?"

"I don't want to meet this guy, Michael." Now I noted nervousness in her voice.

"No, I just want you to change the meeting to someplace more public, a café or something. Yeah, a café. Tell him you want to meet him at Ladurée, but don't use that name, just tell him the café across from Gucci on the corner of rue Royale and Faubourg Saint-Honoré. Yeah, that's perfect."

Yeah, perfect. That way I could intercept. Which, of course, begged the question—what would I do then? I guess I could figure that out later.

"All right, I'll call him and call you back." She hung up.

Hmmm. Luc the Leech was trying to make a major chunk o' change on *my* investment. That wasn't going to happen. Unfortunately, I had no clue what was going to happen. I felt underqualified for my predicament—I needed a weekend seminar at the FBI. And some gumshoes. What *are* gumshoes, anyway?

The phone rang—Alana. Everything was set. Monday at four o'clock at Ladurée. I told her I owed her a nice dinner and Champagne.

"Alana, when I get the bag back, are you interested?" I figured I'd ask.

"Um, no, I don't think so, Michael. Bad bag karma, I think."

"Okay, that's fine, I understand."

Bad bag karma? Oh boy. I didn't really blame her; it would be hard for her to look at it without thinking about this whole mess. I personally never wanted to see a *bleu roi* Birkin again—after I got this one back, that is.

I immediately called Sarah for advice. I brought her up to speed on my conversation with Alana.

"Michael, I hope you're planning on having a couple of bodyguards." I laughed. "I'm totally fucking serious," she said. "How do you know he's going to show up alone? He thinks he's going to get twenty-five grand, I bet he's not going to show up alone. Michael, you cannot go there by yourself, no way! You've got something like a twenty-thousand-dollar investment you've got to protect, not to mention yourself." Sarah sounded like she'd been watching a *CSI* marathon.

"Well, what do I do, call 1-800-bodyguards?" I tried to keep my tone light, no need for both of us to panic.

"No, don't you know anyone in Paris, someone you can call who can help you?"

"Well, the only one I really know in Paris, other than Luc, is Serge, my salesperson at Hermès, and I can't very well call him and tell him about this—can you fucking imagine if I told him this?"

Sarah howled with laughter as she pictured Serge's face upon realizing I was a reseller. This whole thing *was* funny, but it would be a lot funnier if it were happening to someone else, which from Sarah's angle, it was.

"What about if you call Pierre—you know, that guy that you met—one of my buyers? You said you guys got along." Sarah was trying to help me, I could tell.

"Yeah, we did. But he's a casual acquaintance, Sarah. I can't call and ask him if he knows any bodyguards I can hire!" I didn't mean to be snarky, but I didn't see how this guy was really relevant just because he lived in Paris and didn't seem like an axe murderer.

"I don't see where you have many options. It's Saturday now, and you have to meet this shithead on Monday," Sarah said. "And you can't go alone, you know that would be stupid." She had a point.

"Okay, let me get off the phone and arrange a flight and book my hotel—I think I better get to Paris tomorrow no matter what. I'll try calling Pierre." I promised Sarah I'd keep her posted.

I phoned Pierre and awkwardly explained who I was. He laughed and reassured me that he remembered me. Okay, step one accomplished. I spilled out the whole story and subtly incriminated Sarah for involving him in my mess.

Pierre, as a fellow reseller, was deeply unsettled by my story. When I told him about my rendezvous with Luc at Ladurée, he reacted strongly.

"Don't be crazy, you cannot do that," he insisted. "What if he's not alone?" Now I had two people telling me what a bad plan it was for me to go there by myself.

"Sarah thinks I should have some bodyguards go with me, like a couple of really big muscle guys." I figured I might as well get to the point. And I noticed that even though no one wanted me to go alone, no one was exactly lining up to go with me. Pierre laughed (everyone found my predicament so goddamned amusing) and said, "You know, maybe I do have someone for you. He's just a friend of a friend, but I think he used to be in security at a major fashion house. Now he's doing strong-arm work for banks. He might be able to help you. I'll try to track him down and call you back."

It was getting close to midnight by the time Pierre and I spoke again. Pierre said that he was still trying to reach the guy. I told Pierre I was going to call it a day, but I was flying up to Paris tomorrow morning regardless, and staying at the Mansart (of course).

I lay awake for a while, thinking about this bizarre predicament. I couldn't believe that Luc would steal $22,000 from me. But I knew my determination to prevail in this standoff wasn't all about the money. Yes, that was a lot of money, and I did want it back, but it was chiefly a

matter of pride. Luc, with his spoiled attitude and ungrateful heart, was not going to get the better of me. I would get this bag back if I had to travel to the ends of the earth, magnifying glass in my hand and a pipe clenched in my teeth. But I sure wished I had a Watson—or at least one of those cool hats with the earflaps. I always wanted one of those.

33

Fellini Film Noir

PACKING LIST

1. Clothes
2. Toiletries
3. Groucho Marx nose/glasses
4. Baseball hat/bat
5. Night-vision goggles
6. Gumshoes
7. Cell phone
8. Bullets
9. BlackBerry
10. AK-47

I was definitely more than a little nervous packing for my trip to Paris for this impromptu intervention. I knew my plane was leaving in a few hours, and I wasn't really sure if I wanted to be on it. Maybe this whole idea of trying to shake down Luc for my Birkin was a stupid one. Really, between hiring thugs and being blackmailed, it was all starting to be way too *Godfather* for me. (More the first film than the second;

definitely not the third—that movie blew.) I kept reminding myself that my plane ticket was bought, the hotel was booked, and I was going. And I *had* read somewhere that dying people always said they regretted more the things they didn't do than the things they did. I was hoping that using thugs to strong-arm a pompous French asshole to get a handbag back was covered under that little homily.

I didn't tell Juan a thing about what was going down. He was a worrywart as it was, especially since the anemia incident. (He always kept trying to feed me lemons—he and his parents had this almost supernatural faith in the healing power of lemons. Another Catalan thing, I guess. My mouth puckered every morning when I watched him eat his "daily dose." Thanks, but no thanks.) I knew he would absolutely tweak if he thought I was going to some bagfight at the Ladurée Corral. No way I needed that stress, and certainly he didn't. And it wasn't unusual for me to unexpectedly run off to Paris for some hot Birkin prospect, so I knew that wasn't going to raise any kind of red flag. He was happily immersed in Spanish cooking shows that Saturday morning, Dali cuddled at his side, when I kissed them both and left. To assuage my conscience, I decided I would tell him the whole story—as soon as I had the bag back. And I'd tell Dali too. He was getting big, and you can't shield them forever.

When I checked in at the Mansart, I already had messages waiting for me: Pierre, naturally. When I called him back, I got the whole scoop. Pierre and his friend Sandrine had found the thug last night (at two A.M.) while they were out barhopping. I guess I should thank God everyone I know is a boozehound. Pierre also informed me, "This is going to cost you a small fortune, since the guy works on commission." My greatest fear was coming true: the Italian way had seeped into France. Actually, on second thought, that wasn't a fair comparison— the thug was performing a service for me, which I desperately needed, not taking bribes on selling handbags. I supposed it made sense for the value of the item to factor in. Just so long as I got my baby bleu roi back, I didn't really care. It wasn't like hiring the thug was going to cost more

than the handbag. (And what a sad state of affairs that revealed, eh?) I also realized that I had better stop calling the thug "the thug," or else I might slip up when I met him, and that would be bad.

Pierre showed up in a silver BMW, which was nice. If you're about to hire a strong-arm, it's best to arrive in style. I actually was already feeling a lot more positive because I'd hired someone—or was about to hire someone. I come from a school of thought where if something is broken, you hire a professional to fix it. Broken toilet, call a plumber. So I guess if your Birkin is being held hostage, you call someone who used to guard haute couture handbags. I was eager to meet the guy.

From: BirkinBoy1@yahoo.com
To: DeluxeDivaMe@yahoo.com

ok, so here is your update, but you will never believe the day i had! and don't worry, i'm totally fine. first off, the thug that pierre helped me find, or as i like to refer to him now, "the associate," was the size of a superbowl linebacker (and he had on these fantastic bikkembergs sneakers i just adored, too) but then he totally starts firing questions at me first off, he wants to know if Luc knows i stay at the mansart and when i tell him yeah, he says i have to change hotels that night! so i'm in the birkin witness protection program now. then he gives me like the third goddamn degree about if i bought the bag, how much was the bag, where Luc lived, if he did drugs, how i knew him, where he worked, all this shit. i mean, he was asking mostly about Luc, but he is like DRILLING me with the questions. i wanted to order a bottle of Cognac and call it a day, it totally sucked. but then it hit me, he had been making sure i was on the up and up and whatever, and not just hiring him to steal somebody's shit for me. i guess he believed me finally, bc we left and he and Pierre were blah blah blah and we set the whole thing up for tomorrow. the associate made all these notes in this notebook. can you believe this shit??? sarah, this is way the hell out of control. so now i am packing and getting ready for them to pick me up and swap hotels, they are really worried Luc will

see me and realize something is up. i can't believe i can't stay at the
mansart, i love this place, it's so weird to stay anywhere else while im
in paris . . . whatever, tho, long as i get the bag, right. tomorrow is the
big day, think good thoughts. I'll keep you posted.

mt

I was a little concerned about checking out of the Mansart a day
early, since practically everyone there knew me by name and knew I
never stayed in the city for just one night. It wasn't a huge deal or any-
thing, but I didn't want to make up some big story, or have them think
that I wasn't happy with the hotel. Luckily, while I was checking out,
right when the desk clerk would have logically asked me why I was cut-
ting short my stay, the concierge walked over and interrupted.

"Mr. Hermès," he said with a smile. This is what some of the staff
called me now, due to the prodigious number of orange bags I carried
in and out of the lobby. "I have a question for you . . . Do you know an
Oprah Winefree? She is big in the States, no?"

"I think you mean Oprah Winfrey, and yeah, she's very famous in
America. She's one of the wealthiest women in the world, and she hosts
this hugely successful talk show. She's, like, a big deal. Why do you ask?"

"Your friends at Hermès didn't know her, I guess . . . They didn't
let her in the store yesterday around closing time. Her, and another
woman, Gayle? Her friend. Well, they didn't recognize her, it's all over
the television. They didn't let them in, and a lot of people think it's be-
cause, well, because . . ." Here he paused, hesitant to continue.

"Because she's black?" It had to be what he was getting to.

He nodded, looking uncomfortable.

"Do you think they are like that there?" he asked after a second.

"Racist? Um, no . . . not that I know of. But she is superfamous,
so it is kinda bad they didn't let her in. I wonder what will happen . . .
wow." I thought it was funny that my kidnapping drama was unfold-
ing right along with some other big Hermès/Oprah drama. Timing is
a funny thing.

Speaking of which, Pierre honked outside from the loading zone, and I was able to make an escape without revealing why I was leaving so abruptly, or, more likely, lying about why. There really was no easy way to explain my situation, you see.

I still can't believe Pierre didn't let me check in under my own name at the new hotel. I felt like an abused woman on the run from her asshole husband. And once I had settled in, Pierre, nice guy that he was, asked if I'd be okay on my own for the night. Why wouldn't I be okay? What was going to happen? Huh? And then, as if that wasn't enough, he told me to stick close by the hotel. This whole thing seemed to be getting more and more bizarre, rather than less and less bizarre, as I had naively hoped. But I decided, stubborn soul that I am, that I wasn't going to let Luc control my life. I was going out to dinner, and that was final. I got as far as the hotel lobby and decided to return to the room and grab my Red Sox cap and sunglasses to help conceal my identity. Better safe than sorry.

I ate that night at the Royal Madeleine Bistro. Very Old World, lots of wood and zinc. There was a tiny awkward moment when the hostess tried to seat me by the plate-glass window (sorry, ma'am, I need a table in the back, I'm trying to elude a male hustler who stole one of my Birkins). My panic-stricken face said it all, and she immediately took me to a table in the bowels of the restaurant. As an added bonus, from there I was able to do surveillance of the front door. (Alas, I had forgotten my night-vision goggles at the hotel.) I didn't need them to spot the giant silver urn with the Taittinger bottles. Along with the *coup de Champagne*, the waiter also brought me the *Herald Tribune*. I wondered if he sensed my need for camouflage.

I was starving—being on the lam really tires one out. I went with foie gras, onion soup, Dover sole, and a bottle of Côte-Rôtie. How's that for a Last Supper? I also figured, since who knew what tomorrow would bring, that I might as well get really bombed. So . . . tarte tatin and some Armagnac. Waiter, make it a double. Don't mind if I do.

When I got back to the hotel, there was an e-mail from Sarah waiting for me. I blearily looked at it through my Champagne goggles.

From: DeluxeDivaMe@yahoo.com
To: BirkinBoy1@yahoo.com

Holy Fucking SHIT! This is so nuts, too funny. It's like a goddamn heist movie, I am on the edge of my seat, lol! Luc is such a dick to make you go thru all this. It's just a fucking bag, I hope this is worth it. yeah, i know, probably is, it's a shitload of money. good luck, and i know you will get it back, no way Luc will stand up to that guy. say hey to Pierre for me, haven't chatted with him lately. keep in touch and tell me everything, i want all the details. and also so that I know you are alive, hahaha

sarah

PS did you hear about Oprah? i didn't even think she went to Hermès, never "seen" her with a birkin anyway

From: BirkinBoy1@yahoo.com
To: DeluxeDivaMe@yahoo.com

hey, wanted to say hi, yes i'm still alive . . . i'm back at the "new" hotel, CNN on the tube (all oprah all the time, haha, what a fucking PR minefield that whole thing is for Hermès, huh? can you believe it?)

pierre told me not to go out to dinner bc of Luc but i did anyway. didn't see him, i was always good at hide and seek, LOL.

toooo much champagne at dinner, im kinda drunk, can you blame me, haha. nighty nite.

mt

Pierre woke me with his phone call at way too early o'clock. I was (oddly enough) nursing a slight hangover. He told me he was coming to get me at one thirty, which gave me about four hours to lie around and be useless. I did have an assignment, however. I had to write down

everything I could remember about Luc, his house, car, and so on, so that the Associate would be as prepared as possible. Writing anything down right now was about as appealing to me as a game of cricket, but I saw the sense of it. I groped for a piece of hotel stationery, a pen, and my copy of *Vanity Fair* as writing desk.

Luc Menu

- about 5′10″, dark brown eyes, defined build, dark brown hair

- 13 rue Manet, 2nd floor (on right), subway entrance outside of building

- lives alone (has sugar daddy in USA)

- VW Golf, dark gray, not new, 2-door, parks on street, often misplaces car

- very well dressed, dark colors, perhaps dark suit

- carrying large orange Hermès shopping bag??

- very good-looking and very vain (wouldn't want his face hurt)

Between catching a catnap, dosing myself with more aspirin, taking a hot shower, and drinking copious cups of tea, I was reasonably back to normal by the time Pierre picked me up. The Associate sat shotgun, and I handed him my list. I found out that "we" had decided not to go with the Ladurée plan. The Associate opined it was "too out in the open for any sort of scene or rough stuff to go down." I was like, what rough stuff? I could imagine Luc on a bullhorn: "Everyone stay calm, and the handbag won't get hurt."

Now the plan was for the Associate and *his* two associates that he was meeting (this guy was pretty together—he had his own people) to get the bag back before Luc even got into his car. Actually, the *master* plan was that it would all go down right in Luc's apartment building, so there was a minimal chance of anyone being around to interfere. I gave him the dirt on where Luc's door was in the building, all that.

Pierre and I would go to a café right near Luc's house, easily reachable via the "hotline" cell phone that the Associate had given Pierre in case of any "complications." I remembered what Sarah said in her e-mail, about this being a heist flick, and I decided that would only be an accurate comparison if Fellini were directing it. Come on—three purse-pursuing thugs? A gay guy trying to "fence" a crocodile handbag? A special "hotline" cell phone for if there are any "complications" recovering a Birkin? Had the world gone crazy?

After we dropped the Associate back near Luc's, we settled in at the café. The afternoon ticked by. I looked at my watch constantly, and fiddled with my *chaîne d'ancre* (I had worn it because today counted as a Birkin-getting day, albeit an unconventional one).

2:29 Pierre coffee, me tea.

2:34 Pierre's phone rings, startling me out of my stupor. I don't know who he's talking to, but he's not happy.

2:38 Pierre smokes frantically and gives me the dish: some married woman he's sleeping with. She wants to rendezvous in Marrakesh, he doesn't. He's angry. So's she.

2:39 She calls again.

2:40 She calls again.

2:41 She calls again.

2:42 She calls again. Pierre goes ballistic. I barely know what he says but I know they're never going to talk again. Pierre actually *turns off* his phone.

2:43 Pierre beer, me tea.

2:47 "Hotline" cell phone rings. The Associate wants to know if Luc's building has parking, and whether he uses it. No, he *always* parks on the street.

2:54 "Hotline" again. Does Luc have a shaved head? Of course not, he's way too vain. Hadn't the Associate read my "menu"? I decide to keep that thought to myself.

2:55 The Associate calls again with an "interesting development." Two young dudes have entered Luc's building. He says that if those two are involved then the price is five hundred more. Great.

2:59 Pierre beer, me beer.

3:09 "Hotline" rings. My mission: go to pay phone across street, call Luc. I am told very sternly by Pierre to be *sure* to dial 067 first to block caller ID. I'm supposed to see if he answers, and if he does, hang up. Which he does. Which I do.

3:11 Pierre calls the Associate, gives him the GO sign. Associate calls again, in the building and confused. I give him the scoop again:

– Enter front door

– Mailboxes ahead, 15 feet

– Turn left

– Wide old wooden stairs, turn right, go up

– At second landing, double doors to your right

– (Consult Birkin-o-meter now . . .
needle should be in red zone)

Associate no longer confused.

3:19 Take a leak, and worry the whole time in
the bathroom I will miss something.

3:27 "Hotline." Associate worries that Luc has
given them the slip. Back to pay phone . . .

3:28 So weird: I talk to Luc. Not much is said . . . he
"has to go." Yeah, no shit, important purse-fencing
appointment at four o'clock. God, what an asshole.

3:29 Luc's presence in apartment is confirmed to Associate.

3:33–3:42 Repeated calls to Associate, no answer.
Pierre chain-smokes, I guzzle beer. I realize
I am about to be shit-faced again. I decide
I might be an alcoholic. I blame Luc.

3:43 A heavy hand falls on my shoulder, startling me.
Thankfully, it's none other than Mr. Associate, who
has an orange shopping bag dangling in his other
hand and an amused smile on his face. Two other
behemoths stand behind him, both with huge grins on
their otherwise imposing countenances. It is clear that
they can't believe all this fuss over a handbag. I want to
explain, but when I open my mouth, I realize I really
don't understand either. I order everyone a beer instead.

From: BirkinBoy1@yahoo.com
To: DeluxeDivaMe@yahoo.com

Mission accomplished! i didn't see the whole thing go down, but i got the whole story from "my guys." when Luc came out of his apt to go meet "Alana," the associate and his two dudes (yup, i ended up with 3 tough guys) followed them. (Luc had two friends with him BTW—it was all "supposed" to go down in the apt building, but they got sketched by those other dudes being there) anyway, after Luc got to his shitbox "my guys" stood there and trapped them in the car (i picture mice in a cage, haha). then they asked Luc if he had "something of michael's" i wish i could have been there for that, imagine Luc's face!! so then they made Luc hand it through the window, and that was that. candy from a baby, right? of course, pierre and I are sitting at the café this whole time, sweating it out, making phone calls, all this shit. but i have it. although my little bleu roi will need all sorts of therapy to handle its post traumatic stress disorder, hahaha.

be home to barcy tomorrow. this is a crazy ass job we have, isn't it? and, did you still want the bag?

m~

The *bleu roi*, in case you are concerned, recovered nicely. Sarah passed on it, but Carole Bayer Sager gave it a lovely home and plenty of attention, and it has truly flourished. And I'm mostly recovered from the Luc incident too, although I still cringe anytime anyone signs their e-mail with a kiss.

34

Found Money, Hidden Grace

Juan had decided we were rich. Actually, I can't even imagine how much money in savings I would need to have for his parsimonious little soul to feel completely at ease, but he did find out we made a lot more money than he thought we did. He had finally gotten to the boiling point with the store receipts and credit card statements and money-order carbons and bank notices and FedEx forms and other miscellaneous pieces of paper that were choking half of our kitchen table. When I came in the door after yet another handbag excursion, he was sitting cross-legged in the middle of the living room, surrounded by stacks of paper. Dali was "helping" him by acting as feline paperweight, somehow always managing to pick the pile Juan needed to get at. He had a calculator, a notebook, and an incredulous expression.

"Michael, do you know how much Hermès you *bought* last year?"

"Um, no, not really. How much?" I had a feeling it might be a big number. That was mostly due to the change in my merchandise focus—my specialization, if you will. Because in an average *leather* Birkin Hermès outing, I dropped $8,000, minimum; a croc, and it was up to $25,000. And I was a crocodile king now. (Is that a song? No wait, that's "Crocodile

Rock." Right.) Plus I had gotten Juan, and even some of his fellow teachers, into the act. Juan himself had bought bags, many of them crocodile, in Madrid, Barcelona, Dublin, London, Paris, Berlin, Cologne, Prague, and Naples. (His teacher friends generally stuck to the Spanish stores.) So if you factored in all his bags, all the *other* shoppers' bags, the bags bought by yours truly, the "formula" enactment items everyone had to buy to get the bags, the bags bought with charge ships, and the miscellaneous items I bought at auction . . . well . . .

"$1.6 million." His eyes searched mine, to see if I was surprised.

I was. I hadn't really expected that.

"Wow, that's a . . . lot." It *was* a lot. Of course, that was what I spent, not what I made, but still . . . That's a boatload of Birkins. And *chaînes d'ancre*. And Ulysses. And cashmere shawls. And scarves. And scarves. And scarves.

"That's what *I* thought." Juan's voice sounded like he needed some sort of explanation.

"Well, it's an expensive job, Juan, I have a million frequent-flier miles now, but that wasn't the case when I started, and then there are the hotels, and I have to eat." I felt as if I needed to justify this somehow, God knows why. Probably because I had a suspicion that—

"Where is it, Mikey? Where is all the money? We have a lot, but I thought we would have, you know, more . . . if you bought all that." He wasn't mad, thank God, he sounded more frustrated and, more than anything, confused.

I wasn't confused at all. The thing with Birkin money was that it spent real easy. On food, on flights, on hotels, on clothes, on a million and one different "business expenses." My life on the road was my life, or at least half of my life. It was all well and good that Juan could eat Subway for dinner and be happy, and when I was home, so could I, but when I was alone in a foreign city, the fourth foreign city that week, going out for a nice meal at the end of the day was all that kept me from madness. Plus, on a more pragmatic level, at any given time I had $50,000 or $60,000 tied up in "assets," e.g., items I was selling on eBay.

That was money in the bank, as far as I was concerned. As far as Juan was concerned, though . . .

"And we have stacks and stacks of it in the guest room that we haven't even sold yet, Mikey, and you buy more and more and more. I don't understand." Juan's voice was getting a little louder.

"Juan, that isn't fair. This is what I do. I spend a lot of money at Hermès, yes, but I make a lot of money too. And we went to Japan, and we are leaving for New York this weekend. You tell me you want to go to Thailand—that's all going to cost money, and you don't seem to mind spending that money, do you?" My voice wasn't all that quiet right now either.

"Of course, we are going to travel together, spend money together, Michael. Don't be so ridiculous. That's not what this is about."

I noticed I was no longer Mikey, which upset me, and that he was calling me ridiculous, which enraged me.

"I'm ridiculous? *I* am? I make all this money and take you all these places, and all you can do is bitch that it 'costs' a lot to make it?? That I spend too much of my money? I don't know if you took any business courses, but you have to spend to earn." I sounded pretty good to myself there.

"You are right, I see now, Michael, I was wrong to say anything. I didn't realize it was *your* money. I thought it was *our* money." With that, he walked out, stopping short of slamming the door (Dali freaked if we did that).

I didn't sound so good to myself anymore. I moped around the living room, picking up the stacks of evidence, and then, restless and upset, I turned to Grace for advice.

From: BirkinBoy1@yahoo.com
To: GraceoftheGarden@yahoo.com

grace-

i am so bummed right now. i have this big trip planned with juan for next week to NYC and we just got in a big fight! over money of all

things, he figured out what i spent last year at Hermès, it was lot, of course, and he thinks that i should have more/save more and that i spend too much on the road, and it got kinda bad. we will be ok but i hate fighting with him . . . and i don't know what to say, it is what it is, yknow? anyway i just wanted to say hey and see if you had any advice. ☺

mt

Moments later I got a response.

From: GraceoftheGarden@yahoo.com
To: BirkinBoy1@yahoo.com

Michael-

I am sorry to hear of your argument with Juan. I think the main thing that you have to remember is that what you do is very unusual. You are dealing with what could be seen (by many/most people) as remarkable quantities of money. I am sure it will blow over in time for your trip, you two are too smart to let something like money come in between you. I also have an offer to make you in regards to your vacation (one which Juan may be pleased by, also, in light of your recent disagreement). As you know, I loathe the hot summer months in NYC, and I will be taking my customary August sabbatical from Manhattan, and fleeing to the cooler air of Montauk. Did you wish the use of my apartment for your week here? It *is* quite a convenient location (as I am sure you realize from shipping me the odd scarf here and there.) I would be thrilled for you to use it, so please accept. Let me know soon so I can make the arrangements.

Best,

Grace

Grace will forever be the master of the understatement. Her "convenient location" was on the Upper East Side, across the street from

Carl Schurz Park. One of the most desirable locations in the city. I was surprised at the generosity of her offer, although knowing what I did, I shouldn't have been. Grace had told me about some of her charity work, which included cooking huge gourmet dinners every Friday night for a homeless shelter. That kind of thing impressed me, since it was an investment chiefly of time, not money. She was clearly a "real" person, despite her considerable wealth.

From: BirkinBoy1@yahoo.com
To: GraceoftheGarden@yahoo.com

Grace-

of course i will accept, if you are certain you don't mind! that sounds great. so now i will even see your apt before i ever see you, haha. make sure you don't leave any photo albums out, i might not be able to control myself. let me know if you need anything from me.

mt

Juan and I were hot and sweaty from the humid August weather, as well as weary from our flight, when we reached the door of Grace's Manhattan apartment later that week. (We had exchanged apologies and called a truce, although I had a sneaking suspicion the discussion wasn't totally over, just delayed.) I fumbled at the lock with keys that the doorman had handed me in the lobby. Grace was on the top floor of a huge old brick apartment building that had the added charm of a rooftop garden, but right now all that loveliness was lost on us. We wanted showers, and pajamas, and a nice rest; nothing more, nothing less. When I finally got the door open, a blast of cold air hit both of us. Juan and I looked at each other, both slightly taken off guard by *how* air-conditioned the place was. It couldn't have been more than sixty-five degrees in there, which made it almost thirty degrees cooler than outside. At the moment, though, it felt great, and we gratefully shuffled in, dropping our burdensome luggage as the door swung shut behind us.

The entranceway was dominated by a ten-foot-long mahogany table, filled with dozens of framed photographs. In the very center of that table I saw a note on heavy cream paper, and I recognized Grace's elegant script. (She sent me "hard copy" Christmas and birthday cards every year now.)

Michael and Juan~

Welcome! I hope your trip was not too strenuous. A few last minute tidbits of information for you:

I have a car service that you can use if you so desire, please feel free, they are very good, the number is (212) 555-5555.

I am a "regular" at Elaine's, which is right around the corner. If you are wishing to dine there (and I highly recommend you do), you should make the reservation under my name, as it can be difficult to get in.

I have a selection of wine in the living room—you will see the cabinet. Please help yourself to whatever you want. The same goes for anything you can "scrounge up" in the kitchen.

Keep the temperature of the apartment at what suits you, I know I keep it cooler than most, but please turn each of the room thermostats back down to sixty-three before you go.

Most important, I hope you have a great time in the city, and make yourselves at home. My housekeeper will be in after your departure, so do not trouble yourselves overmuch with any of those details.

Best,
Grace

P.S. Michael, I think our relationship being strictly through email has been what has made it special, and I see no reason to "sully" it now. So as per our longstanding tradition of visual anonymity, I have removed all photographs in the apartment that contain me, save one. It is a group shot—which resides somewhere on this table. If your curiosity is too much for you, well, happy hunting!

Loved that. And I loved the apartment too. Dark, narrow-boarded wood floors, lacey drapes on the floor-to-ceiling windows to let in plenty of light, many oil paintings, and a host of antiques. Some of the paintings were Grace's, as she also dabbled in art (she had an adorable little studio right in the apartment, replete with easel and skylights). The dining room was my favorite, though, with its domed stained-glass ceiling. The colored light it created dappled across the sideboard and its large collection of mismatched sterling silver and plain white china. The kitchen had state-of-the-art everything, with white walls and copper pots that were obviously there for use, not show. Grace had actually taken some classes at the Divina Cucina in Florence and Ritz Escoffier School in Paris, so she was all about cooking. (I saw the institutional-sized pots she must use for her charity work.) William Yeoward crystal filled a glass-fronted cabinet in the living room, and the choices in her "wine closet" ranged from a $15 Chilean wine to a $200 French Bordeaux. A second case displayed her two hundred–plus rabbit collectibles, housing both a dime-store ceramic Thumper and a bejeweled blue bunny presumably worth thousands. Juan was suitably taken aback by the breadth of this collection, but I knew about her "rabbit habit" going in, since Grace had confided in me all about her (late) pet rabbit Pate and her general affinity for things with bright shiny noses and powder-puff tails. Pate had been her constant companion for years, and stayed at the Ritz Paris with her so many times that the concierge had become semi-attached and insisted on handling his feedings personally. Later that week I saw the closet that had housed Pate, with his tiny bed as yet unremoved.

The overall impression I got from my initial tour is that Grace liked what she liked, and it didn't really matter much to her what the price tag said. She did have her high-end indulgences, of course, which ranged from her beloved Hermès scarves to the Rigaud Cyprès candles scattered throughout the place. When I peeked in her gigantic walk-in closet, I saw stacks and stacks of orange scarf boxes reminding me of

Ellen Yeats. However, Grace was "all scarves all the time," which made her stockpile neater, if not any less grandiose.

Juan and I spent the stereotypical week in New York City and enjoyed every second of it. We dined at Elaine's under Grace's name, and got VIP treatment there as a result. (The food wasn't anything extraordinary, but the clientele was pure New York literary scene, which made it fun.) We saw *The Lion King, Cabaret,* and Eugene O'Neill's *A Long Day's Journey into Night.* This last was my choice, as it was starring Vanessa Redgrave, whom I knew from an assignment back in my hair and makeup days. She had taken a liking to me, and we had spent an afternoon shopping and lunching together on Newbury Street. She was unbelievably kind and down-to-earth, unlike many of the other celebrities I had met through TEAM. This was eight or so years ago, and since then I had sent her "backstage" notes at several productions, which were always answered by a handwritten thank-you note. This time I decided to send her some flowers as well, something that could go on her dressing room table. My generosity may have been partially inspired by Grace's—leafing through the *Playbill* a few nights prior, at *The Lion King,* Juan had spotted her name on the patrons page for a Shakespeare production. It seemed her philanthropic interests were all over the place.

We had a notable week in another way, as well. For some reason, we saw celebrities everywhere we ate. I mean, yes, we were dining at places like Daniel and Gramercy Tavern, but still, in one week, we had vacation "cameos" from Kevin Bacon, Liam Neeson, Ellen Barkin, Macaulay Culkin, Tony Bennett, Ethan Hawke, and Michael Imperioli (Chris from *The Sopranos*). Bizarre, right? However, even more bizarre for me was not going to Hermès while I was in New York. I had decided that I didn't want to reopen any sort of argument with Juan, so I never even suggested it. Although it was hard not to mention that we owed this whole stay in this stylish Upper East Side apartment to my job, I managed to keep my mouth shut. With Grace, however, I couldn't resist belaboring one particular point, and I left her a note of her own:

Grace~

Loved the place, absolutely great, we had an unbelievable week. (Elaine's was yummy!) Thank you so much. I will be in touch, of course.

~Michael (and Juan)

PS I'm not sure if I picked you out from your pictures, but I did manage to hide one of me somewhere in the apartment. Cheers!

I hadn't really, but she didn't know that. I wonder how many scarf boxes she would go through before she called it a day.

35

A Birkin for Mom

The rest of the summer and early fall were uneventful, marked by only a handful of trips and even more reliance on my shoppers. I was trying to stick closer to home. Juan and I had reached a truce, cemented by the addition of a playmate for Dali. Gala (named after Salvador's wife) was another Bengal kitty, and watching the two of them frolic was a highlight of the days I was working from home.

It was on such a day in November that my phone rang, startling the ever-timid Dali off of his perch near my laptop, and causing Gala to glare imperiously, furious she had been awakened from her nap. I ignored them both. The caller ID said Mom.

"Hey, Mom, how are ya?"

"Oh, I'm all right. I'm sort of down right now."

That was unusual; my mother was as stable as they come.

"Really, why? Something wrong?"

"Well, my back has been giving me a lot of trouble lately, and now I can't even golf like I have been. I'm down to a couple times a week, and even then it's bad. Your poor father has had to take care of all the shipping and everything, I'm afraid bending and carrying those bulky boxes is a little much for me most days."

"Dad doesn't have to do it. I can take care of everything here—don't even worry about it."

"No, no, Michael, don't be silly; he actually enjoys it. I'm just cranky, I think, and frustrated. They've given me muscle relaxers, and I've been using a heating pad, and none of it seems to help. And Thanksgiving is next week, and you know, it's hard not feeling good around the holidays."

"Oh, I know, there's nothing worse than back pain, too. I'm sure you just need to rest. I'm not sure if you should be golfing at all." I mean, duh, Mom. But I knew how much she loved to golf. You might as well tell her not to read, which is how she spent the other half of most days.

"Well, I might stop for a while," she said, startling me.

"Good, you should." I didn't allow her to hear my surprise at her easy surrender.

We chatted about this and that, and by the time I got off the phone, I wasn't really thinking about my mom's back trouble so much as about a couple of incoming calls I had missed on my BlackBerry while we were talking, and brand-new e-mails I needed to deal with. Lately, working out of my apartment meant I was always working.

The phone rang on a similar morning a couple of weeks later. Same startled Dali and pissed-off Gala. Same caller ID.

"Hey, Mom. How are you? Feeling any better?"

"Hi Mike, it's Dad." That was odd; my dad wasn't generally in charge of phone calls.

"What's up?"

"Well, your mother's back—you know it's been bothering her. And one day it's her shoulders, next day it's her hips. We don't know what the hell to think. We went in and had some X-rays done over the last couple weeks. You know, a series of them, and . . ."

"And what? What? Did they find something?" Oh no.

"Well, they say there are cloudy spots. Cloudy areas, they said. They need to do more tests. But what the hell is that, *cloudy areas*? What do you think of that, Michael? What does that *mean*?" His voice pleaded, as though I could tell him it was nothing to worry about, happened all the time, those cloudy areas. And, of course, the truth was that I knew not one single thing about any of it.

"Well, I'm not sure, Dad. I would wait to make any kind of guess; the doctors will know more after the tests. Might be nothing." Might it be? I didn't know.

"Well, yeah, maybe it's nothing. A pinched nerve or infection or something like that." He sounded like he was trying to convince himself. I let him.

"Yeah, who knows? Take it easy. Just take care of her, don't let her do too much. How is she taking the news? Is she okay?"

"Oh, you know her, Michael. She didn't even want to say anything to you guys. But I thought you and Dottie should know. Don't say anything about me telling you, for right now. I don't want her thinking I'm worried." They were sort of cute, the two of them, always protecting each other from, well, each other. Like my mother wouldn't be able to tell my father was worried after the fifty-odd years they had been married. Funny.

"Okay, no problem, Dad. I'm sure it is nothing, really. Take care, okay?"

I immediately called Dottie, my sister. She lived right near them, with her husband, Eddie, and daughter, Riane (the light of my mother's life).

If anyone knew what was up, it was Dottie. After our greeting and idle talk, I asked about Mom, which we both knew was why I had called.

"Michael, she looks very tired, not good at all. I don't know what that test means, we need to wait and see. But I'm making her go in for a complete physical next week, regardless. We need to get to the bottom of this." Dottie tended to worry at times, but I was grateful she was leaving no stone unturned. She continued on.

"I think maybe you should come home for Christmas. You know, it would give her a lift to see you, Michael. She missed seeing you this August." She was right. I had felt bad about canceling my annual summer trip, anyway. I could make it up to her now.

"You're right, I'll look into plane tickets today."

This was not the best news I'd ever heard, not only because I was sick with worry that my mother was ill, but also because Juan and I were planning a Christmas trip to Thailand, and now I had to tell him it was a no-go. This was completely needless worry on my part, as Juan didn't even mention the trip when I called him two minutes later to procure his blessing on the change of yuletide venue. When *I* brought up Thailand, he acted like I was nuts for even thinking twice about it. ("It's your mom, Mikey, of course we will go.") One less thing to worry about, thank God.

Finding transcontinental flights right before Christmas was always a treat, and I spent the better part of the afternoon looking for tickets. I finally found two seats, but they were on two different planes, and one of them had a lengthy layover at JFK. I decided to book Juan on the more direct flight and put myself on the New York one. In a moment of inspiration, I booked my connecting flight to Miami for the following day, which would give me a night in the big city. I could do my Christmas shopping there, and see one of my old friends, Geoffrey, in the process. He knew my mother pretty well, and, for some reason, that seemed important right then.

Two weeks later, I was on a flight to New York, more miserable than I could ever remember feeling. The test results had come in, and my

mother had cancer. Lung cancer, to be exact, even though she had given up smoking fifty years earlier. Her family history of cancer likely had more to do with it than anything. The cancer was moving fast, and the oncologist had not been too optimistic about her prognosis, although he tried to avoid saying so outright. And, as my family kept telling one another, there was always hope, and she was in the best hands, and we were sure something could be done. At least that's what we said. What we thought, at least in my case, was a different matter altogether. I was terrified. And I still didn't know what to get her for Christmas. On the plane, as I was blinking back tears, it occurred to me—so obvious it was strange I hadn't thought of it before—that I would get her a Birkin. After all, she had shipped hundreds, and it was only her due.

Geoffrey was waiting at the terminal, not our normal MO for my sporadic visits, but he somehow knew I would need him to be at the airport this time. He was right. He greeted me with a big hug, and I almost started crying right there. I was losing it. He saw I was a little, um, fragile, and took charge. He carried my bag, got us a cab to his apartment, canceled the reservation he had made at Le Bernardin, settled me into the living room with a glass of red wine, and cooked me a comfort meal of chicken and mashed potatoes. He listened to me ramble, continuously refilled my wineglass, and made sure I ate at least enough to keep me going. I dropped into bed with the heavy exhaustion I had been feeling since my mother got sick. It was more leaden than the normal kind of tired I was used to, more numbing and almost physically heavy. And no matter how long I slept, when I woke up, I felt the exact same amount of tired. This time was no different, and that morning I got ready for the least energetic bout of Christmas shopping I could have imagined.

I did feel somewhat better as I shopped. Christmas in New York is inescapable in its cheer, and I love buying presents anyway. So I forgot about my misery for a while and allowed myself to enjoy the skaters in Rockefeller Center, and the windows at Saks Fifth Avenue. Before I knew it, I was laden with shopping bags, and it was time for my last

stop. Hermès. Always my most important stop, but today, much more important than ever before. I was getting my mother's Christmas present. That trumped everything else I'd ever bought there.

I walked in, and for some reason, the cheer went out of me. I didn't know why, exactly; it wasn't anything against their holiday decorating, which was fairly festive, albeit in a typically understated way. Maybe it was that being in an Hermès store was so *normal* for me, and I remembered how *not normal* was the reason I was here today. I still had to work my Birkin magic, though, so I shrugged off my gloom the best I could. I found an Incurable Romantic salesman, and did the usual song and dance, though without my usual flair. The whole time I felt like a robot—I couldn't really flirt back with my salesman or talk about my mom's wish list, like I usually did. I was numb, and all I wanted was to get the hell out of there. Nonetheless, I amassed my usual pile of merchandise, mumbling something about Christmas gifts, and finally popped the question.

"Oh, I'm sorry, sir, we don't have any right now. We can put you on a list, perhaps . . ." Oh no. This couldn't be happening. I had bought how many of these things, and now, when it mattered, I couldn't get one? I was utterly defeated. I could barely get the words out.

"Well, I really want to get everything in one place. I can go by the Bal Harbor or perhaps the Palm Beach store once I get to Florida, one of them will have a bag for me I'm sure." I eased away from him, hoping he didn't notice my voice was slightly choked up.

I didn't leave the store for some reason, though, not right away. I wanted to pull myself together, and I wasn't sure what to do. Should I buy her something else? A "less desirable" Hermès handbag? They certainly had plenty of them. While I lingered in the handbag department, I saw a couple come in, a man and woman of indeterminate age, nothing flashy in their appearance, both with rather strong Russian accents. I watched, somewhat intrigued, as they piled up three pieces of luggage, plus crocodile shoes and matching croc belt. Easily more than $30,000 worth of merchandise. While her husband made transport

arrangements for the luggage pieces, the woman stood casually at one of the display cases, seemingly waiting for him. But as it turned out, she was waiting for something else, because while I stood watching, a saleswoman walked over to her with two Birkins for her to choose from. I don't know why I was so angry, but at that moment, I was. And more than angry: I felt betrayed. Betrayed by my salesperson, betrayed by my formula, but mostly betrayed by myself. I was a loser, a loser for not having enough money to drop in Hermès NYC and get my mom her Christmas gift. Why hadn't I gotten a Birkin? It was simple—I hadn't spent enough. Here in Manhattan, the stakes were higher. Why hadn't I thought of that? And what good was it that I had gotten Birkins all over the world, and couldn't get one now, when it mattered? The "it boy" of the "it bag"? What a joke that was. I was nobody, at least here in New York. And nobodies didn't get Birkins. I should have known that by now.

I didn't get my mom anything that day. In fact, once I calmed down and got out of my self-hating funk, I realized she never would have wanted a Birkin. She found the price of the bags sort of ridiculous, actually, even though she could have afforded one. My mother never cared what other people wanted, and the idea of a "coveted" purse was alien to her. I don't know exactly why I had thought otherwise, except that Birkins were so desirable to everyone I dealt with that I somehow forgot not *everyone* longed for one. Certainly not my mother. And I *had* been a complete emotional wreck, so perhaps I hadn't been thinking clearly.

I decided to go with the less expensive Berlingot, a sportier bag that Sarah happened to have in stock at the time. Since she wintered in Palm Beach, the DeluxeDiva herself made an "emergency holiday delivery" to my parents' house outside of West Palm. Of course, my mom never knew that wasn't the original plan. She was thrilled with the Berlingot, her very own Hermès handbag, and stood up proudly, albeit unsteadily, to model it on Christmas morning. That was the only time I ever saw her holding it. My mother went into the hospital the day after Christmas, and she never really came home, the rest of her life a blur of hospitals, nursing homes, and, at the end, hospice. I was

at her side as much as I could be, and that was a lot, thanks to my unconventional work life. She passed away a scant but endless six weeks later, in February. I remember wishing that we were up north, instead of in Florida, so that the weather outside would have matched the gray bleakness I felt inside on the day we lost her. Instead, I had to shield my eyes from the tropical sun, as well as from everyone around me. I was inconsolable. We all were.

After the quiet memorial service my family had decided on, Juan and I returned to Barcelona. (He too had been to Spain and back numerous times, once flying in for just two days. He was a keeper, for sure.) I tried to get back to normal, but as a few weeks passed, one thing became very clear to me. I didn't like my job anymore. It all seemed so frivolous, the way things can after you lose a loved one, only maybe even worse in my case. I tried to rally, and went on a couple of bag-buying missions, but nothing was the same. I didn't know if my malaise was a phase, or what. Juan was worried about me, not just because of my grief, which was normal, but because I had confided to him that I had difficulty dealing with even the most rudimentary tasks of my business. I ignored e-mails and phone calls all the time now, totally out of character. I was miserable. Even the cats couldn't cheer me up.

Then, one day, I received a faxed letter, from Serge, of all people. (He knew nothing of my mom's passing, because I hadn't gone to Paris since I lost her.)

Dear Sir:

Owing to serious problems with the supply of skin qualities necessary to the manufacture of your items as well as of production, we are really sorry to inform you that we have today no other options than canceling your orders, i.e.:

1 Fuchsia lizard Kelly clutch bag
1 White bull calf, 30cm, Birkin bag
1 Fuchsia goatskin, 36cm, Haut à Courroie bag.

With our most sincere apologies for not being able to give you satis-
faction and thanking you in advance for your understanding, we remain,

Sincerely yours,

Serge de Bourge
Leather Department

Repeated calls over the next couple of weeks to the store (as well as
to Serge's cell phone and home phone) got me nowhere. No return call,
no response at all. I somehow doubted that Hermès was out of leather. I
did figure out that I wasn't completely busted as a Birkin reseller, since I
went and bought a couple of bags in France the week after I got his mis-
sive. It was likely that it was just the Faubourg that had finally figured
things out. Either way, it didn't help my state of mind. Serge had been
a friend, not an enemy, and I had never done a thing to hurt him. The
coldness, his refusal to even talk to me, stung somehow. I wanted to call
someone as down-to-earth as they come, and as Mom was no longer an
option, I went with the next best thing: Kate.

She had been my bedrock friend during my mother's illness, her
patience and understanding likely owing to her own experience with
the untimely death of her brother. During those hellish weeks, she re-
minded me to eat, and sleep, and breathe, and calmed me down when I
railed against the doctors, and reassured me when I confessed my own
feelings of helplessness. And when I spoke with her now, as usual, her
advice was simple. She told me I needed to drop everything, at least
temporarily, and get out of Dodge. No Birkins, no BlackBerry, no eBay.
And no Juan, since he was working, anyway. As we talked, she extolled
the benefits of such a journey. Mulling it over after we hung up, I de-
cided she was right. But I needed to pick carefully where to go.

Back in my life Before Hermès (B.H.), right when my hair and
makeup company had started to take off, I took a celebratory vacation
in Greece. I explored Athens for a few days, and then took a five-hour
ferry ride for a stopover on the island of Sifnos. As soon as my foot hit

the island, the rest of my travel itinerary went out the window, as did my desire to go back to work—I stayed there for three weeks, basking in the near-heavenly natural environment and reveling in the low cost of just about everything.

I didn't want to go back to Sifnos, because I didn't want to take any chance of marring my almost overidealized memories of that first vacation. I did realize, however, that the Greek Island pastiche of soothing green waters and amnesia-inducing sunshine was exactly what I needed. I also had a secret fantasy that if I stared long enough at the side of one of the brilliantly white buildings dotting the islands, my future would appear on it as a slide show, bright and clear in my mind's eye, like some sort of Zen trick.

I settled on Mykonos. It was less isolated than Sifnos and had something of an urban vibe. The prospect of a larger cross section of cuisine, as well as a decent shopping district, also appealed to me for this trip (I didn't know how long I would stay, and I didn't want to go stir-crazy). For my living quarters, I wanted privacy. And privacy I got, preserved not by some ugly barbed wire fence, but by 110 stone steps—the stairs you had to traverse to reach my hilltop cottage, which overlooked the sea and the village from a peacefully removed distance. (When the realtor showed me the place, she advertised the 110-stair walk down to the village, but cautioned me on the 110-stair walk back up.) The view was unreal, the nights quiet, and the solitude unsullied. I'd made the right choice for my sabbatical.

I limited my outings to one a day, for obvious reasons. I went down the hill in the early evening, to dine at whatever restaurant I'd plucked from the guidebook that afternoon. It was always a minor miracle if I found my pick—usually, I confusedly wandered one of the many narrow streets that wound their way through the town, until eventually I ate somewhere out of sheer hunger. (It's no wonder those Greek heroes were superb at labyrinths, let me tell you. They live that shit on a daily basis.) It was on one of these twilight-time sojourns that the blessed anonymity of my vacation was forcibly, if

temporarily, shattered. In staunch defiance against all odds governing probability, I ran into someone I knew. And, unfortunately, it was not someone I was longing to reconnect with.

I recognized him from behind, at a distance of nearly fifty feet, not something I can usually do with a casual acquaintance. However, in the very particular case of Lakis Gavalas, it was a pretty simple matter. It wasn't that he was really fat or really tall or something else physically arresting like that. No, Lakis was just really . . . decorated. Exactly like the last time I saw him, he was a mobile Hermès accessories department. I watched him teetering down the street in his mincing way, tethered to a teeny-weeny Hermès backpack. "Backpack" was really a misnomer; although technically it was something one could carry on the *back*, it wasn't something one could actually *pack*—not unless you were packing, say, a toothpick, a tampon, and a Tic Tac. Maybe that's why he also held a (much roomier) pale gray croc Birkin in the crook of his arm, which I spotted as I drew nearer. My faster pace meant I would soon overtake him on the road, and I braced myself for the meeting. I considered briefly putting on my sunglasses, as I remembered being blinded by his teeth the first time we met. I finally drew up alongside him and greeted him politely. (To finish off the accessories collection, he wore a croc belt, but his ruby-and-diamond dragonfly brooch was probably not Hermès—I guess he wanted to diversify.) Fortunately, Lakis wasn't all that excited to see me either, judging by the limp hand he extended me and the brevity of our chat. His only real comment was on the shopping bag I carried from my gift-buying foray into Lalaounis (a jewelry store made famous by Jackie Onassis).

"Ooooh, I bet you bought something beyootiful . . . I love their things . . . I have the entire collection," he bragged. "Well, this is my shop, you see, and I am expected . . . nice to see you again, Michael . . ." With that, he sashayed into the handbag-and-clothing boutique we were in front of, where the mannequins modeling his designs peeked out at us from behind the windows.

I looked up at the storefront and read the sign: LAK. (Surprising he would name it after himself—he was generally so unassuming . . . yeah.) I breathed deeply, willing myself calm, concentrating solely on the sweet puffs of island breeze and lingering warmth of sunset hour. I couldn't understand why I was so riled up by my chance meeting with Lakis. After a couple of glasses of ouzo at my chosen eatery, I finally relaxed enough to realize what it was. He was a prime example of what wearied me in this whole Birkin world. Here was a man, truly a talented designer, so insecure in himself that he lived like a walking billboard. He had more than two hundred of the bags alone, not to mention all the other Hermès items of adornment he collected—and why? To what end?

I had met some exceptional people over the last few years, some of them with collections to rival his, some of whom I considered close friends. But for every sweet Ellen, or entertaining Sarah, or brilliant Grace, there was a person whose obsession with Birkins and scarves bordered on sheer narcissism. Every day I fielded frantic phone calls and pleading e-mails from people who lacked for nothing, but who longed for more. I wasn't going to be one of them. I wasn't going to spend my time making money I couldn't enjoy the way I wanted to, wasn't going to live my life away from my home and boyfriend. What was the point of that? Losing my mom had brought about this revelation faster, but I think it would have come eventually.

The truth of it was, I couldn't do it anymore. I couldn't keep the Lakises of the world happy, no matter what I did—after all, Hermès would always keep making new Birkins, new scarves, new *stuff*. I was sick of having the often thankless duty of window washer in the Hermès skyscraper. It was definitely over for me.

I had no regrets—it had been a lucrative, if lunatic, way to earn a living. I had also traveled to many of the world's most desirable cities, eaten some unbelievable cuisine, drank a lot of expensive wine, and had millions of dollars of luxury merchandise pass through my hands. All because I knew how to do one important thing—I knew how to bring

home the Birkins. But I was ready—ready to hand off the orange crown to the next eager globe-trotting bag buyer, whoever that might be. And I had a couple of stories to tell at cocktail parties, that's for sure. Hey, maybe I should write some of the crazier ones down before I forgot them—what else did I have to do, drink ouzo?

Epilogue

Now, since you presumably just read it, you know the deal—*Bringing Home the Birkin* is about how Spain, eBay, love, Hermès, serendipity, and Birkins turned my life upside down. By the time those five years had their way with me, the "truth is stranger than fiction" cliché had new meaning. Writing a book about the whole thing seemed only logical. Well, what I didn't realize at the time is how goddamn difficult writing a book is. I mean, we are talking blood, sweat, and tears here (heavy on the tears.) The thing is, no one warned me. Not that there were many possible people who could have—honestly, how many authors do you know personally? I, at the time, knew none. If I had, and they had been able to paint an accurate portrait of the "creative process," I'm pretty sure I would have gone the ouzo route for sure. But, well . . . I didn't. And here I am, three years after that fateful day in Mykonos. That leads to the next question that epilogues are intended to answer—what am I doing now? And, probably more to the point—what about everyone else?

The good news is everyone (including *moi*) is still doing pretty well. The usual suspects:

SARAH: She is still running CreateursdeLuxe, and has even referenced *Bringing Home the Birkin* on her Web site as part of

her "cred." I don't know who gets her all that crocodile now, but judging from all the listings on her site, she has a new "reptile" expert working the Hermès scene.

ELLEN YEATS: Thankfully, she has traded her love for Hermès for a much more substantial love—her new husband. She and I got together last year and did perhaps the most expensive closet cleaning of all time. Yup, almost all those orange boxes and their contents went on the eBay shopping block.

LUC: Watch out, New York. Yup, that's right, Luc is now living it up in Manhattan (courtesy of some sugar daddy or another, no doubt). Did I mention how much I love living in Spain?

WARD: You know, the guy who was supposed to hire me, and then couldn't? Well, he's doing great, and has just launched another jewelry line at Bergdorf Goodman. Still no factory in Barcelona, though. Man, I would *still* be waiting for that job.

GRACE: Still in New York. Still amazing. Still have never met her.

DAD: Will always miss my mom, but can finally hold his head high on the golf course. *Everyone* knows what a writer is.

BERNARD: I dunno. Never heard from him again. My guess is he is still at the Faubourg.

LAKIS GAVALAS: Who knows? Who cares?

Juan and I (and Gala and Dali) are still living in Barcelona, on Las Ramblas. He is still teaching, and I am . . . well, I'm writing another book. I know—I can't really believe it myself. I'm clearly a glutton for punishment. All kidding aside, though, I feel truly blessed to be where I am. From Birkin buyer to memoirist? Things could be a hell of a lot worse.

One last thing I have to say about the trade paperback edition of *Bringing Home the Birkin* coming out is . . . thank God. Now, I don't

mean that in the way major league baseball players say it when they get a home run and win the pennant, apparently courtesy of Jesus. I mean it more how people say it when they are finally able to get the bartender's attention at a crowded club. Because if there is one question I cannot stand to answer, even one more time, it's this one—"So, um, is it in paperback?" Now I can finally say . . . *Yes!* It is! Buy it!!

Although I can't say that to you, because you already did. And I thank you for that.

Everbest—
mt

Glossary of Hermès Terms

25CM, 30CM, 35CM, 40CM: the Birkin is produced in a variety of sizes; the numbers refer to the length in centimeters across the bottom of the bag

BAGMATI: a large cashmere shawl, tissue-thin, light as a feather, and costing about $1,000

BARENIA: a fatty natural leather with an untreated surface. Considered a classic Hermès leather and always seems to be in short supply

BIRKIN: a leather handbag produced in a variety of skins, designed to be a carryall for working or traveling women. Named for the actress Jane Birkin, who codesigned this bag along with Jean-Louis Dumas Hermès in 1984

BLEU ROI: French for royal blue

BLUE JEAN: light sky blue

BOLIDE: a name for a particular handbag model with a zipper that runs across the full length of the arched top. Originally called Bugatti but later changed for legal reasons

BRAISE: a bright, rich red color of dyed crocodile used in the making of handbags and small leather goods

CHÈVRE: goatskin

CITES: Convention on International Trade in Endangered Species of Wild Fauna and Flora. An international agreement between governments; its aim is to ensure that international trade in specimens of wild animals and plants does not threaten their survival. Hermès furnishes customers who live outside the country of purchase with a CITES document when they buy an item made of crocodile, alligator, lizard, or ostrich

CLOCHETTE: the small bell-shaped leather cover that hangs from a thin leather strap (usually hung from the handle of a bag) and houses the key for the handbag's lock

CLOU: metal foot on the bottom of an Hermès handbag

CROC: short for crocodile (also used as slang for any crocodile or alligator species)

ÉTRUSQUE: medium reddish brown color for leather goods

FAUBOURG: the location of the original and flagship Hermès store in Paris, in the Eighth Arrondissement. The actual address is 24 rue du Faubourg Saint-Honoré

GEORGE-V: the avenue where one of the three Hermès shops in Paris is located

KELLY: a handbag made famous by Grace Kelly after a photo of her carrying the bag appeared on the cover of *Life* magazine back in 1956. The Kelly has one handle (whereas the Birkin has two) and can be carried on the shoulder with an optional shoulder strap (whereas the Birkin cannot)

HARDWARE: the locks, zippers, and other metal fittings on the handbags

HAUT À COURROIE: the original and taller version of the Birkin, this bag was designed in the early 1900s to carry a horse saddle. It is also produced today in a variety of handbag sizes

PALLADIUM: silver-colored metal hardware on the handbags

PARIS BOMBAY: a handbag that looks similar to a fat baguette

PASHMINA: typically a blend of approximately 70 percent cashmere and 30 percent silk, used in the making of shawls

PLAQUÉ: metal plates at the end of the leather *sangles* (straps). One plaque is inscribed with "Hermès Paris"

POIGNÉES: handles

PONTET: metal belt loop on the front of a Birkin that holds the *sangles* (straps) in place

POUDRE: a creamy beige color of dyed crocodile used in the making of handbags and small leather goods

RUTHENIUM: a gunmetal-colored shade of hardware used on leather goods

SANGLES: leather strap; term used both for Hermès saddles and handbags

TIRET: leather cord that attaches the *clochette* to the handbag

TOGO: leather with a small pebblelike grain to it

TOURET: small metal wheel that the lock attaches to

ULYSSE: a small leather notebook that comes in several sizes and has refillable pages

VERMILLON: red with an orange undertone, used for leather goods

Acknowledgments

To Laura Yorke and Cassie Jones for getting it from the get-go (and to Johnathan Wilber for helping to ice the cake).

To Dad, who gave me, among all other things, my sixth sense: humor.

To JCT, who will be on my side forevermore.

To Eddie for reading and Dottie for waiting.

To Kara Blood for her words.

To Riane, the youngest fan in the clan.

To Peach, who babysat the writer—twice.

To Gene and Elaine, for giving me the tools for writing.

To Barbara Smith, who always believed.

To Mica R. Bonner, for being the diamond in my *clochette*.

To Gala and Dali, the cutest paperweights a boy could have.

And a most grateful thank-you to Anne Blake, Carole Bayer Sager, Créateurs de Luxe, David Tobin, Dean Silvers, Debbie Stier, DeMane Davis, Galina Slinin, Geoffrey Proulx, Hiromi Tsukada, the Hotel Mansart staff, JPG, James Wadsworth, Jill Melhado, Kate Hunt, Lakis Gavalas, Mary Jane, Melissa Jane Bradley, "Mom and Dad" Canal, MGS, Muntsa Vicente, Patricia Petal, Pime, Rick Johnson, Sharyn Rosenblum, Simonetta Lussu, Ward Kelvin, Willow Bay, www.LuxuryShops.com, everyone at William Morrow who helped with this book . . . and Hermès.